Like the printing press, radio, and television in the past, today's communication technologies are vastly reshaping the political landscape. Bowers has been in the middle of this revolution, while Kerbel has had a front-row seat. Together, they place current changes in historical context and persuasively suggest what this era of the Internet means for liberals, conservatives, and the future of American politics.

Markos Moulitsas, Founder of Daily Kos

Matthew R. Kerbel and Christopher J. Bowers have written the seminal account of the ascendance of the netroots and the progressive movement that has accompanied it. *Next Generation Netroots* describes the struggle of the forces on the left to first gain a foothold in the Democratic Party and, more recently, to use the mobilization powers of the Internet to assert a stronger voice in setting policy. This book is crucial to the understanding of the conflicting forces at work at a time when the direction of the country is deeply uncertain.

Thomas B. Edsall, Columbia University

Next Generation Netroots is the book online activists didn't know they were waiting for. Matthew Kerbel and Chris Bowers explain why everything we thought we knew about how to expand the progressive netroots is wrong, and why it's time for a new approach. When what you're doing doesn't work, read this book.

Susan Madrak, Senior Political Writer at Blue Nation Review

NEXT GENERATION NETROOTS

From the early demise of Trent Lott at the hands of bloggers to the agonized scream of Howard Dean; from *Daily Kos* and the blogosphere to the rise of Twitter and Facebook, politics and new media have co-existed and evolved in rapid succession. Here, an academic and practitioner team up to consider how new and old media technologies mix with combustible politics to determine, in real time, the shape of the emerging political order. Our political moment shares with other realigning periods the sense that political parties are failing to address the public interest. In an era defined by the collapse of the political center, extreme income inequality, rapidly changing demography, and new methods of communicating and organizing, a second-generation online progressive movement fueled by email and social media is coming into its own.

In this highly readable text, the authors—one a scholar of Internet politics, the other a leading voice of the first generation netroots—draw on unique data and on-the-ground experience to answer key questions at the core of our tumultuous politics. How has Internet activism changed in form and function? How have the left and right changed with it? How does this affect American political power?

Matthew R. Kerbel is Professor and Chair of the Political Science Department at Villanova University.

Christopher J. Bowers is the Senior Campaign Director for *Daily Kos* and an experienced consultant for a wide range of campaigns and organizations.

NEXT GENERATION NETROOTS

Realignment and the Rise of the Internet Left

Matthew R. Kerbel and Christopher J. Bowers

NEW YORK AND LONDON

First published 2016
by Routledge
711 Third Avenue, New York, NY 10017

and by Routledge
2 Park Square, Milton Park, Abingdon, Oxon OX14 4RN

Routledge is an imprint of the Taylor & Francis Group, an informa business

© 2016 Taylor & Francis

The right of Matthew R. Kerbel and Christopher J. Bowers to be identified as authors of this work has been asserted by them in accordance with sections 77 and 78 of the Copyright, Designs and Patents Act 1988.

All rights reserved. No part of this book may be reprinted or reproduced or utilised in any form or by any electronic, mechanical, or other means, now known or hereafter invented, including photocopying and recording, or in any information storage or retrieval system, without permission in writing from the publishers.

Trademark notice: Product or corporate names may be trademarks or registered trademarks, and are used only for identification and explanation without intent to infringe.

Published 2016

Library of Congress Cataloging in Publication Data
Names: Kerbel, Matthew Robert, 1958- author. | Bowers, Christopher J., author.
 Title: Next generation netroots : realignment and the rise of the Internet left / Matthew R. Kerbel, Villanova University, and Christopher J. Bowers, Daily Kos.
 Description: First edition. | New York, NY : Routledge, 2016. | Includes bibliographical references.
 Identifiers: LCCN 2015041948| ISBN 9781138652477 (hardback) | ISBN 9781138652484 (pbk.) | ISBN 9781315624235 (ebook)
 Subjects: LCSH: Internet–Political aspects–United States. | Information society–Political aspects–United States. | Communication in politics–Technological innovations–United States. | Political participation–Technological innovations–United States. | Liberalism–United States. | Political culture–United States.
 Classification: LCC JK468.A8 K46 2016 | DDC 302.23/10973–dc23
LC record available at http://lccn.loc.gov/2015041948

ISBN: 9781138652477 (hbk)
ISBN: 9781138652484 (pbk)
ISBN: 9781315624235 (ebk)

Typeset in Bembo
by Taylor & Francis Books

To our spouses, children and parents

Adrienne and Gabrielle Kerbel
Doris and Sheldon Kerbel
Natasha and Linus Chart
Maureen and James Bowers

CONTENTS

List of illustrations   *x*
Acknowledgments   *xi*
List of contributors   *xii*

Introduction   1

1   There is No Center   7

2   On Coalitions, Movements and Regime Change   34

3   Netroots Rising   56

4   Television, Message Control, Money and Republican Dominance   84

5   Objectivity and Transparency   100

6   The Limits of Netroots Influence   115

7   Resolution   131

Index   *150*

LIST OF ILLUSTRATIONS

Figures

6.1 Cumulative change in real hourly wages of all workers, by wage percentile, 1979–2013	116
6.2 Third Way Board of Trustees	121

Tables

1.1 Major presidential campaign spending on television during the Reagan coalition era, in millions	16
2.1 Fourteen key similarities between the conservative and progressive movements	43
3.1 Top 25 sources of traffic to Daily Kos, November 14, 2005–January 17, 2006	68
3.2 Average monthly television and Internet use by age (hours)	79
4.1 Traffic, "Likes" and "Talking About This" figures for leading conservative and progressive Facebook pages, November 2014	88
6.1 New York State traffic to Daily Kos during the 2014 New York State Gubernatorial Primary	124

ACKNOWLEDGMENTS

Collaboration is always more than two writers working together, and we were fortunate to benefit from the wisdom and experience of our editor, Jennifer Knerr, and from the editorial assistance of Ze'ev Sudry. As we developed our manuscript, we received critical feedback on the content of our argument from a host of individuals with insight into the dynamics of Internet politics in general and the Internet Left in particular. We are especially indebted to David Karpf, John Kenneth White, Natasha Chart, Markos Moulitsas, Will Rockafellow, Susie Madrak, Michael Langenmayr, Ilya Sheyman and Tim Tagaris.

Any undertaking of this magnitude takes time and invariably requires long nights of writing under the pressure of looming deadlines. For one of us, this was the first time through the process of writing and revising a manuscript; for the other, it was the ninth. Regardless, we were both sustained by the patience of our families and by their support for our commitment to this project. They are partners in our work, and with a deep sense of appreciation and gratitude we dedicate this book to them.

LIST OF CONTRIBUTORS

Matthew R. Kerbel is Professor and Chair of the Political Science Department at Villanova University. An early student of the Internet, he is the author or editor of nine books on American politics, including *Netroots: Online Progressives and the Transformation of American Politics*, and *If It Bleeds, It Leads: An Anatomy of Television News*. In *Netroots*, he considers the possibility that Internet politics will rekindle the relationship between politicians and ordinary citizens that was largely lost in the television age. His interest in media politics stems from his experience in radio and television news, including work as a news writer for the Public Broadcasting Service in New York. He lives in Wayne, Pennsylvania with his wife Adrienne and daughter Gabrielle.

Christopher J. Bowers is the Senior Campaign Director for Daily Kos. From May 2004 through June 2007, he was lead writer at MyDD.com. In July 2007, he co-founded Openleft.com and served as the managing editor until August 2010. He has been involved in seminal netroots events, including organizing the Liberal Blog Advertising Network in 2005 and the Senate public option whip count in 2009. Additionally, he has served as a consultant for a wide range of campaigns and organizations, including online powerhouses MoveOn.org, the Progressive Change Campaign Committee, and the New Organizing Institute. He lives in Rochester, NY with his wife Natasha Chart and son Linus.

INTRODUCTION

> I want my country back! We want our country back! I am tired of being divided![1]
> *Governor Howard Dean to the California Democratic Convention, March 15, 2003*
>
> America has made their decision, they've decided, we are going to take our country back![2]
> *Rep. Michele Bachmann to Iowa voters, March 26, 2011*

Take our country back from whom? While the context of these two statements could not be more different, with Howard Dean embracing a pluralistic view of America in opposition to the economic and foreign policies of the George W. Bush administration, and Michele Bachmann railing against big government and the social policies of the Obama administration, the rhetorical similarity—and the sentiment behind it—is striking. Increasingly over the past decade, rhetoric on the right and left has reflected profound feelings of unease, suggesting that something significant is changing in our political and social relationships. We only want our country back if we feel it has been stolen from us, if we believe that something fundamental has changed. And although the left and right have divergent ideas about what has been taken away, a broad sense of national discontent is being driven by an overwhelming set of economic, cultural and technological forces to which the political power structure in the United States has been slow to adapt.

Our objective in this book is to identify how our current politics operates from the vantage point of the historical ebb and flow of political regimes and the emergence of new media of communication. We contend that the seemingly intractable, hallmark red state/blue state divisions of twenty-first-century politics cannot endure these pressures, and will succumb eventually to a new political alignment. We have already seen significant changes in how the electorate is divided, as the coin-flip elections of 2000 and 2004 that produced almost evenly divided government have yielded to a sine-wave pattern of Democratic dominance of presidential years and Republican dominance of midterm years, generating push–pull governance reflecting the priorities of two mutually exclusive electorates. Like a top spinning evenly before wobbling wildly and then tipping over, the 50/50 electorate has become a contentious, zero-sum electorate that cannot be sustained indefinitely. Seemingly intractable battles of the kind that characterize our age foreshadow a moment of transition, resonant with previous periods when once-dominant regimes lost their intellectual energy and coalition partners, leaving them vulnerable to electoral defeat in the wake of new, more robust coalitions.

Each of these previous moments—the emergence of Jacksonian democracy, the disintegration of the Whigs and fragmentation of the Democrats over slavery and secession, the formation of the New Deal coalition and its eventual demise—coincided with the successful political application of new communication technologies (inexpensive printing, the telegraph, radio and television, respectively). Today, the Internet is becoming a politically viable medium at a point when the center-right Republican coalition that governed national politics since 1969 is showing signs of severe strain. The Internet has been essential to the rise of a progressive movement that is playing a pivotal role in an emerging post-50/50 America. The interplay of these two forces—Republican regime decay and Internet activism—driven by important large-scale social and economic trends, will determine the shape of the regime to follow.

Progressive bloggers, email campaigners, social media curators and social justice activists organized online will be at the epicenter of the political changes ahead. But this does not guarantee that the next regime phase will be a liberal one, as some of the forces promoting political change are working against the left. Conservatives have a well developed messaging machine integrated with Republican governing elites that has been refined over decades to shape public opinion, and as the 2012 and 2014 political cycles demonstrated, a significant spending advantage in a post-*Citizens United* world.[3] As the dominant coalition in the waning political alignment, the right enjoys important institutional advantages assembled over its years in power. However, the right's messaging apparatus is a top-down system modeled on and built around television, which itself is changing in the wake of pressure from the decentralized, bottom-up Internet. In this respect, the right and the left are in a race with technology over how long it will be possible for conservatives to dominate politics with a big-money, big-media model before the small-dollar, individualized politics of digital media replaces it. The outcome of that race, unknown and unpredictable, will help determine whether today's political instability will produce a realignment of the right or left.

We plan to tell the story of this precarious moment in American political history by intertwining two narratives: the emergence, strengths and limitations of online progressive political action; and the ebb and flow of political regimes. The first narrative recounts the rapid development of political blogging and email campaigning from free-form exercise to professional venture that grew in accordance with the horizontal, decentralized structure of the Internet to become a force for large-scale movement activism. The second narrative places contemporary politics in historical context, drawing comparisons with previous moments brought about by movements as diverse as Andrew Jackson's populism and Barry Goldwater's conservatism, when long-established coalitions eventually succumbed to powerful new political forces aided by new methods of political organizing. The narratives intertwine in the present day, where the work of the netroots—still widely misunderstood or downplayed by political and media figures who rose to prominence in an earlier era—and professional digital campaigners is presented as an increasingly fundamental component of politics at a tenuous point in American political life.

In the process, we will address a range of questions central to understanding the arc of contemporary politics: How has Internet activism changed in form and function from the first decade of the twenty-first century to the second? How has the left changed with it to develop an online platform that serves as the basis for a new progressive movement? What is the potential—and potential limitation—of this platform? Is there historical precedent for the outlandish claim that emerging digital media can contribute to changing the trajectory of American political power? How will the convergence of television and the Internet potentially amplify the effectiveness of online politics? What is the evidence that we are in a realigning era, moving permanently away from the politics of the past 40 years and, not coincidentally, from the television-centered strategies that bolstered it? How does the changing media landscape factor into that realignment?

The authors of this book bring complementary academic and applied perspectives to the telling of these narratives. One is a student of Internet politics whose previous work chronicled the emergence of the Internet as a political tool and its utilization by the left to develop and deploy a movement modeled on early twentieth-century progressive values. The other has been in the thick of that movement since its earliest days, initially as one of the prominent voices of the first-iteration progressive blogosphere, now as executive campaign director for the largest online progressive news and activism community in the United States.

Our story begins in the present day, with the assertion that politicians who seek a way to unite the left and right fail to appreciate that the center is missing. In Chapter 1, we examine factors which, along with dramatically changing modes of communication, are contributing to today's political instability: rapid age, attitudinal and demographic shifts in the population; increasing polarization between the political parties; rising income inequality; and emerging radical dominance of the Republican Party. The chapter introduces our core argument that these factors point to a breakdown in the forces driving consensus-building institutions in an asymmetrical manner characterized by a struggle over power and participatory democracy on the left—where Internet activists are at ground zero—and ideology on the right, leading to the question: without a political center, what happens next?

In Chapter 2, we begin to address this question through the lens of partisan realignment, which allows us to view the present political environment as more than a series of election cycles resulting in seemingly ad hoc shifts to the left and right. This allows us to think of elections as events related to the rise and fall of political regimes rather than as the idiosyncratic occurrences they appear to be in mainstream media coverage, and to think of realigning periods as transitional moments between regimes. We examine past transitional moments and consider the role that changes in the media landscape have played during each inflection point, as illustrated by inexpensive printing technology during the Jackson realignment, the telegraph during the Civil War, radio at the emergence of the New Deal coalition, and television during the Nixon–Reagan regime. We apply lessons from the past to the present day in order to extrapolate from past media revolutions what we might expect to see in today's transitional politics.

To this end, in Chapter 3 we examine the emergence and development of the modern progressive movement, which owes its existence to the Internet. Mainstream political observers may still regard the netroots as secondary actors in today's politics because, despite many years of struggle, they have not been able to displace neoliberal influences in the Democratic Party. However, the movement is large, growing and a key force in the push for a progressive realignment. We explain how the modern progressive movement developed in two iterations—the first built around blogging, the second around email and social media—and how it has become the left's most potent political weapon. Progressive Internet-based political and media organizations are rapidly gaining in reach, providing the left with sophisticated messaging and mobilization tools. We provide a history of this evolution and explore how the expansion of progressive grassroots participation in the political process is beginning to challenge the status quo.

If the progressive movement has expanded grassroots participation through continued mastery of the Internet, conservative movement politics is still largely dependent on the big-money, television-centered politics of the television era. The period 1968–2008 was a time of center-right governance noted for the success of a well funded movement conservatism suited to television politics which, for all its effectiveness, faces challenges as the Internet becomes a predominant media force and as television itself assumes the decentralized, on-demand qualities of the Internet. In Chapter 4, we consider the degree to which the changing media environment may pose challenges to the cash and organizational advantages of the conservative movement.

Against the backdrop of a changing media landscape, the economic model that governed television and newspaper reporting for decades is faltering, rendering traditional media unable to tell the story of the political moment. This poses an additional obstacle to progressive activists as well as an opportunity, as we see in Chapter 5. While declining audiences challenge conventional media, they remain a present and prevalent part of the political process, and the conventional model of reporting rooted in objectivity prevents traditional journalists from communicating the ideological and small-d democratic battle lines of contemporary politics—to the detriment of the netroots.

If progressives have organized effectively online and have started realizing policy victories against entrenched factions in the Democratic Party, they nonetheless face significant limitations in their quest to realign politics in their direction. As we see in Chapter 6, despite the advantages progressives enjoy through Internet-based movement organizing, and even in the midst of a populist and grassroots outpouring marked by the rise of the netroots, the political process remains responsive to the wishes of large, organized, corporate and moneyed interests long in the crosshairs of progressives. Continued elite dominance, even within the Democratic Party, provides a counterweight to the success of the progressive netroots and tells a cautionary tale about the potential limits of online grassroots activism in the face of concentrated wealth.

At the same time, while conservative activists are relatively well integrated with one another on socioeconomic and cultural levels, the same cannot be said for the left. This, too, presents a challenge for online progressives. Netroots communities, even though they number in the millions, skew toward white, male and better educated, while largely failing to reach the more diverse and more economically distressed core of President Obama's 2008 coalition. The inability of the progressive movement to unite these demographics limits the ability of progressive political power to overtake corporate interests inside and outside the Democratic Party.

The prospects for fundamental long-term realignment are discussed in a concluding chapter that brings together the book's twin narratives of grassroots Internet politics and regime change, centered on the power struggle between progressive activists and Democratic elites, and the ideological takeover of the Republican Party by latter-day movement conservatives animated by an out-of-the-mainstream, libertarian-tinged conservatism. As reactionary influences in the Republican base have forced an end to a decades-long consensus over the scope of political conflict between center-left social welfare liberals and center-right market conservatives, movement progressives seek to reorganize the Democratic Party as a bottom-up participatory organization in order to displace what they regard as corporate dominance. We contend that the result of these two parallel struggles will determine whether the electorate realigns in a rightward or leftward direction. A key wild card is the changing electorate itself, which skews heavily in a progressive direction but is composed of voters without a history of participation.

We consider two outcomes: a conservative transformation bankrolled by corporate interests, powered by right-wing populism, and locked in by gerrymandered legislative maps and voting restrictions; or a progressive realignment bolstered by new media, where progressives become the majority partner in the

Democratic Party and energize a changing electorate with an inclusive, progressive, populist message. These possibilities will play out against the political instability of the present moment, which resembles past periods of realignment, and the rising influence of the new media, without which progressives would not be able to engage in their struggle against entrenched Democratic Party elites.

Terminology

This book uses four terms to describe the progressive online politics and media universe. Three of them—blogosphere, netroots and Professional Left—are semi-obscure political terms, while the fourth—Internet Left—is a term coined by the authors for use in this book:

Blogosphere	The network of partisan progressive blogs such as *Daily Kos* that focus on national political news with original content from a progressive perspective.
Netroots	The progressive blogosphere in combination with progressive, mass-membership, digital-native-activist organizations such as MoveOn.org.
Internet Left	The netroots in combination with the constellation of progressive but non-partisan digital media operations. *Upworthy*, *Alternet* and *Salon* are examples of media outlets that are part of the Internet Left but are not considered part of the netroots.
Professional Left	The paid staff of netroots organizations as well as the paid staff and consultants who handle the digital operations for Democratic campaigns and traditional progressive advocacy organizations.

Notes

1 Dean, Howard, Address to California State Democratic Convention, Sacramento, March 15, 2003. Retrieved from www.gwu.edu/~action/2004/cdp0303/dean031503spt.html.
2 Schneider, Matt, "Rep. Michele Bachmann in Iowa: 'I'm In, You're In, We Will Take This Country Back in 2012.'" 2011. *Mediaite*, March 2. Retrieved from www.mediaite.com/tv/rep-michele-bachmann-in-iowa-im-in-youre-in-we-will-take-this-country-back-in-2012.
3 In 2012, outside groups spent $63 million on over 112,000 campaign ads in support of Republican Senate candidates, compared with $15.7 million spent in support of Democrats. Through the final weeks of the 2014 campaign, Republicans enjoyed closer to a 2–1 advantage over Democrats. See "Heated Battle for U.S. Senate Draws Deluge of Outside Ads, Most Are Dark Money." 2014. *Wesleyan Media Project*, September 4. Retrieved from http://mediaproject.wesleyan.edu/releases/heated-battle-for-u-s-senate-draws-deluge-of-outside-group-ads-most-are-dark-money.

1

THERE IS NO CENTER

The homepage of AmericansElect.org trumpeted "the first national online primary" to make politics work for people frustrated with the fruits of the two-party system. They envisioned the 2012 presidential race being enriched by a nationwide online vote for someone who would defy the country's familiar red–blue divisions and offer an alternative the likes of which the major parties reliably fail to produce: someone who could represent the great purple middle of American politics. Boasting technological savvy and millions of dollars from deep-pocketed contributors, the nonprofit spent $35 million to secure ballot access for their would-be candidate in 27 states.[1] But they never got their candidate. Under the organization's rules, viable nominees needed 1,000 supporters in at least ten states. Nobody even came close to achieving that benchmark.[2]

The first national online primary was shut down on May 15, 2012 for lack of interest. And the Americans Elect site, which once triumphantly predicted it would change history, was reduced to saying sheepishly, "See you in 2013" after acknowledging the failure of its grand presidential experiment. Somehow, the likes of Buddy Roemer (the former Louisiana governor whose 6,000 votes made him the most popular declared candidate) didn't trigger an electoral groundswell.

Postmortems on the effort questioned the wisdom of bankrolling a people's movement with hedge fund money,[3] rules that favored insider candidates[4] and the mistaken belief that people would rally around a process rather than a person.[5] Notwithstanding these significant considerations, Americans Elect suffered from a huge conceptual misunderstanding of contemporary politics in assuming there is a definable political space in the center of the spectrum for a "candidate of the people" to occupy. If such a vast middle exists, what would it look like? Would it be a place where health insurance is a right or a privilege? A place where the government guarantees a social safety net or where markets are in the business of providing Social Security and Medicare? A place where taxes can be increased or where they are never raised?

Those old enough to remember what politics looked like in the second half of the twentieth century may recall that none of these zero-sum contingencies was at issue. Without question there were hotly contested, impassioned debates over economic and social policies ranging from health care to welfare reform. But all parties to those debates accepted the fundamental premise of a welfare state that would provide some set of basic services to the general public in exchange for some amount of public revenue. There were ideological differences over whether to fix the health care system with market-based or government-run programs, but the goal of universal health care had broad bipartisan support. We may have disagreed on how much we should collect in taxes, but the question of *whether* we should tax was relegated to the fringe. This is no longer the case. There may still be a right and a left in American politics but there is no identifiable center between them.

Instead, our political era is defined by an asymmetrical contest waged by two camps operating parallel to one another. On the left, neoliberals find themselves under attack by a new breed of progressives contesting what they regard as the outsized influence of financial and corporate interests in Democratic Party politics that renders the party impotent to advance the concerns of the poor and middle class. On the right, a conservative reaction bankrolled by corporate dollars has pulled the Republican Party out of the political consensus it shared with Democrats since the New Deal by standing in ideological opposition to the New Deal itself and to any policies that would strengthen that share of the welfare state enjoyed by the poor and disadvantaged. As progressives battle neoliberals for control of the Democratic Party in a power struggle dating back to Howard Dean's 2003 presidential campaign, ascendant right-wing elites and their foot soldiers in the Republican base ensure ideological fealty to an anti-New Deal platform through a string of successful victories in Republican primaries, including several against long-serving officials deemed too soft or too willing to compromise with the opposition.[6]

Although progressives on the left and conservatives on the right are commonly viewed as mirror images of one another, this inside-out vantage point overlooks the way the two groups are quite different in structure and purpose. The progressive clash with entrenched neoliberal interests in the Democratic Party is best understood as a battle about participatory democracy aimed at reducing the power wielded by corporate patrons by reinvigorating democratic processes. In the mold of progressives from the first Gilded Age, their ultimate goal is reforming what they see as a damaged political process to make the political class responsive to the interests of those who can't afford to write large checks for political campaigns. It is fundamentally a process-oriented struggle because progressives view organizational power as a prerequisite to making policy shifts that would help the middle class and the poor.

The outcome of this battle remains in doubt. Neoliberal interests are deeply entrenched in Democratic Party politics, and the rules of political engagement favor the wealthy. But progressives are not without significant assets, most notably in the form of an extensive and growing grassroots movement supported by a network of online institutions. For over a decade, activists on the left have been working to open the political process to the grassroots, and their influence has grown along with the Internet. In scope and reach, they are far ahead of where they were several years ago when Internet politics was emerging.

For a movement associated with prominent issues such as opposition to the Iraq War and advocacy for a public health insurance option in the Affordable Care Act, it may not be intuitive to think of progressives in non-ideological terms. However, a quick survey of some of the largest campaigns conducted by progressives in recent years reveals a consistent emphasis on democratic processes. These include:

- filibuster reform and democratizing the rules of the U.S. Senate;
- increasing voter participation through an ever-escalating investment in get-out-the-vote efforts;
- limiting the role of money in politics, including the delivery of over 3,000,000 petition signatures to Congress demanding a Constitutional Amendment to reverse the *Citizens United* Supreme Court decision; and
- preserving net neutrality to maintain the Internet as an egalitarian medium.

Through campaigns such as these, online progressives seek to democratize the rules of the game in order to get more people to play it, believing that substantive policy change is possible only through meaningful changes to the political process.

The intramural battle raging in the Republican Party looks quite different. There, an energized base is at war with a traditional conservative establishment over the party's direction and commitments. This struggle is more ideological than pragmatic because the base is advancing an agenda that is pulling the Republican Party outside a decades-old consensus over political boundaries. Deep-pocketed economic interests whose objectives align with the rebels supply fuel for the effort, which in its intensity is akin to a religious war driven by unshakable beliefs. Unlike the left they are focused on outcomes rather than processes. They do not have to worry about expanding political participation or altering the rules of the game because they have been engaged for years as the voters that sustained the dominant position of the Republican Party. But now they have split with their leadership over the nature of conservatism, demanding the party take a radical turn. And more often than not they are winning.

Viewing the struggle on the left through a procedural lens and the struggle on the right through an ideological one helps to clarify the reasons for the breakdown of political consensus, the disappearance of the political center and the decay of the once dominant center-right Reagan coalition. Although each side attacks the other ferociously, the balance of power at this moment lies not in an imaginary center between left and right but in the fluid contests to define both sides of the spectrum. The next political alignment will be shaped by the outcome of the twin battles being waged between progressives and neoliberals on the left and conservatives and radicals on the right. It will depend on the ability of progressives and radicals to remake their respective political parties and then gain the control of political institutions necessary to implement their vision.

In the meantime, the long-term objectives of these groups are mutually exclusive but the governing process requires compromise. So either the system will yield eventually to the well financed demands of the right and usher in an era of Tea Party governance, or progressives will succeed in their organizational fight with Democratic Party elites and restructure the party along the lines of a diverse, grassroots, participatory mass movement, offering voters an alternative to corporate-sponsored conservatism *and* corporate-sponsored neoliberalism. The third choice is continued stalemate. But that is a dynamically unstable proposition.

The political revolutions of the right and left are playing out against a backdrop of social and demographic changes that are making the politics of a divided America increasingly untenable even as they fuel red/blue divisions. The political process is destabilized by changes in the way people associate and organize through technology, generational shifts in social attitudes, the rapid emergence of majority–minority communities and associated demographic shifts, and a long march toward dramatic income inequality, in addition to declining moderate self-identification, declining ticket splitting and the increased polarization of the parties in response to the right-wing Republican purge. Destabilization is indicative of decaying political alignments, in this case the dominant center-right alignment dating back at least to Ronald Reagan and arguably to Richard Nixon. It is a sign that the coalitions supporting the status quo are weakening as the parties as constituted fail to deal sufficiently with fundamental political and social problems. It means that some form of political realignment—a shuffling of the political deck—is in the offing.

Whether this broken stalemate results in a lasting regime of the Tea Party right or a second progressive era, history tells us that information technology will figure foremost among the agents pressing for change. Almost every regime transformation in American history has been accompanied by the maturation of a new medium of communication that figured prominently in the emergence of the new majority coalition. If communication technology has never been the reason for political realignment, it has played an important role in the successful strategies of new regime leaders. In the case of radio and television, it defined their eras and their coalitions. Who could imagine the New Deal coalition without Franklin D. Roosevelt's deft use of radio, or the Republican regime that followed without Ronald Reagan's slick use of television? Abraham Lincoln expanded executive power and cemented Republican control of government with a political strategy that included expansive use of the telegraph and wire services. And what inexpensive printing was to Andrew Jackson's populist coalition in 1828, the Internet is to progressives seeking to infiltrate entrenched interests—a means of identifying, organizing and mobilizing a disparate political constituency.

Like these earlier technologies, the Internet is neither entirely new nor fully developed. Since Howard Dean proved you could run an Internet insurgency in 2003, we have seen the transformation of online politics through the emergence of sites like Facebook, YouTube and Twitter; a revolution in information-on-demand capabilities so great that Google became a verb; and hardware and software advances that make possible the rapid download of data-rich content on a scale unthinkable ten years ago. The first generation of online activism marked by community blogging and grassroots activism has morphed into a second generation defined by social media and professional digital campaigning. But the Internet growth curve has yet to flatten, as market pressure for personalized content is forcing television to reinvent itself as an on-demand medium. The more our media environment is driven by the Internet's atomized structure rather than by television's mass structure, the greater the threat to the one-to-many communication model that defined the Republican politics of the late twentieth century. But whatever will replace it remains a work in progress.

Politically engaged individuals from both camps are at the heart of that work in progress—most notably those who were pioneers in the digital-native progressive grassroots media and activist organizations known as the "netroots" whose efforts birthed the progressive movement in the early years of the twenty-first century (the term "netroots" is a neologism combing the words "Internet" and "grassroots"). Some of these are bloggers, members of a self-selected group who, through talent or determination or the good fortune of being there first, occupy the hubs in that decentralized place called the blogosphere where political networking happens. Some are professional digital activists—the Professional Left—who have emerged as second-generation online leaders, taking advantage of the email campaigning and social media explosions, and the path cleared for them by those who came before. Bloggers matured and shone in the free-form Internet era. The Professional Left emerged as the Internet was becoming more routinized and the nascent political structures of the progressive movement had started to mature. In conjunction with a nexus of large progressive publishers that do not engage directly in electoral activism, they form what we call the "Internet Left." If technology is once again to play an essential role in the transformation between political epochs, it should be uncontroversial to assume bloggers and online activists will be in the mix.

Our understanding of this particular moment, ripe with the prospect of uncertain change, takes place at the intersection of regime transformation and Internet activism. To understand how we ended up on that particular corner, let's take a closer look at the factors contributing to political instability to understand better why we believe we are approaching a realignment; the concept of realignment to see how applicable it is to today's politics; the way media technology has factored into past realignments; and how Internet technology could play a role in sorting out today's political instability.

Toward the End of Blue versus Red

Beneath the surface of today's dysfunctional politics resides a cauldron of forces threatening to break through and upend the political landscape. Political polarization is gobbling up the center as the right wing consumes the Republican Party, undermining our faith in the institutions we traditionally rely on for direction and solutions. An ascendant generation with social views quite unlike their parents', together with a rapidly growing non-white population, is producing demographic shifts large enough to rock our politics. Vast income inequality threatens a social backlash, while the influence of money in the political process grows to Gilded Age levels (Hacker and Pierson 2010; Gilens 2012). As all this is happening, technology is changing our relationships to one another to a degree that challenges eternal preconceptions about time and space.

Polarization and right-wing dominance

It is a professional dictate of the mainstream press to find equivalence in the actions of the right and left in order to avoid siding with either. And it is not uncommon for online activists to object.[7] This dynamic between the old and new media, which we discuss in detail in Chapter 5, demonstrates how far our political debate has drifted from the days of the New Deal consensus over domestic policy and the Cold War consensus over foreign policy, when journalists could claim to be objective by balancing their coverage without doing violence to reality.

The critical distinction is that all sides were once constrained by the same set of facts. From the Great Depression through the turn of the century, disagreements turned on how to solve problems within the widely shared contexts of Cold War and post-Cold War politics abroad and welfare state politics at home. Solutions posed by social welfare liberals, or what in the United States has typically passed for the center-left, were ascendant for roughly the first half of this period. Solutions posed by market conservatives, the policies of the American center-right, were ascendant during the second half.[8] For much of this period, both sides agreed on an expansionist foreign policy in the name of containing communism, even when they disagreed on how much to spend to support it, or whether to pursue military or diplomatic avenues to advance it. Despite holding different attitudes toward government and different preferred solutions, they agreed on the domain in which their disagreements would play out.

Not today. On meaningful issues, today's progressives and conservatives operate from a different and mutually exclusive set of beliefs about the world, manifested in and reinforced by unique sets of facts. If your knowledge of the world were derived entirely from Daily Kos or MSNBC, you would assume President Obama is a sympathetic actor who in good faith did what he could to pull America from the brink of economic collapse through a set of liberal (but by no means progressive) policies. If, however, you knew only what you read on right-wing blogs, heard on conservative talk radio or saw on Fox News, you would assume Obama to be an alien threat to American life, an illegitimate president most probably born in Kenya, sporting a secret socialist agenda that is bringing the country to the brink of ruin. Strip away the hyperbole and you have two incompatible views of the president that align with similarly incompatible views of just about everything else. As a *factual* matter, progressives will tell you there are no death panels in the Affordable Care Act; conservatives will tell you there are. Conservatives will tell you President Obama apologized to the world for past American policies; progressives will say he did nothing of the sort. Progressives will tell you global warming is real. Conservatives will tell you it is a hoax. And they both have the facts to prove it.

The implications of these core differences go well beyond the inability and unwillingness of mainstream reporters to arbitrate between the two mutually exclusive sets of factual claims (although, as we will see in Chapter 5, their continued insistence on maintaining neutrality is a significant part of our story). Irreconcilable world views nullify the governing model of the two previous party regimes, stretching from FDR to George W. Bush, by making compromise akin to treason, or at least to the foolish abandonment of common sense. In so doing, the polarization of today's politics represents the end of a longstanding period of political regime stability, even if by its extreme nature it is not likely a stable alternative.[9] We believe the success of today's far-right activists may be regarded as the fulfillment of the conservative movement's 50-year struggle to pull the Republican Party out of the New Deal consensus. The inability of mainstream conservatives to keep them in check is a sign of a political coalition in twilight succumbing to excesses borne of its own longevity, much as Democrats found themselves captive to core interests as liberalism lost its appeal in the 1970s and 1980s.[10] It is the brilliant supernova prior to implosion.

Minorities and generations

One need look no further than the 2010 census to find a glaring reason for conservatism's potential decline and a key source of pressure on existing political coalitions. Between 2000 and 2010, the number of Americans calling themselves white grew by only 1.2% as the overall population increased by 9.7%. In stark contrast, African-Americans in the population grew by 12.3%, individuals of mixed race by 32%, Latinos by 43% and Asian-Americans by 43.3%. As a result, whites in the population receded by 5.4 percentage points as these other groups grew, with Latinos accounting for more than half the growth during the first decade of the century (Humes et al. 2011). Every state in the union experienced an increase in its minority population. With particularly explosive growth among young minorities entering their childbearing years, the transformation of America into a majority–minority nation is on a fast track.[11]

These changes are a body blow to a political coalition dependent on white voters. Had only whites been eligible to vote in 2012, Mitt Romney would have won in a 20-point landslide. Barack Obama received only 39% of the white vote, several points less than the share Al Gore received in 2000 en route to a virtual tie in the Electoral College. But in 2012, it was good enough for a 51–48% win. The difference: whites made up 81% of the electorate in 2000 but only 72% twelve years later.[12]

Swift generational changes are occurring in tandem with these racial shifts to reorient the electorate away from the values and preferences of the center-right. The under-35 Millennial Generation hold a markedly different set of values from their parents and grandparents. Eighty million strong, they are, according to the Pew Research Center, "confident, self-expressive, liberal, upbeat and open to change" (Taylor and Keeter 2010). More educated and less religious than their predecessors—fully 26% claim no religious affiliation, compared with 13% of Baby Boomers at a comparable age[13]—Millennials are wary about people but more willing to trust government to address social problems and more likely to believe government should take action when problems arise. They are less likely than older generations to support a muscular foreign policy and more likely to embrace social moderation. They contain a larger share of self-identified liberals than their elders and, not surprisingly, they are more likely to affiliate with the Democratic Party (Taylor and Keeter 2010).

Rapid demographic change is the cornerstone of the argument made more than a decade ago by journalist John B. Judis and political scientist Ruy Teixeira (2002) that Democrats stand to gain permanently at the expense of the old Republican coalition as the population shifts in their direction. The Democratic majority they saw emerging at the turn of the century would rest on a post-industrial coalition of socially conscious, educated professionals living in new-economy metroplexes they call "Ideopolises," along with ethnic minorities, gays, single women and young people drawn to the Democratic Party for its openness to social diversity—essentially the coalition that Democrats had been *losing* with for 20 years. In time, Judis and Teixeira predicted the cultural values of an idea- and service-based economy would take hold, and the "bohemian" ethos of multicultural academic–commercial clusters centered around urban cores dominated by research universities and research-based industries would replace the liberal–conservative urban–suburban split of the postwar era (Judis and Teixeira 2002, 73). They predicted Democrats would dominate this demographic alignment.

Although it took longer than the authors anticipated, by 2008 evidence of their forecast was starting to emerge. Obama's surprising Virginia and North Carolina victories could be attributed to strength in post-industrial clusters in northern Virginia and North Carolina's Research Triangle, while he ran poorly in areas untouched by the new economy like Appalachia, or resistant to post-industrial values like metropolitan Salt Lake City. Indeed, when Obama bested Hillary Clinton for the Democratic nomination, he became the first Democrat of recent vintage with strength among professionals and intellectuals to emerge victorious over a primary opponent backed by traditional blue-collar constituencies. Similarly situated candidates in previous cycles—Howard Dean in 2004, Bill Bradley in 2000, Paul Tsongas in 1992, Gary Hart in 1984 and Ted Kennedy in 1980—were turned away, respectively, by John Kerry, Al Gore, Bill Clinton, Walter Mondale and Jimmy Carter, all with strength in the working-class electorate. To the extent that Obama appears alien to conservative working class whites, we have a measure of the vast cultural and experiential difference between them and the new economy voters who embraced Obama's call for hope and change.

Judis and Teixeira did not anticipate the collapse of the political middle, believing instead that the new Democratic majority would be a coalition of "progressive centrists." Accordingly, they missed the rise of the progressive movement circa 2003 and consequently did not address that movement's animating desire to break up the concentrated power that comes with concentrated wealth. However, progressive ideas should resonate naturally with the ethos of post-industrial Ideopolises and should particularly resonate with the core groups in the emerging coalition they describe: minorities, women and professionals who are part of the new information economy. Demographic changes could herald a Democratic majority that is also a progressive majority, if demographic changes alone were shaping our politics. But political demography is not the only force exerting exorbitant pressure on old political alignments.

Money

The right may be on the wrong side of population changes, but shrinking constituencies have not translated into empty coffers. In the post-*Citizens United* world, conservative candidates up and down the ballot have been able to rely on an outpouring of funds to support often aggressively negative advertising designed to shape political narratives and move public opinion in their direction. Mitt Romney and three affiliated advocacy groups supported by the likes of former Bush advisor Karl Rove and businessmen David and Charles Koch spent a total of $115 million on negative ads to advance Romney's candidacy—*before* the fall general election campaign began. Their combined expenditures dwarfed the $53 million spent by the Obama campaign and the pro-Obama political action committee Priorities USA on negative advertising during the same period.[14] Even in a divided country where many people have already chosen sides, negative messaging can serve to rally the faithful while persuading the nonaligned, particularly those who pay little attention to politics and are likely to absorb limited amounts of information.

It is also an approach with deep ties to the old media. Even as advertising strategies have grown to incorporate social media, saturating a market with the same message in order to reach the largest number of people is a twentieth-century idea. It is what television does best: indiscriminately flooding large populations with small, simple and repetitive bits of information from a single source. That we see hundreds of millions of dollars devoted to such efforts is a useful measure of how much power television still has—or how much those who make their livings from the proceeds of ad buys believe, or want to believe, it still has. In any event, television is still the largest expenditure for campaign money,[15] and as Table 1.1 indicates, campaign dollars flowing to television have increased exponentially during the life of the Reagan regime. As long as television continues to influence mass audiences as it did in the pre-Internet days, conservatives will have a potent vehicle to combat unfavorable demography.

There is, however, another side to big money, and that is the vast economic inequality that defines our time and poses a challenge to a center-right political coalition built around a preference for free market principles over active government. Income inequality declined from the end of World War II until the demise of the New Deal coalition, falling 7.4% between 1947 and 1968. Thereafter, it began to rise, returning to postwar levels by 1982 before blowing past them (Weinberg 1996; Ruffing 2013). The inflection point in income inequality coincided with the shift from center-left to center-right governance, and continued unabated through four decades of center-right administrations.

If conservatives were comfortable with this trend, consistent as it is with a free-market philosophy, they were relentless about blaming Washington for economic ills in an era of growing disparity. Every enduring political coalition has an adversary to rally its supporters, and in the Nixon–Reagan–Bush era that adversary has been government itself. When Ronald Reagan famously pronounced in his first inaugural that "government is not the solution to our problem; government is the problem," he was delineating the major fault line in American politics

TABLE 1.1 Major presidential campaign spending on television during the Reagan coalition era, in millions

Year	Republican	Democrat	Independent	Total
1984	25.0	25.0	–	50.0
1988	35.0	30.0	–	65.0
1992	38.5	35.0	40.0	113.5
1996	78.2	56.0	22.0	156.2
2000	63.0	45.0	–	108.0
2004	200.0	146.6	–	346.6
2008	128.0	250.0	–	378.0

Sources: Devlin (1985, 1989, 1993, 1997, 2001, 2005); Kaid (2009).

Note: Excludes spending by political parties and affiliated groups.

and positioning himself on the winning side, no less than when Bill Clinton, constrained by the same dynamics that propelled Reagan, somewhat disingenuously declared in his 1996 State of the Union address that "the era of big government is over." For better than three decades, with trust in government on the decline, private institutions were held in higher regard than public institutions and public solutions.

These attitudes had not changed appreciably when Barack Obama convinced Congress to pass the Affordable Care Act in 2010. Even though the legislation did not replace private insurance markets with government coverage, its detractors readily dubbed it a "big government solution," and their derision resonated with those whose skepticism about big government solutions had been shaped over decades of conservative governance and rhetoric. Anyone looking for ad hoc but compelling evidence that a revolution in public attitudes had not occurred could trumpet the unpopularity of the program among those who saw it as a case of government overreach.

But if decades of anti-government attitudes remained sticky, evidence of the political cost of economic inequality built over that same period exploded during the brief but dislocating experience of the Occupy Wall Street movement in the fall of 2011. Simmering resentment toward economic elites stemming from the crash of 2008, which contributed to the Tea Party movement a year earlier, was given a left-wing voice by protesters who demanded that attention be paid to how those with extreme wealth can write, perpetuate and live by a different set of rules to the detriment of everyone else. Although focusing more on the problem than on solutions, their collectivist sensibility did not preclude, and at times embraced, the possibility of new laws and regulations to address the glaring inequities that emerged during the Reagan regime.

Although reluctant to engage the electoral process, the Occupy movement reframed the political debate in the one way the right could not defend by giving the public a new adversary they dubbed the "one percent"—the super-rich who almost exclusively receive the benefits of the new economy. By default, this construct leaves everyone else—the 99 percent—in common cause against a new enemy. Efforts by conservatives to reframe the debate as a middle-class group of "53 percent" (the percentage of Americans who pay federal income taxes) pitted against the freeloading poor who, in the words of one advocacy group, have no "skin in the game," proved less enduring,[16] to say nothing of the self-imposed headaches this framing later caused Mitt Romney after he was caught on camera excoriating the selfish behavior of the other 47 percent. As winter set in and occupations were broken up across the country, Occupy Wall Street faded from the headlines, but the "99 percent" framing endured, taking its place alongside long established anti-government sentiment. America was now expressing anger about the excesses of both government and the marketplace.

In this context, Romney's emergence as the Republican Party's 2012 presidential nominee could not have been more ill timed. A venture capitalist with offshore accounts and a dogged determination not to let the public know the details of his personal wealth, Romney battled hard against the impression that he was alien to ordinary people, an "other" of a different sort than the African-American president with the odd-sounding name. In fact, if Obama generated cultural anxiety in older and whiter corners of the electorate, it is easy to see how Romney could have generated dissonance among those who found resonance in Occupy Wall Street's economic message. It is ironic, then, that the millions of dollars in negative messaging spent on behalf of Mitt Romney in the 2012 campaign were aimed at convincing working-class Americans to support the poster child for the one percent. Subtext reigned supreme in this presidential contest between a product of the country's changing demographics and a product of its economic inequities, two of the biggest drivers of political anxiety and instability.

Technology, time and space

In 2005, 8% of adult Internet users were on social networking sites. Within eight years, that figure had ballooned to 73%, including 90% of adults age 18–29.[17] Forty percent, and two-thirds of adults under 30, accessed social networking sites from their smartphones.[18] So much has been written about how technology is changing the way we relate to each other that it has become almost platitudinous to say that our understanding of time and distance has been turned on its head through the emergence of cell phones, webcams and related hardware, along with text messaging, social networking websites and related software.[19] In the information economy workplace, instant communication over great distances makes it possible to be at work without being physically present while blurring the distinction between work and private time. Words, voices or images of loved ones who are physically distant can be summoned at a moment's notice to appear on a host of screens. GPS devices ensure we are never lost but also never fully private.

Among political elites, these developments promote instability by upending long-established modalities for campaigning and governing. In Chapter 3, we will see how the emergence of social networking reshaped the Internet and spurred the development of an online political environment more far-reaching and sophisticated than anything we saw during the century's first decade, making twentieth-century assumptions about how to run political campaigns and govern the nation increasingly antiquated. As political practitioners learn how to apply new technology to old functions such as fundraising, advertising, messaging and mobilizing supporters, politics never takes a vacation.

Among the general population, Internet use and social networking are reshaping how people relate to the political process. In 2011, the Pew Research Internet Project found that Internet users are more likely to vote, attempt to influence the vote of a friend or relative, and attend political meetings than people who are not online. Facebook users—a group that now includes a supermajority of the adult population—are even more politically engaged than Internet users who do not frequent social media sites. This is especially true for frequent Facebook users, who at the time the study was conducted were still disproportionately young and female, two key groups in Obama's winning coalition (Hampton et al. 2011).

This uptick in political engagement stands in sharp contrast to the hallmark disaffection of the television age, which, as we discuss in Chapter 4, was the default condition during decades of center-right ascendancy. Although demobilizing the electorate may or may not have been a strategic imperative of the right in its early years, television viewing is correlated with diminished political and social engagement (Kerbel 1998), and the Nixon–Reagan–Bush political alignment was based heavily on television. Shifting patterns of media use and the behavioral changes they bring are forcing the right to adjust to a set of technological and social circumstances that are bearing down on an aging coalition.

The Case for Realignment

Political alignments are always under pressure from within and without, but they endure when they succeed in addressing the concerns of their core constituencies while maintaining broad-based appeal. They start to falter over time when confronted with new issues with which they are ill-prepared to engage, when they lose key partners or when they run out of ideas. The New Deal coalition held together during a protracted depression, a world war, the Korean War and the early Civil Rights movement, but lost energy as the South deserted over civil rights policies and the white working class over Vietnam-era domestic disorder and a push to equalize economic and social outcomes. The Reagan coalition survived the fall of the Soviet Union, record budget deficits, the high-tech boom and the September 11, 2001 terror attacks. However, the strain on political alignments caused by the disappearance of the political center, right-wing dominance of the Republican Party, demographic changes, generational shifts, vast income inequality and the accelerating effects of technology have undermined the ability of Republicans to function as a governing party, and threaten their national viability in a changing electorate.

From this perspective, the electoral system is ripe for realignment—if it is in fact justifiable to think in such terms. Political scientists have long believed that some elections serve as inflection points in the alignment of groups that determine political outcomes, but they are divided over the causes of these shifts, whether they occur during single elections or over time and if they happen with predictable regularity. Sixty years ago, V. O. Key (1955) offered a theory of critical elections characterized by a sharp break in the voting patterns of the past that persisted for several subsequent electoral cycles. Walter Dean Burnham (1970) suggested that critical realignments have occurred infrequently but regularly throughout American history at times when the coalitions composing the major parties found themselves unable to confront serious social or economic problems they were not originally constituted to address.

Five elections occurring at surprisingly regular intervals over time could be said to have fulfilled these requirements. Andrew Jackson's 1828 election ushered in the first era of mass politics and ended the process of presidential selection by congressional elites. Abraham Lincoln's 1860 election saw the demise of the Whigs, the reshaping of the Democratic Party and the rise of the Republican Party in response to secession and slavery. William McKinley's 1896 election reaffirmed Republican dominance as the party of industrialization in a triumph over agrarian interests on tariffs and the gold standard. Franklin D. Roosevelt's 1932 election arose from the Great Depression and toppled the Republicans in a contest over government's response to economic crisis (Brady 1982). Ronald Reagan's 1980 election, born of a stagnant economy and years of social unrest, ended the New Deal coalition as a national electoral force and ushered in a long period of center-right governance (Meffert, Norpoth and Ruhil 2001).

But there is no prototype critical election among these five; each has unique characteristics that defy generalization. Lincoln's election was the only one to catapult a minor party to major party status; McKinley's did not even realize a change in the dominant party. The McKinley electorate was highly polarized, whereas the electorate in 1932 was not, and Roosevelt's realignment did not evidence the same geographic divisions as its predecessors (Brady 1982). Turnout wasn't particularly high in 1932, but FDR's election did lead to dramatic policy change; on the other hand, turnout was high in 1896, but McKinley's election reinforced more than it changed existing policy (Mayhew 2002). Reagan's election came 14 years before Republicans were able to fashion a House majority, did not coincide with a dramatic event like civil war or depression and was not associated with a steep boost in Republican self-identification in the electorate.

Furthermore, scholars disagree over whether critical realignments are national phenomena or are driven by lasting regional changes (Nardulli 1995), and whether realignments occur after critical elections when the victorious party has an opportunity to consolidate its gains (Weatherford 2002; Hurley 1991) or over a series of cycles leading up to the critical election (Campbell 2006; Waterman 1990). Critics of the critical election model, such as political scientists David Mayhew (2002) and Richard L. McCormick (1986), feel the concept straightjackets the ability to recognize gradual movement in the electorate that contributes to lasting change.

The idea that a party system can experience a "secular realignment"—an enduring shift over several election cycles without a critical election—loosens the conceptual straightjacket and goes a long way toward explaining what happened in the 1960s and 1970s and what is happening again today with the disappearance of the political center. The electorate of the late 1960s was amenable to electing New Deal liberals, as it had done in seven of the previous nine presidential contests before Richard Nixon narrowly defeated Hubert Humphrey in 1968 in an election marred by violence abroad and at home. So close was the election and so turbulent the circumstances, it would be reasonable to attribute Humphrey's loss to the problems of the moment rather than to see it as a harbinger of a lasting shift to the right. After all, Democrats maintained control of Congress and remained strong at the state level in the wake of Humphrey's slender defeat.

Hindsight permits us to view 1968 as the year the New Deal coalition had run out of steam at the presidential level. If not a critical election, it was a tipping point. Democrats continued nominating candidates in the New Deal mold for years afterwards, running on platforms supportive of government programs and attendant taxation, but voters rejected them by wide margins. Yet, Democrats maintained control of the House for another 26 years. When Republicans finally conquered Congress in 1994, it was in part because they were victorious in a majority of southern districts for the first time. A "staggered realignment" that had started at the presidential level in the late 1960s was finally complete (Campbell 2006), a product of two decades of weakening party ties (Abramowitz and Saunders 1998; Ladd 1991).

Post-Reagan, the parties gradually became more ideologically distinct than they had been during the New Deal years as Republicans became increasingly conservative. This had a clarifying effect on party identification, as voters were better able to select a party based on their ideological leanings and policy choices, facilitating a sorting of partisan preferences that extended the long secular realignment to the right (Abramowitz and Saunders 1998). Because of the time involved and the uneven nature of the realignment, the pendulum shift to the right is easier to identify in hindsight than when it was happening. The same is probably true today, although in Chapter 2 we will engage our understanding of what happened to the New Deal coalition to clarify our present pendulum position in the long arc of political change.

Realignment and Technology

The 1968 election wasn't simply noteworthy as the year the New Deal coalition unraveled. It was also the year that Richard Nixon completed his unlikely comeback with the help of a sophisticated television campaign, making it the year that television—a fixture in politics since 1952—came into its own as a political medium. This delay between the introduction of new media technology and the perfection of its political use has repeated throughout history in an uncanny cycle coinciding with the coalition shifts associated with most critical elections. There is a noteworthy correlation between the maturation of communication technology and the Jackson, Lincoln, Roosevelt and Nixon elections. Each of these elections and the regimes they ushered in was facilitated by the use of a new technology in a novel and creative way that would later define how that technology is used in politics: Jackson and mass printing; Lincoln and the telegraph; FDR and radio; Nixon and television. In subsequent chapters we will consider whether we can add Obama and the Internet to this list.[20]

Jackson and mass printing

The Jacksonian realignment of 1828 pre-dated the age of mass communication and was as much the product of successful institutional development as technological change. But it was precipitated by improved printing technology that led to falling printing costs and the consequent explosion of newspaper publishing at a time of growing literacy and expanding suffrage. Jackson understood better than his adversaries how to harness these changes for maximum political effect.

After being denied the presidency in 1824 despite having won the most popular and electoral votes, Jackson recognized the need to upend a presidential selection process driven by a closed congressional elite of which he was not a member. His solution was to tap into the expanding franchise and rising literacy rates by building a mass-based party with a national network of partisan newspapers as its nerve center (Baldasty 1992). Americans in the early nineteenth century loved to read, and literacy rates higher than those of any European nation drove technology costs down while making printing more efficient (Leonard 1995). In the 1820s, improved printing technology enabled newspapers to spread to the most remote frontier towns in what could be regarded as the country's first information revolution (Starr 2004). In keeping with the custom of the time, most of these newspapers openly declared their partisanship, so it was unremarkable that Jackson would seek to purchase or establish dozens of papers run by supportive editors. What made Jackson's efforts revolutionary was his understanding of how to turn a multitude of local newspapers built on cheap, efficient printing technology into the basis for a national political party organization.

Jackson's strategic novelty rested with the technique of "management"—using affiliated newspapers to coordinate communication among the state party organizations and grassroots officials that formed the backbone of Jackson's national political network (Shaw 1981; Smith 1977). Jackson used his newspapers to synchronize campaign operations, circulate a unified campaign message, generate grassroots excitement and mobilize voters, building an apparatus capable of performing the core political functions of a first-of-its-kind mass democratic party (Keller 2007), and he did it in the absence of a true mass medium of communication.

This makes Andrew Jackson a low-tech precursor to the netroots: shut out of an elite national power structure, he faced the daunting dilemma of trying to obtain power from the outside. He had at his disposal a recent technological advance, which—like the Internet circa 2003—was broadly available to anyone else who wished to use it for political purposes. But nobody had. Like early twenty-first-century bloggers, Jackson was a first mover, and in part by using technology to successfully implement his vision he was able to define his political time.

Lincoln and the telegraph

Samuel Morse ushered in the age of mass communication in 1844 when he electronically telegraphed the words "What Hath God Wrought?" over an experimental line between Washington and Baltimore, but almost two decades would pass before Abraham Lincoln became the first president to figure out how to use the telegraph to maximum political advantage. In the intervening years, the telegraph had facilitated dramatic changes in news dissemination, marked by the decline of the partisan press of Jackson's time and the rise of a commercial press characterized by cheap newspapers powered by advertising revenues, the formation of the Associated Press wire service that permitted widespread and cost-efficient information dissemination, and the rudimentary professionalization of journalism that included the separation of reporting and editorial functions (Kaplan 2002; Douglas 1999; Summers 1994; Baldasty 1992).

No longer partisan mouthpieces, editors and reporters were becoming independent agents of news reporting. Their value to the political class was undiminished, but techniques were now required to win their influence. Where Jackson used the technology available to him to organize the decentralized grassroots, Lincoln used the technology of his day to amplify the power of the presidency. His approach, recognizable to anyone familiar with contemporary politics, was top-down: monopolize the flow of information available to the public in order to exercise command over the messages people received.

His reason for doing this, of course, was the Civil War. Other presidents had served during the telegraph era, but none faced anything resembling the challenges posed by secession and unprecedented military mobilization. To this end, Lincoln became the first president to employ the telegraph and the wire service that had developed around it to get a favorable message to as many people as possible while blocking his political opponents from doing the same (Carwardine 2006). In the process, he built the Republican regime that would dominate politics for decades after the Civil War.

Lincoln's insight into the political ramifications of the telegraph was that the president could have a monopoly over information provided he exercised a comparable monopoly over the technology of information dissemination. Where future presidents would employ less draconian means to this end, Lincoln, through his war powers, took statutory control of the American Telegraph Company, permitting the administration tremendous command over news coming from Civil War battlefields. Because Lincoln's opposition did not control its own telegraph, Associated Press stories became the official version of events.

To ensure those stories were reported the way he wished, Lincoln employed an access strategy that would also be emulated by a number of his successors. Lincoln engaged in what could be regarded as a kind of nineteenth-century attempt at spin control built around maintaining good relations with top-level Associated Press reporters. He cozied up to Associated Press Washington Bureau Chief Lawrence Gobright, offering him exclusives in the knowledge that they would be favorably reported and telegraphed nationwide to appear prominently in newspapers (Carwardine 2006). Lincoln understood how the combination of mass media technology and an independent or quasi-independent press necessitates media control strategies, and shrewdly used the prevailing technology to monopolize the flow of information about his administration as no-one had before.

FDR and radio

Three presidents had made radio broadcasts prior to Franklin D. Roosevelt. Warren Harding was the first, but his broadcasts were of little consequence because radio in the early 1920s was the domain of hobbyists and mariners rather than mass audiences (Ponder 1998). His successor's term coincided with the rapid growth of commercial radio and, despite his reputation for stoic silence, Calvin Coolidge was actually quite the radio star, with a resonant voice that made him one of the most liked radio personalities of his day (Winfield 1990). But Coolidge saw radio as a new medium that could serve traditional political purposes rather than as a transformational medium that could create new political opportunities, so his radio appearances took the form of formal addresses and prepared speeches (Delli Carpini 1993). He succeeded in reaching a lot of people with his voice, but nothing more.

If there was ever a president who needed a breakthrough medium to help him out of political trouble, it was Coolidge's successor Herbert Hoover. Ironically, despite having had a key role in early government regulatory decisions about radio when he was Commerce Secretary in the Coolidge administration, Hoover had limited understanding of the medium as a tool of mass communication, and radio was unkind to him (Jansky 1957). Hoover actually made more radio broadcasts in his single term than FDR would make during his first four years, yet radio was never part of Hoover's governing strategy and he gave no indication that he understood how radio could be a vehicle to mobilize the country behind him (Liebovich 1994; Delli Carpini 1993).

But his successor knew. Franklin D. Roosevelt had used radio during his stints as New York governor and Assistant Secretary of the Navy. So when he reached the Oval Office he knew precisely how to reap the political benefits awaiting the first person to figure out that radio was a medium that could move people—and lots of them—by manufacturing a sense of intimacy with the listener. The political magic behind FDR's signature "fireside chats" came from the informal, direct way Roosevelt spoke with his audience. This no doubt sounds simplistic to generations raised on electronic media but it was revolutionary in its day. No president in history had ever presented himself the way Roosevelt did on the radio. Presidents had been distant figures who spoke in official settings using formal language. Roosevelt addressed his radio listeners as "my friends."

Radio broadcasts were employed as part of a larger media strategy which sought the same objectives as every media strategy employed by every astute president who ever served in a mass media regime: control your message; transmit it effectively; and dominate the national agenda. To borrow language from the television age, Roosevelt's fireside chats were "media events"—public rituals manufactured by FDR and his advisers to sell the president's agenda by building a bond of trust between the public and the president (Ryfe 1999; Steele 1985). The timing of his addresses was carefully chosen and the frequency carefully guarded so as not to risk overexposure. Administration surrogates including cabinet secretaries and First Lady Eleanor Roosevelt reinforced the president's message through carefully crafted public statements (Ryfe 1999). The result was a degree of message coordination and control unparalleled in the history of American politics at that time.

Recognizing that radio exists in the realm of illusion (a recognition that fuels the success of contemporary political talk radio), FDR was able to craft an on-air persona around the deception that a disembodied voice can be an intimate companion. Radio professionals understood this dynamic, but Roosevelt was the first national leader to apply it to politics. By recognizing that paradoxically only a mass medium could create a sense of intimacy, Roosevelt found in the emotional pull of radio broadcasts a powerful political resource for rallying the public behind his agenda and solidifying the New Deal realignment.

Nixon and television

Dwight Eisenhower was the first president to embrace television. John F. Kennedy was the first telegenic president. But Richard Nixon—dour and serious—was the first to reinvent himself on television and in the process unlock the medium's transformational qualities while laying the groundwork for the coming period of Republican dominance. This took place 16 years after Ike had run his first television ad campaign.

A failed presidential candidate in 1960 and the victim of television's unforgiving lens during his ill-fated televised debates with John F. Kennedy, Richard Nixon in 1968 was damaged goods. As political handlers are inclined to say, he had high negatives—people disliked him and didn't trust him. His ambition unabated, if Nixon wanted to stage a political comeback he would have to do it as a different person than the dark, shadowy figure people remembered from the 1960 contest and his years as Eisenhower's vice president. Television gave him the vehicle to do exactly that.

Nixon's strategy centered on convincing voters that he had fundamentally changed—that he had become a "New Nixon," a more accessible, agreeable version of his former self—and to do it without actually changing anything save for the way he would be perceived. The strategy was at its core a dishonest one, because the New Nixon projected on television screens was deeply at odds with the person behind it. But Nixon and his shrewd advisors understood that television invites deception and untruths can be spun convincingly with the proper degree of control over production values.

The "New Nixon" was a creation of the television studio, where the candidate was sequestered so that every element of his appearance could be customized to conform to the fabrication he was creating for the American voter. This strategy was the product of a group of hardened advisers—advertising men, lawyers, media consultants and speechwriters—who understood the dynamics of television marketing and weren't afraid to treat the political campaign like the roll-out of a repackaged but fundamentally unchanged product. In order to create a relaxed, spontaneous Nixon, they paradoxically had to exercise control over every element of his image, which meant throwing out the book on how to run for president and writing a new one suited to the potentialities of television. Open campaign forums were banned. Rallies and speeches to large crowds were dropped. Reporters, with their potentially challenging questions, were locked out. Everything was stage-managed (Donovan and Scherer 1992). But nothing about the candidate fundamentally changed. He remained as cranky as ever.

The success of the Nixon campaign shaped the way campaigns and officials would act during the television era, for Nixon and his advisers had demonstrated that television affords skillful politicians the opportunity to turn statecraft into stagecraft and manipulate public opinion. During this period, the public would become increasingly likely to make political judgments based on the personal qualities of candidates, believing through the sensory realism of the medium that the image they saw of the candidates projected over the air captured the reality of the person (Keeter 1987; and Lang 1956, 1968). Elections would more than ever turn on matters of candidate character, but not their real character as much as television's version of their character, which the successful ones knew how to manage.

Television did not invent image-making but it did necessitate it, so the television era rewarded politicians who could tell a resonant story, regardless of the facts. More often than not, those stories advanced the center-right objectives of lower taxes, less regulation, muscular foreign policy and "family values." Ronald Reagan, the most natural television practitioner and one of the most carefully scripted presidents in history (Han 2001), was a master at stage-managing television images with the intention of manipulating public perceptions of political reality (Covington 1993; Donovan and Scherer 1992; Paletz and Guthriel 1987; Glaros and Miroff 1983). So when Reagan wanted to avoid political fallout for cutting health care funds for the elderly, he appeared at a ribbon-cutting ceremony at a retirement home and basked in the televised imagery that communicated how much he cared for the welfare of seniors. As a result, you couldn't convince people that Reagan had cut the funding, because when what we see contradicts what we hear the pictures win out. As researchers Kurt and Gladys Lang noted from work conducted during television's early days, "With all its magic, television remains a mass and not a face-to-face medium of communication; yet the belief in the intimacy of television has its own far-reaching consequences … The viewer cannot comprehend the 'real' personal qualities of the familiar face with which he is confronted, but he may believe he can" (Lang and Lang 1956, 112).

It is not entirely surprising, then, to find that in the years since Nixon's breakthrough the American public has been, in Seymour Martin Lipset's (1985) terminology, programmatically more liberal than most of the people it elected to the presidency. Voters who disagreed with elements of Reagan's policy agenda twice contributed to his electoral victories, once in a landslide (Alger 1987). So it is that Nixon should be credited as the transformational figure whose mastery of television produced the blueprint for two generations of conservative governance. Ronald Reagan may have had a more natural feel for show business and have been better in front of the camera, but he owes a debt of gratitude to Nixon, who demonstrated how to use television to sell something that wasn't there.

Obama and the Internet?

Whether or not the 2008 election inflected American politics permanently to the left, it marked the arrival of the Internet as a campaign medium as powerful as those that came before. History will remember Obama's Internet presence as a watershed in media technology on a par with Nixon's ruthless embrace of television, FDR's strategic understanding of radio, Lincoln's mastery of the telegraph and Jackson's shrewd use of inexpensive printing. Without the Internet, it is hard to imagine how Obama would have twice mobilized a young, multicultural electorate. For that matter, without the Internet it is hard to see how he would have outlasted Hillary Clinton and won the Democratic nomination in the first place.

We don't know yet if Obama's experience belongs on this short list of technology-assisted realignments. We will offer an argument in Chapter 2 for why Obama might rightfully claim a qualified place on this list. However, even if Obama's election turns out to be an aberration rather than the start of a realignment, the remarkable success of Obama for America should be appreciated as a piece of a larger revolution in online politics. The nature of the medium mandates as much.

Until the Internet, the long march of media technology perfected the ability of a small number of agents to communicate a message to large populations. The telegraph introduced instantaneous transmission, radio added sound and television added pictures. But the Internet is built on an entirely different architecture. It is the first mass medium since the Industrial Revolution to operate on a decentralized platform, making possible a panoply of interactions: one-to-one through email, instant messaging and texts; one-to-many through email blasts, blogs and personal websites; many-to-many through community websites and social media. This architecture guarantees widespread interaction. Unlike the false intimacy of television, the Internet encourages social action through networks of virtual relationships.

Online activist communities have developed on both sides of the ideological spectrum, but the progressive netroots—pioneers in what has grown into the nexus of online political activists and organizations that constitute the Internet Left—proved a particularly good match to the Internet's decentralized structure. They embraced the Internet's open architecture and built multiple overlapping communities organically and from the bottom up. They were first movers before Obama: the netroots were organizing for political action before most people knew who Barack Obama was, and as we will see in Chapter 3, the Obama campaign was in important ways an outgrowth of Howard Dean's rudimentary netroots effort. The netroots were blogging about politics long before Twitter, mobilizing supporters before Facebook. Although they often share goals with the president, their relationship with him has not always been easy. Any claim Obama might make to being a transformational figure would arguably be shared to some degree with the work of these activists before and during his presidency.

Where Jackson recognized that the secret to inexpensive printing was its ability to support a national political organization, where Lincoln understood that the secret of the telegraph rested with how it permitted him to dominate national discourse, where Roosevelt knew that the secret of radio resided in its ability to communicate intimacy and mobilize a nation, and where Nixon comprehended that the secret of television lay in its capacity to sell false images, the progressive netroots, like Barack Obama, know that the secret of the Internet is its ability to decentralize power and build networks, as they have been doing for over a decade.

The Internet remains a young medium. It still competes with television for political prominence. And the shape of the next dominant political coalition remains uncertain. But if we are in a realigning period when a new politics will replace the vacancy in the center, there should be no question that the Internet puts an emerging progressive movement in the middle of the action.

Notes

1 Thompson, Krissah. 2012. "Americans Elect Calls It Quits." *Washington Post Election 2012 Blog*, May 17. Retrieved from www.washingtonpost.com/.../post.../post/americans-elect-calls-it-quits/2012/05/17/glQAxSSsWU_blog.html (no longer available online).
2 Vogel, Kenneth P. 2012. "Americans Elect Without a Nominee." *Politico*, May 15. Retrieved from www.politico.com/story/2012/05/americans-elect-without-a-nominee-076306; and Weigel, Dave. 2012. "Nobody for President." *Slate*, May 15. Retrieved from www.slate.com/articles/news_and_politics/politics/2012/05/americans_elect_an_inevitable_35_million_failure_.html.
3 Weigel (2012) advised Americans Elect's founders, "Do not launch by telling the *New York Times* you've got 'serious hedge fund' money."
4 Vogel (2012) quotes Democratic Party operative David Axlerod as calling the process "uber-democracy meets back room bosses."
5 Americans Elect spent resources obtaining ballot access before it had a candidate and presupposed grassroots excitement would develop once it did. See Cillizza, Chris and Aaron Blake. 2012. "Americans Elect and the Death of the Third Party Movement."

The Washington Post, May 18. Retrieved from www.washingtonpost.com/blogs/the-fix/post/americans-elect-and-the-death-of-the-third-party-movement/2012/05/17/gIQAIzNKXU_blog.html.

6 When six-term Senator Richard Lugar lost his 2012 primary to a conservative activist, CNN reported that Indiana Republicans were "punishing him for the qualities he considered assets: seniority, expertise in foreign policy and a penchant for bipartisan cooperation." See Walsh, Deirdre and Dana Bash. "Longest-serving GOP Senator Loses Primary Fight." *CNN*, May 9. Retrieved from www.cnn.com/2012/05/08/politics/indiana-republican-primary.

7 Progressive bloggers in particular have a long-running in-joke about a reporting philosophy they refer to as "broderism." Referencing David Broder, the late "dean" of the Washington, DC press corps, it refers to any extreme example of false equivalence made by mainstream reporters. In 2007, "broderism" was entered in urbandictionary.com and defined as "the worship of bipartisanship for its own sake, combined with a fake 'pox on both their houses' attitude." See urbandictionary.com, at www.urbandictionary.com/define.php?term=broderism.

8 This period covers the arc of the last two enduring American political coalitions. The period 1933–1968, bracketed by the New Deal presidency of Franklin D. Roosevelt and the Great Society presidency of Lyndon Johnson, saw the emergence and expansion of an advanced social welfare state and what Dwight D. Eisenhower termed the military–industrial complex. The period 1969–2008 witnessed a center-right reaction to the New Deal, which reached its rhetorical zenith during the Reagan administration when the president recast the image of the federal government as a behemoth to be tamed in the interest of unleashing individual initiative rather than as a source of solutions to collective problems.

9 Significantly, polarized worldviews do not need to imply programmatic polarization among the general public. The breakdown of consensus among political elites has not coincided with mass breakdown of consensus on political issues, just as the endurance of majority political opinion on key issues has not undermined the emergence of incompatible elite worldviews. For instance, an April 2013 *Washington Post*–ABC News Poll revealed majority support for a path to citizenship for undocumented immigrants, a ban on assault weapons and opposition to budget cuts brought about by the sequester. That same poll found seven in ten Americans believed the Republican Party was out of touch with the concerns of most people. But these attitudes did not register in the actions or publicly expressed attitudes of those who composed the Republican Party-in-government. See *The Washington Post* at www.washingtonpost.com/page/2010-2019/WashingtonPost/2013/04/16/National-Politics/Polling/release_226.xml.

10 It is interesting to note that the disintegration of the conservative coalition mirrors—in reverse—the rise of that coalition in the 1980s. Southern whites were the initial group to defect from the New Deal coalition over the issue of race, followed by a broader group of white managerial and working-class voters who soured on big government solutions to social and economic problems. Now, many of those voters have abandoned the Republican Party, leaving Republicans increasingly dependent on white southerners and their lingering adherence to old social and economic structures.

11 See Brownstein, Ronald. 2011. "The Next America." *National Journal Online*, April 1. Retrieved from www.nationaljournal.com/next-america.

12 NBC News. 2012. Election Results. Retrieved from elections.nbcnews.com/ns/politics/2012/all/president/. See also Pew Research Center. 2012. "Inside Obama's Sweeping Victory." Retrieved from www.pewresearch.org/2008/11/05/inside-obamas-sweeping-victory.

13 Millennials are also less likely than older Americans to attend religious services or claim that religion is important in their lives. See Pew Research Center. 2010. "Religion Among the Millennials: Less Religiously Active Than Older Americans, But Fairly Traditional In

Other Ways." Retrieved from www.pewforum.org/2010/02/17/religion-among-the-millennials.
14 Figures are as of August 1, 2012 and are from Kantar Media/CMAG as reported in *The Washington Post* at www.washingtonpost.com/wp-srv/special/politics/track-presidential-campaign-ads-2012/.
15 The Federal Election Commission reports that through October 2012, the Obama and Romney campaigns combined spent 44% of their funds on media placement and production, far greater than online advertising, payroll, direct mail, travel and supplies.
16 The quote is attributed to Ronald Morternsen of citizensfortaxfairness.org. See McKitrick, Cathy. 2011. "'53 Percent' Takes on '99 Percent' Occupy Movement." *Salt Lake Tribune*, November 3. Retrieved from www.sltrib.com/sltrib/money/52826016-79/percent-tax-income-pay.html.csp. Perhaps more ominous for conservatives was the intensity of the reaction against Mitt Romney's secretly recorded diatribe about the non-Federal taxpaying 47 percent of the population derided by the candidate as dependents of the state.
17 Figures are from the Pew Research Center Internet Project Social Networking Fact Sheet, Library Survey, July 18–September 30, 2013. Retrieved from www.pewinternet.org/fact-sheets/social-networking-fact-sheet/.
18 Figures are from the Pew Research Center Internet Project Social Networking Fact Sheet, Pew Internet Spring Tracking Survey, March 15–April 3, 2012. Retrieved from www.pewinternet.org/fact-sheets/social-networking-fact-sheet/.
19 Social networking effects are most dramatic for young people and span every facet of social activity from political participation and civic involvement to friendships and dating. For a thorough overview of the relationship between young people and social media, see Lenhart et al. (2010). Other research has found that frequent use of social networking sites for interpersonal communication is associated with greater wellbeing and stronger social identity, and can be instrumental in the formation of social identities. See Wang et al. (2014); Jenkins-Guarnieri et al. (2013); Anderson et al. (2012).
20 A more detailed version of this argument may be found in Kerbel (2009, 15–38). Portions of that discussion are excerpted here.

References

Abramowitz, Alan I. and Kyle L. Saunders. 1998. "Ideological Realignment in the U.S. Electorate." *Journal of Politics* 60: 634–652.

Alger, Dean. 1987. "Television, Perceptions of Reality and the Presidential Election of '84." *PS: Political Science & Politics* 20: 49–57.

Anderson, Beth, Patrick Fagan, Tom Woodnutt, Thomas Chamorro-Premuzic. 2012. "Facebook Psychology: Popular Questions Answered by Research." *Psychology of Popular Media Culture* 1: 23–37.

Baldasty, Gerald J. 1992. *The Commercialization of News in the Nineteenth Century*. Madison, WI: University of Wisconsin Press.

Brady, David. 1982. "Congressional Party Realignment and Transformation of Public Policy in Three Realignment Eras." *American Journal of Political Science* 26: 333–360.

Burnham, Walter Dean. 1970. *Critical Elections and the Mainsprings of American Politics*. New York: Norton.

Campbell, James E. 2006. "Party Systems and Realignments in the United States, 1868–2004." *Social Science History* 30: 359–386.

Carwardine, Richard. 2006. "Abraham Lincoln and the Fourth Estate: The White House and the Press during the American Civil War." *American Nineteenth-Century History* 7: 1–27.

Covington, Cary R., Kent Kroeger, J.D. Woodard. 1993. "Shaping a Candidate's Image in the Press: Ronald Reagan and the 1980 Presidential Election." *Political Research Quarterly* 46: 783–798.

Delli Carpini, Michael X. 1993. "Radio's Political Past." *Media Studies Journal* 7: 23–35.

Devlin, L. Patrick. 1985. "Campaign Commercials." *Political Persuasion* 45: 45–50.

Devlin, L. Patrick. 1989. "Contrasts in Presidential Campaign Commercials of 1988." *American Behavioral Scientist* 32: 389–414.

Devlin, L. Patrick. 1993. "Contrasts in Presidential Campaign Commercials of 1992." *American Behavioral Scientist* 37: 272–290.

Devlin, L. Patrick. 1997. "Contrasts in Presidential Campaign Commercials of 1996." *American Behavioral Scientist* 40: 1058–1084.

Devlin, L. Patrick. 2001. "Contrasts in Presidential Campaign Commercials of 2000." *American Behavioral Scientist* 44: 2338–2369.

Devlin, L. Patrick. 2005. "Contrasts in Presidential Campaign Commercials of 2004." *American Behavioral Scientist* 49: 279–313.

Donovan, Robert J. and Ray Scherer. 1992. *Unsilent Revolution: Television News and American Public Life, 1948–1991*. New York: Cambridge University Press.

Douglas, George H. 1999. *The Golden Age of Newspapers*. Westport, CT: Greenwood.

Gilens, Martin. 2012. *Affluence and Influence: Economic Inequality and Political Power in America*. Princeton, NJ: Princeton University Press.

Glaros, Roberta and Bruce Miroff. 1983. "Watching Ronald Reagan: Viewers' Reactions to the President on Television." *Congress and the Presidency* 10: 25–46.

Hacker, Jacob S. and Paul Pierson. 2010. *Winner-Take-All Politics: How Washington Made the Rich Richer—And Turned Its Back on the Middle Class*. New York: Simon & Schuster.

Hampton, Keith, Lauren Sessions Goulet, Lee Rainie and Kristen Purcell. 2011. "Social Networking Sites and Our Lives." Washington, DC: Pew Research Center, Pew Research Internet Project. Retrieved from www.pewinternet.org/2011/06/16/social-networking-sites-and-our-lives.

Han, Lori Cox. 2001. *Governing From Center Stage: White House Communications Strategies during the Television Age of Politics*. Cresskill, NJ: Hampton.

Humes, Karen R., Nicholas A. Jones and Roberto R. Ramirez. 2011. "Overview of Race and Hispanic Origin: 2010." *U.S. Census Bureau 2010 Census Briefs*: 1–5.

Hurley, Patricia A. 1991. "Partisan Representation, Realignment, and the Senate in the 1980s." *Journal of Politics* 53: 3–33.

Jansky, C. M., Jr. 1957. "The Contribution of Herbert Hoover to Broadcasting." *Journal of Broadcasting* 3: 241–249.

Jenkins-Guarnieri, Michael, Stephen L. Wright and Brian D. Johnson. 2013. "The Interrelationships among Attachment Style, Personality Traits, Interpersonal Competency, and Facebook Use." *Psychology of Popular Media Culture* 2: 117–131.

Judis, John B. and Ruy Teixeira. 2002. *The Emerging Democratic Majority*. New York: Scribner.

Kaid, Lynda Lee. 2009. "Changing and Staying the Same: Communication in Campaign 2008." *Journalism Studies* 10: 417–423.

Kaplan, Richard L. 2002. *Politics and the American Press: The Rise of Objectivity, 1865–1920*. New York: Cambridge University Press.

Keeter, Scott. 1987. "The Illusion of Intimacy: Television and the Role of Candidate Personal Qualities in Voter Choice." *Public Opinion Quarterly* 51: 344–358.

Keller, Morton. 2007. *America's Three Regimes: A New Political History*. New York: Oxford University Press.

Kerbel, Matthew R. 1998. *Remote and Controlled: Media Politics in a Cynical Age*. Boulder, CO: Westview.

Kerbel, Matthew R. 2009. *Netroots: Online Progressives and the Transformation of American Politics*. Boulder, CO: Paradigm.

Key, V. O., Jr. 1955. "A Theory of Critical Elections." *Journal of Politics* 17: 3–18.

Ladd, Everett Carll. 1991. "Like Waiting for Godot: The Uselessness of 'Realignment' for Understanding Change in Contemporary American Politics." In *The End of Realignment?: Interpreting American Electoral Eras*, edited by Byron E. Shafer, 24–36. Madison, WI: University of Wisconsin Press.

Lang, Kurt and Gladys Engel Lang. 1956. "The Television Personality in Politics: Some Considerations." *Public Opinion Quarterly* 20: 103–112.

Lang, Kurt and Gladys Engel Lang. 1968. *Politics and Television*. Chicago, IL: Quadrangle.

Lenhart, Amanda, Kristen Purcell, Aaron Smith and Kathryn Zickuhr. 2010. "Social Media and Mobile Internet Use Among Teens and Young Adults." Washington, DC: Pew Research Center, The Pew Internet and American Life Project. Retrieved from www.pewinternet.org/files/old-media/Files/Reports/2010/PIP_Social_Media_and_Young_Adults_Report_Final_with_toplines.pdf.

Leonard, Thomas C. 1995. *News for All: America's Coming-of-Age with the Press*. New York: Oxford University Press.

Liebovich, Louis. 1994. *Bylines in Despair: Herbert Hoover, the Great Depression, and the U.S. News Media*. Westport, CT: Praeger.

Lipset, Seymour Martin. 1985. "The Elections, the Economy, and Public Opinion: 1984." *PS* 18: 28–38.

Mayhew, David. 2002. *Electoral Realignments: A Critique of an American Genre*. New Haven, CT: Yale University Press.

McCormick, Richard L. 1986. "Walter Dean Burnham and 'The System of 1896.'" *Social Science History* 10: 245–262.

Meffert, Michael F., Helmut Norpoth and Anirudh V. S. Ruhil. 2001. "Realignment and Macropartisanship." *American Political Science Review* 95: 953–962.

Nardulli, Peter F. 1995. "The Concept of a Critical Realignment, Electoral Behavior, and Political Change." *American Political Science Review* 89: 10–22.

Paletz, David L. and K. Kendall Guthriel. 1987. "Three Faces of Ronald Reagan." *Journal of Communication* 37: 7–23.

Ponder, Stephen. 1998. *Managing the Press: Origins of the Media Presidency, 1897–1933*. New York: St. Martin's.

Ruffing, Kathy. 2013. *'Gini Index' From Census Confirms Rising Inequality Over Four Decades*. Research Report. Washington, DC: Center on Budget and Policy Priorities. Retrieved from www.cbpp.org/blog/gini-index-from-census-confirms-rising-inequality-over-four-decades.

Ryfe, David. 1999. "Franklin Roosevelt and the Fireside Chats." *Journal of Communication* 49: 80–103.

Shaw, Donald Lewis. 1981. "At the Crossroads: Change and Continuity in American Press News, 1820–1860." *Journalism History* 8: 38–50.

Smith, Culver G. 1977. *The Press, Politics, and Patronage*. Athens, GA: University of Georgia Press.

Starr, Paul. 2004. *The Creation of the Media: The Origins of Modern Communication*. New York: Basic Books.

Steele, Richard W. 1985. *Propaganda in an Open Society: The Roosevelt Administration and the Media, 1933–1941*. Westport, CT: Greenwood.

Summers, Mark Wahlgren. 1994. *The Press Gang: Newspapers and Politics, 1850–1878*. Chapel Hill, NC: University of North Carolina Press.
Taylor, Paul and Scott Keeter, eds. 2010. *Millennials: Confident, Connected, Open to Change*. Research Report. Washington, DC: Pew Research Center. Retrieved from www.pewsocialtrends.org/2010/02/24/millennials-confident-connected-open-to-change.
Wang, Jin-Liang, Linda A. Jackson, Gaskin James, Haizhen Wang. 2014. "The Effects of Social Networking Site (SNS) Use on College Students' Friendship and Well-being." *Computers in Human Behavior* 37: 299–336.
Waterman, Richard W. 1990. "Institutional Realignment: The Composition of the U.S. Congress." *Western Political Quarterly* 43: 81–92.
Weatherford, M. Stephen. 2002. "After the Critical Election: Presidential Leadership, Competition and the Consolidation of the New Deal Realignment." *British Journal of Political Science* 32: 221–257.
Weinberg, Daniel H. 1996. *A Brief Look at Postwar U.S. Income Inequality*. Current Population Reports. Washington, DC: United States Census Bureau. Retrieved from www.census.gov/prod/1/pop/p60-191.pdf.
Winfield, Betty Houchin. 1990. *FDR and the News Media*. Urbana, IL: University of Illinois Press.

2

ON COALITIONS, MOVEMENTS AND REGIME CHANGE

On the surface, Barack Obama appears to have little in common with Richard Nixon. But when the history of his administration is written, it may turn out that political circumstances relegated Obama to something less than the transformational place in history to which he aspires, leaving him with a legacy in relation to shaping the political future that is closer to Nixon than Lincoln. Despite his being the first African-American president and a gifted speaker, Obama's presidency has been symbolically and rhetorically dramatic, his role in the grand process of regime development—and therefore his claim to transformational status—remains cloudy. The evidence from his first term suggests Obama is less likely to be remembered as midwifing a lasting progressive regime than presiding over an inflection point away from conservative governance that could lay the groundwork for future progressive governance or, alternatively, function as an interregnum between two conservative eras.

In this regard, he may end up occupying a place in relation to the dominant conservative period preceding his administration similar to the one Nixon occupies in relation to the dominant liberal period preceding his. Recall that, in our understanding of secular realignment, Nixon's 1968 election served as a tipping point away from the New Deal coalition that reached fruition at the presidential level with Ronald Reagan's election 12 years later and at the congressional level with the ascension of Newt Gingrich to the House speakership in 1994. Nixon was no more a movement conservative than Obama is a movement progressive, and like Obama he was not entirely trusted to advance movement objectives against the wishes of supporters of the political status quo. Nixon appropriated wage and price control policy from Democrats and presided over the expansion of federal environmental protections. Obama appropriated market-based health care reform from Republicans and advocated for deficit reduction that included

Medicare and Social Security changes detested by progressives. The institutional limitations of the presidency made it easier to talk about change than effect it, except in those rare instances where presidential authority gave them latitude to act. So, Nixon appointed conservative justices to the Supreme Court and Obama appointed progressives, in each case reversing a longstanding trend, but both faced stiff and successful opposition on the particulars of their broad visions. Nixon called for a New Federalism that would shift responsibility to the state and local levels, but Democratic congresses resisted his efforts. Obama championed a vision for America built around progressive values, most notably in his second inaugural address. But, like Nixon, an opposition Congress stood in the way of turning his vision into reality.

Perhaps their most definitive contributions were electoral. Nixon had shown conservatives the way to forge a national majority with southern white voters, peeling away a core New Deal constituency that had been long ready to abandon the Democrats over Civil Rights; no Democrat in the New Deal mold would sit in the White House again after his narrow 1968 victory. But whether Nixon's presidency signaled an enduring rightward turn or simply a chance for liberals to regroup was uncertain at the time and muddier still following Jimmy Carter's victory in the post-Watergate 1976 election. Likewise, it is impossible to state with certainty that Republicans will never again elect a movement president like Reagan, although Obama twice proved that Democrats could win the White House convincingly with a diverse coalition featuring non-white, secular, young and female voters.

Whether Democrats can duplicate his success remains a question for future elections, but the potential exists in much the same way as it existed for Republicans in the 1980s. This is because the political and ideological condition of the conservative movement in the Obama era bears an eerie similarity to the state of New Deal liberalism in the Nixon years, which in turn is of a piece with why both Nixon and Obama were frustrated in their efforts to bring about a greater turn, respectively, to the right and left. Presidents, like all of us, are to some degree hostages to circumstances they did not create and cannot control, and both Nixon and Obama came to power in opposition to an existing regime that was running out of ideas and hemorrhaging voters but which maintained enough institutional advantages to resist being repudiated by a president intent on purposeful and lasting changes in political direction.

Nixon was, in political scientist Stephen Skowronek's terminology, a preemptive leader, limited in his ability to disrupt the status quo by the durability of the New Deal regime. Skowronek (2008) contends that presidential leadership is constrained or enabled by where a president serves in the lifecycle of his regime, and that presidents serving under similar regime conditions face comparable leadership opportunities, their range of options determined by whether they are affiliated with, or opposed to, the prevailing regime and whether that regime is ideologically and programmatically viable.

At the end of a regime cycle, when the public has largely rejected the majority party's philosophy of government and its solutions to major policy problems, the status quo is vulnerable to what Skowronek terms reconstructive leaders, presidents who successfully use the authority of their office to repudiate the aging regime and permanently move the country in a different direction. Reconstructive presidents loom large in American history, for they are remembered as historic figures; Jefferson, Jackson, Lincoln, FDR and Reagan all came to power in opposition to a bankrupt regime and established a new regime in their image. The problem Nixon faced in 1968 was that, while segments of the public were open to arguments against New Deal liberalism, and while he won election by chipping at the looser edges of the New Deal coalition, the existing order was resilient enough to constrain Nixon from pushing the country too far to the right without risking his legitimacy. An opposition Congress, Democratic voter registration advantages and a mainstream press operating on generations-old assumptions about the center-left locus of political debate all worked to hem him in. The best Nixon could do was pre-empt: appropriate the still-popular ideas of the existing order but give them a conservative spin.

In time, the New Deal coalition would run its course, its exhaustion evident in Jimmy Carter's inability to reconcile its warring factions,[1] and it would fall to Reagan to repudiate it, in the process winning over one-time coalition supporters like blue collar whites (the so-called "Reagan Democrats"). By 1984, Walter Mondale would learn the hard way that running on a platform of guaranteed tax increases was no longer such a great idea. But Democrats were still entrenched in the House and at the state and local levels outside the South, so it was easy for them to dismiss Reagan as an anomaly. Much of this was attributable to institutional factors such as incumbency advantages that masked shifting political allegiances. By the end of the 1980s, Democrats were essentially not viable as a national party; Republican claims to the once solidly Democratic South, when added to traditional Republican strongholds like California and the mountain West, meant Republicans started every presidential campaign on the threshold of triumph. Bill Clinton's 1992 victory in a three-way race that split the Reagan coalition gave him the presidency but not a license to repudiate Reaganism. Twenty-four years after Nixon's pre-emptive Republican administration, Clinton was a pre-emptive Democrat engaged in "third way" governance, triangulating his more liberal tendencies with the prevailing center-right assumptions of the day. Two years after his election, Congress fell to Gingrich's insurgents. The regime Nixon anticipated and Reagan initiated had been consummated.

Despite criticism of Skowronek's work as being too deterministic (Arnold 1995) and simplistic (Hoekstra 1999), it provides a useful framework for understanding the political moment and placing it in the context of other moments of regime flux. Not coincidentally, all of Skowronek's reconstructive leaders coincide with periods of realignment. And it provides a meaningful way to understand the political limitations confronting President Obama while drawing parallels between the rise and fall of the New Deal and Reagan regimes.

The New Deal and the Conservative Movement

If there was ever a pure case of electoral realignment it was the critical election of 1932 that gave rise to the New Deal coalition.[2] In textbook fashion, the dominant party was swept away and replaced by the out party in an enduring shuffling of the electoral deck. Groups such as African-Americans, that previously had voted Republican, began their shift to the Democratic Party, joined in an odd alliance with Southern whites as well as Catholics, Jews, union workers, the poor and urban liberals (Brady 1982). The laissez-faire philosophy championed by the previous regime was replaced in dramatic fashion by an activist administration that gave birth to a social welfare state unprecedented in scope and size.

Although the contours of this new alignment were anticipated by the urban appeal of Al Smith's 1928 presidential candidacy, the 1932 results were dramatic (Waterman 1990). Republicans were locked out of the White House for 20 years. So enduring was the Democratic tilt in the electorate that even an unpopular incumbent like Harry Truman was returned to office despite whatever underlying desire for change may have been evident in the electorate after 16 years of Democratic administrations. It would take no less than the Supreme Allied Commander of the European campaign in World War II to briefly regain the White House for Republicans before Democratic hegemony was reasserted in 1960.

Programmatically, Roosevelt's New Deal and to a lesser extent Truman's Fair Deal redefined the federal government's relationship to the states and individual citizens. Taking on a broken economy, Roosevelt and his congressional allies regulated banks and securities, opened the federal treasury to massive public works projects to spur employment, and invested in farm relief measures before turning their attention to Social Security, unemployment insurance and welfare. FDR appropriated the term "liberal" to describe these policies, leaving to his opponents—formerly free-market laissez-faire classical liberals—the designation "conservative." It was not meant as a compliment.[3] Decades would pass before the pejorative prefix "big government" would be affixed to liberalism. In its day, conservatism evoked a backwards-thinking hands-off approach to the Great Depression symbolic of the weak hand conservatives were left to play.

Initially, conservatives opposed to Roosevelt's initiatives lacked the political strength to block them. By the time congressional Republicans and conservative Democrats found the capacity to put the brakes on some of Truman's more ambitious initiatives, federal regulatory and social welfare policies had become the norm. Questions about *whether* the federal government should engage in regulation, progressive taxation and social spending gave way to questions about *how much* government should regulate, tax and spend. The fundamental premise of the New Deal—that government should actively engage the private sector to create the conditions for economic growth and opportunity—had become the operative foundation for political debate.

Nowhere was this more apparent than in the actions of the first post-New Deal Republican president, Dwight Eisenhower, a triangulator decades before Bill Clinton who positioned himself between New Deal liberals and the conservatives in his party who would abolish their work. Calling himself a "Modern Republican," Eisenhower ran against big government in the abstract but advocated for a government role in protecting society's most vulnerable citizens. Such "third way" positioning, characteristic of a pre-emptive leader opposing a robust regime, had the political effect of marginalizing conservatives and ratifying the New Deal by expanding Social Security, increasing domestic spending and enlarging the bureaucratic apparatus of the welfare state (Stebenne 2006).

Hard-core conservatives were livid. Working out of the fringes of American public opinion, a few began a quixotic quest to dismantle the New Deal and return American politics and public policy to pre-FDR norms. What would become the conservative movement is generally considered by its leaders to have originated in 1955 with the establishment of William F. Buckley's *National Review* as a vehicle, in the words of its long-time editor William A. Rusher, for "dent[ing] the public consciousness" with conservative ideas (Rusher 1993, 82). Lee Edwards, whose decades-long involvement in movement conservatism dates back to its early days, pointedly noted, "Its mission was not just to 'renew the attack against the Left' but to consolidate and mobilize the Right. *National Review* was not a journal of opinion but a political act" (Edwards 1999, 80).

It would be the first significant political act in a quarter-century-long quest to reshape the Republican Party and build a dominant political coalition behind movement objectives. Prior to establishing the *National Review*, conservatives did not have a voice in mainstream political discourse and lacked the organization to mount an offensive against a Republican Party that had decided the most prudent political course was to moderate conservative positions in the wake of the overwhelming popularity of the New Deal. They believed the lack of an organized movement contributed to the 1952 defeat of anti-New Deal conservative Robert Taft for the Republican presidential nomination at the hands of the better organized and more media-savvy Eisenhower, and were determined not to let it happen again (Edwards 1999). They feared Nixon would continue Eisenhower's moderate course if elected in 1960 but lacked the strength to block his nomination. Four years later they succeeded in nominating Barry Goldwater, the paramount political voice of movement conservatism, and although they had briefly conquered the Republican Party their candidate was trounced in the general election. Building a winning coalition would take much longer; however, Lyndon Johnson, the 1964 winner, would unintentionally give the movement an enormous assist by hastening the decline of the New Deal coalition.

Johnson was a complex leader presiding over a troubled time, and some of the damage to the Democratic Party during his tenure was brought about by difficulties inherent in maintaining a governing coalition in late middle age. In

Skowronek's conceptualization, Johnson was affiliated with the New Deal regime in twilight, a "second round innovator" faced with the risky prospect of trying to hold together a fragmenting coalition while making his mark on policy, competing tasks which can cause the president's political authority to "dissolve in its own accomplishments" (Skowronek 2008, 103). This is an apt description of what happened to Johnson, whose ambitious Great Society programs and prosecution of the Vietnam War expedited the departure of white southerners from the New Deal coalition and gave rise to a radicalized New Left.

The objective of the Great Society was to eliminate poverty and alleviate racial discrimination through a raft of new social programs, effectively altering the purpose of the New Deal by putting government in the business of equalizing social outcomes rather than advancing individual opportunity. This marked a quantum step away from the classical liberal understanding of government as an arbiter of the social contract in place before the New Deal to a referee who intervenes to prevent social ills, or, in Theodore Lowi's understanding, from a society made free *for* risk to a society made free *from* risk (Lowi 1995).

The political consequences of this shift were profound. Lowi notes that among adherents of the New Left of the 1960s, morality replaced pragmatism as the foundation for liberal policy through absolutist positions against poverty and racial discrimination. Concurrently, Lowi (1979) argues that the rise of the administrative state necessitated by the collective programs of the New Deal era had by the 1960s shifted governing authority to the bureaucracy and, more profoundly, their affiliated interest groups. These twin effects of the Great Society mobilized conservatives and exploited the stress fractures in what had always been an uneasy coalition. It became easier for the right to characterize the left as out of step with mainstream opinion and beholden to special interest groups. Racial tensions boiled over. The New Deal coalition was coming apart.

Reagan Conservatism and the Progressive Movement

Democrats would have one more chance to elect a president with the coalition that had powered them for over 40 years, but the fact of Jimmy Carter's emergence from a crowded Democratic field and the circumstances surrounding his election are indicative of a regime in its end stages. Carter won the nomination over better-known and more liberal Democrats, including Rep. Morris Udall of Arizona, Indiana Senator Birch Bayh and California Governor Jerry Brown. His southern roots enabled him to carry a region that had been lost to Democrats during the two previous cycles when they ran liberal midwestern standard bearers, and Carter owed his election to his ability to win almost every southern state despite limited strength elsewhere. Even then, he won by only two points against Gerald Ford, the only unelected incumbent in history, in the wake of Ford's unpopular pardon of Richard Nixon for his Watergate involvement and in a bad economy. It would be hard to characterize that as a stellar performance.

The Democrat was left without a base when southern voters deserted their native son four years later. He carried only six states en route to a rout that, in its paucity of Electoral College real estate, recalled McGovern's defeat by Nixon in 1972 and anticipated the sorry performance of Democrats through the 1980s. In hindsight, Carter's 1976 victory appears as an aberration, the curtain call of a spent regime that coincided with its collapse.

Movement conservatives took advantage of the moment by forging a coalition as tentative and unlikely as the New Deal alliance. But where the New Deal coalition was born in response to the previous regime's inability to combat the Great Depression, what would become known as the Reagan coalition was held together by a mutual dislike of liberalism. Movement conservatives opposed to the welfare state remained animated by the desire to get government out of the way of free enterprise through lower taxes, fewer regulations and reduced entitlements. They were joined by a group of disaffected liberal intellectuals who had begun to abandon the Democratic Party following the social dislocation of the 1960s and 1970s. More policy-oriented than political, these "neoconservatives" shared the movement's strong anti-Communist sentiments and provided the budding regime with intellectual energy (Edwards 1999). Collectively, they formed an odd alliance with the other two main coalition partners: evangelicals and economically insecure whites. The former group was motivated by a particular understanding of Christian values that they felt should be embraced by everyone. The latter group, known as Reagan Democrats in the 1980s and as the Tea Party today,[4] was animated by a dislike of multiculturalism and perceived threats posed by immigrants and racial minorities (Lowi 1995).

This uneasy collection of classical liberals, theocons and working-class whites shared an enemy in big government, but for vastly different reasons. As Lowi (1995) points out, economic conservatives were looking to advance a smaller government to promote laissez-faire capitalism; their aims were secular and their understanding of individual liberty was defined in market terms. Evangelicals sought a non-secular order driven by religious dictates; they could accept limited government in economic affairs as long as it advanced their values agenda. Working-class whites came to the coalition with an authoritarian bent, speaking the language of individual liberty but valuing order above all else.

When this alliance came to power in 1980, it marked the culmination of a generation of work by movement conservatives who had started as outcasts. Despite their different goals and perspectives, they were able to function as a governing coalition because, in Lee Edwards' words, they had "a consistent philosophy, a national constituency, requisite financing, a solid organizational base, media support, and a charismatic, principled leader" (Edwards 1999, 241). It also didn't hurt that Reagan chose not to declare war on the welfare state. That wouldn't happen until years later, when the regime was losing public support and, like the New Deal coalition before it, became beholden to the core demands of its constituent groups.

The intervening years produced a regime life similar to the New Deal coalition. Starting in 1980, Republicans won the presidency in five of seven elections, overwhelmingly at first, tenuously later. George H. W. Bush sought and won Reagan's third term by running as a steward of Reaganism and the Reagan legacy (Ladd 1988). Bill Clinton, the only Democrat to serve between 1980 and 2008, was to the Reagan coalition what Eisenhower had been for the New Deal, the pre-emptive leader who validates the assumptions of the prevailing regime through his inability to change it. Although opinion data from this period suggest that liberal attitudes plateaued following Reagan's election, it is an open question whether the country shifted programmatically to the right as thoroughly as the partisan shift away from New Deal liberalism would suggest. Nonetheless, while evidence indicates liberal attitudes continued to dominate on issues related to equal rights, matters of paramount importance to Reagan coalition partners—notably taxes, spending, welfare policy and social control—moved in a conservative direction (Smith 1990).

By the turn of the century, the Reagan coalition found itself where the New Deal coalition had been in the 1960s. George W. Bush lost the popular vote and became president only after the Supreme Court ended the disputed Florida recount with Bush in the lead by the thinnest of margins. He was narrowly re-elected in a time of war. Although Iraq and Afghanistan indulged neo-conservative foreign policy beliefs, Bush was viewed as a profligate spender by laissez-faire conservatives for running up huge deficits and took an accommodating approach to immigration policy. His coalition survived the end of his term, but signs of strain were apparent in the 2008 election. John McCain's tragi-comic choice of Alaska Governor Sarah Palin as his running mate was a harbinger of where the coalition would go once out of power. As the base fawned over the governor as if she were a rock star, swing voters worried about her suitability for high office. Within months of Barack Obama's election, the Tea Party emerged as the dominant coalition partner, forcing the Republican Party out of the policy consensus that had held through two political regimes.

At the start of this long arc of conservative dominance, liberals were defensive and uncertain about how to regain their footing. Unwilling to accept that the public had rejected their governing approach, they kept offering more of the same only to be rebuffed at the polls. Their behavior mirrored free market liberals—now known as conservatives—at the start of the New Deal coalition, until they recognized that their future political viability required them to accept the prevailing terms and conditions of political debate. Democrats reached this point in 1992, at a time when Republicans had succeeded in turning "liberal" into an epithet. Bill Clinton effectively ran against his own party, positioning himself as a "New Democrat" open to free market principles, friendly to business and willing to take on core liberal interests while smoothing over the rougher elements of conservatism. His neoliberal, "third way" approach brought Democrats back to political respectability but at the cost of running away from key elements of the New Deal and Great Society. Organized movement liberals might have pushed back against this positioning, except for the fact that there were no organized movement liberals.

That started to change when the Bush administration invaded Iraq with the support of congressional Democrats under what turned out to be false pretenses, as we will see in Chapter 3. Just as the rise of the New Deal spawned a reaction by those who were unwilling to support what they viewed as the capitulation of the Republican Party, the Bush administration's muscular neocon foreign policy and the Democratic Party's unwillingness to challenge it sparked what would grow to be the modern progressive movement, which would eventually become a player in twenty-first-century politics in an eerie parallel to the growth of the conservative movement 50 years earlier.

The Conservative Movement and the Progressive Movement

The genesis and early growth pattern of the progressive movement is, in key respects, similar to that of its conservative adversaries. Although only a little more than a decade old, the movement has gravitated from the fringes to the mainstream, experiencing similar triumphs and setbacks to movement conservatism during its formative years, while meeting with a similar pattern of reactions from established institutions. In relative terms, progressives are positioned comparably to conservatives during the Nixon administration—they are included in the conversation but they do not drive it. They approach a president with sympathetic leanings who did not emerge from their movement with feelings ranging from satisfaction to disappointment to at times anger, divided in their loyalties between those who find him to be a far preferable alternative to anyone the other side would nominate and those who feel he is too closely wedded to an unacceptable status quo. Movement conservatives would suffer through the fallout of the Watergate scandal before eventually seeing one of their own reach the presidency in 1980. Whether progressives are able to elect a president remains to be seen, but the experience of movement conservatives reads like a template for how it can be done.

Table 2.1 lists 14 substantive similarities between the conservative movement of the 1950s and 1960s and the progressive movement of the past decade. Collectively, they illustrate how two coalitions with dramatically different visions but facing the same set of obstacles approached their impediments in comparable ways. In the parallels to movement conservatism, we can see the path progressives have already followed and may take in the future to try to forge an enduring political alignment.[5]

TABLE 2.1 Fourteen key similarities between the conservative and progressive movements

Conservative movement	Progressive movement
Lacked a media apparatus to combat Democratic messaging during the movement's early years	Lacked a media apparatus to combat Republican messaging during the movement's early years
Mobilized early through *National Review*	Mobilized early through the netroots
Worked to get Democrats out of power while building a farm team of loyal conservatives	Worked to get Republicans out of power while building a farm team of loyal progressives
Developed intellectual infrastructure before making a serious bid for political power	Developed intellectual infrastructure before making a serious bid for political power
Early efforts involved organizing, mobilizing and raising money from grassroots supporters	Early efforts involved organizing, mobilizing and raising money from netroots supporters
Critical of "me-too" Republicans from the party's liberal wing giving cover to Democrats	Critical of "me-too" Democrats from the party's conservative wing giving cover to Republicans
Recognized the threat posed by the movement to mainstream Republicans	Recognized the threat posed by the movement to mainstream Democrats
Mainstream Republicans initially ignored the movement, then ridiculed it, then engaged it	Mainstream Democrats initially ignored the movement, then ridiculed it, then engaged it
Had to contend with extreme elements in the movement	Had to contend with extreme elements in the movement
Complained of an echo-chamber effect by mainstream media looking to crush the movement in its infancy	Complained of an echo-chamber effect by mainstream media looking to crush the movement in its infancy
Found a galvanizing leader in presidential candidate Barry Goldwater, who spoke his mind in an unvarnished manner that rallied supporters but troubled non-supporters	Found a galvanizing leader in presidential candidate Howard Dean, who spoke his mind in an unvarnished manner that rallied supporters but troubled non-supporters
The collapse of the Goldwater presidential campaign was incorrectly interpreted by mainstream media as the end of the movement	The collapse of the Dean presidential campaign was incorrectly interpreted by mainstream media as the end of the movement
The election of Republican Nixon divided movement loyalists between those who found him "conservative enough" and those who felt he did not do enough to challenge the status quo	The election of Democrat Obama divided movement loyalists between those who found him "progressive enough" and those who felt he did not do enough to challenge the status quo
Effectively used a new medium—direct mail—to target small donor supporters and challenge mainstream media messages	Effectively used a new medium—digital media—to target small donor supporters and challenge mainstream media messages

No messaging capability in the early years

Conservatives eventually would build a media empire and progressives would learn how to harness the power of the Internet—but not initially. Each movement started from scratch with no megaphone and a message few in the mainstream wanted to hear, facing off against a set of assumptions about what constituted acceptable political alternatives set by an entrenched regime. The message in each instance was fairly robust and oppositional. Movement conservatism has roots in the anti-Communist crusades of the early 1950s and sought to limit the federal government by reversing the New Deal, which it saw as a perversion of American self-reliance. The progressive movement was launched by the strong anti-Iraq War sentiment of the early 2000s, when the war enjoyed enormous institutional and public support, and by opposing what they believed was a morally bankrupt Bush administration, progressives sought to return the federal government to its version of the rule of law.

In each case, the impulse to organize was driven by the desire to have a voice to express those positions. Conservatives in the early 1950s lacked the ability to combat charges leveled against them by national Democrats, just as progressives were powerless in the face of Republican efforts to marginalize them in the early 2000s. They were shouting from the outside without an amplifier, and few were listening.

First steps: mobilizing through the media

This changed for each movement when they established a media presence that gradually permitted them the opportunity to express their views. In the case of the conservative movement, the vehicle was Buckley's *National Review*, which offered a decidedly conservative alternative to mainstream publications and a vehicle for advancing conservative ideas among an intellectual elite. For the progressive movement, it was the formation of an Internet grassroots or netroots—a web of blogs that served as a central hub of progressive discourse and activism. Each attempted to capitalize on the media structure of their day, with *National Review* taking aim at the power elite through persuasive writing, and the netroots providing a clearinghouse of progressive information for ordinary individuals seeking to become activists in the early days of digital media. Few paid attention at first, but *National Review* by virtue of its intellectual heft, and the netroots by virtue of its reach on the Internet, eventually captured mainstream interest, including a fair amount of pushback and ridicule.

A small media nexus evolved around these pioneering vehicles. Six years after the 1955 founding of *National Review*, its editor William Rusher noted that the movement had "several respectable, though not large, publications to sound its themes and keep informed conservatives in communication with one another. It had two or three grass-roots membership organizations serving the same important purposes" (Rusher 1993, 82). A similar statement could be made about the progressive movement at roughly the same stage of development, although the organic nature of the Internet lent a more fluid quality to these other organizations, some of which pre-dated the emergence of the progressive blogosphere as proto-sites for progressive action. As we will see in Chapter 3, sites like MoveOn.org, which traces its origins to the late twentieth century, linked horizontally with a constellation of progressive blogs, some with national reach, others with smaller groups of followers organized around state, local or policy-centered interests.

Over time, these media outlets would become intellectual engines that would draw attention to each movement's out-of-the-mainstream philosophy. Movement conservatives and progressives benefited from having the intellectual playing field to themselves. When Buckley arrived on the scene, whatever remained of the conservative intellectual tradition had been tossed to the side by New Deal liberalism and considered useless and spent by adherents to the dominant liberal philosophy of the day. The progressive netroots confronted a parallel situation in which liberal solutions to political problems were widely regarded as failed relics of another era, outside the range of acceptable elite consideration. It fell to each movement to use its small corner of the mass media universe to make the case for their alternatives.

At the same time, each movement used the media to attract and engage supporters in the same set of activities: organizing, mobilizing and raising money. Visibility draws interest from like-minded readers who over time become a critical core of supporters even as a broader degree of respectability remains a ways off. As *National Review* won notice and acclaim for articulating a conservative worldview, it drew sympathetic followers who previously had no place to go. Likewise, early progressive blog posts and their attendant comment sections are filled with surprise and gratitude from those who had felt they were the only ones out there seeking progressive outcomes, people who were discovering that the Internet is a gigantic search engine capable of sorting by any imaginable preference. As the progressive movement grew, it leveraged this capability to attract others to what would become a cause.

Party-building and movement-building

Movement conservatives worked to elect Republicans and movement progressives worked to elect Democrats, but not blindly. Because both movements chose to operate within the electoral process, there was a rational preference for the party most affiliated with their ideas, but they were operating outside their chosen parties and therefore had to figure out how to advance partisan goals without undermining their greater ideological objectives. This problem was particularly acute in the early days of each movement. Conservatives who fought Eisenhower at the 1952 Republican convention came around to support his election in order to dislodge Democrats from the White House. Progressives put aside the bitter disappointment of Howard Dean's defeat by John Kerry in the 2004 Democratic primaries and advocated for the latter as a preferable alternative to George W. Bush.

Nonetheless, movement conservatives recognized that simply replacing a Democratic president with a Republican who would accept the premise of the Democrats' governing philosophy would do little to advance movement objectives, and movement progressives recognized that replacing a Republican president with a Democrat who governed within a political space defined by Republicans would also be counterproductive.

This is why movement conservatives took measures over many years to build a farm team of loyal conservative candidates. Although they would seek office under the Republican label, their governing approach and philosophical allegiance would be to the movement. Progressives acted the same way when they waded into the candidate-recruitment process in an effort to find potential officeholders who shared their views and objectives. Markos Moulitsas, founder of Daily Kos, which would grow to become the largest progressive community site, called this approach looking for "better" Democrats—i.e., Democrats who are progressives first, partisans second. Daily Kos blogger Armando elaborated in a December 11, 2011 post, saying:

> Daily Kos is in the progressive flank of the Big Tent Democratic Party. It wants, in my opinion, to pull the Party toward progressive values. Part of pulling the country toward progressive values requires the Democratic Party wining of course … But it also requires, from the progressive standpoint, a "better Democrats" component—in order to have progressive values triumph, the Democratic Party has to get better—it has to become more progressive.

Like conservatives before them, the long-term progressive strategy was to build a movement, then use the strength of that movement to change its affiliated political party. Accordingly, neither movement had much tolerance for partisans who, through words or actions, ratified the governing philosophy of the other side. In recent years, some conservatives have taken to referring to Republican officeholders as "RINOs" (Republicans in Name Only) when they moderate their views or express a penchant for compromise with the Obama administration, while some in the netroots will deride conservative and corporate-friendly Democrats as "DINOs" (Democrats in Name Only). The shared sentiment behind these labels is the sense that an officeholder of the preferred party is taking up space that could be put to more productive use by a movement affiliate—or worse, that they are actively undermining the movement.

Both movements were forced to find a balance between being pragmatic about partisans outside the movement and pushing to change the party's direction. This proved challenging. Conservatives may have chosen to make peace with Eisenhower's nomination, but they were no friends to Eisenhower Republicans. Compelled by circumstances to accept the Nixon presidency as a practical alternative to Ronald Reagan in 1968, some in the movement sought unsuccessfully to mount a primary challenge in 1972 (the *National Review* endorsed conservative Republican Rep. John Ashbrook of Ohio, whose attempt to unseat Nixon went nowhere).

The progressive movement went to war with powerful Democratic Senator Joseph Lieberman, the party's 2000 vice presidential nominee, for being too cozy with the Bush administration and too willing to thwart progressive objectives for someone holding a Senate seat from a liberal state like Connecticut. In 2006, they rallied behind businessman Ned Lamont, a progressive hero who successfully challenged Lieberman for the Democratic Senate nomination in what at the time was seen as a great victory for the fledgling movement. But Lieberman ran as an independent and defeated Lamont in the general election to retain his seat and remain a thorn in the side of progressives, demonstrating the resiliency of the status quo.

Battling mainstream pushback

Neither movement was naïve about the threat its success posed to an establishment that had no use for their ideas or tactics. "Let's grow up, conservatives!" Barry Goldwater proclaimed in his 1960 convention speech. "We want to take this party back, and I think some day we can" (Edwards 1999, 94). But the party that nominated Richard Nixon in Chicago that summer week had no interest in seeing the party taken over by a figure with limited appeal outside his core group, regardless of how much he motivated true believers. It would not have been too difficult to anticipate the debacle that would befall them once Goldwater claimed the party as his own four years later.

To progressive bloggers, a significant point of discussion—and derision—has been establishment Democrats who are perceived to care more about their careers and egos than winning elections. During the Bush years in particular, progressives would lash out against a permanent Washington elite who feasted off a supply of easy campaign money and were rewarded in failure with a steady stream of appearances on television news programs. They reserved their most intense scorn for Bob Schrum, the consultant associated with eight losing Democratic presidential campaigns including John Kerry's. "Our consultants really don't care about winning," blogged Moulitsas on September 16, 2004, just before Kerry's defeat:

> For our side, it's commerce. It's the almighty dollar ... Schrum (and his firm's partners) will be getting a $5 million cut for Kerry's media buys (another $3 million will go to other media firms used by the campaign).

> While some of that is undoubtedly expenses for creating new ads, the vast majority is not. The lion's share of $5 million of your own contributions going not to defeat Bush, but to line Schrum's pockets. Does that feel right to you?[6]

No doubt it felt fine to the consultants, who were no more enamored of the progressives' critique of their gravy train than Eisenhower-era Republicans were eager to see their party overtaken by movement conservatives.

Elites in each era had strikingly similar responses to movement pressure. Initially, liberal Republicans ignored the conservative movement entirely, viewing them as a powerless fringe. When movement conservatives didn't go away, liberals reacted by making fun of them, and attempted to dismiss them by defining the entire movement in terms of its most radical elements. This proved to be a sensitive matter, as the movement attracted what Edwards called "doomsayers and paranoiacs" as it grew, including—in an interesting foreshadowing of the conservative coalition in twilight—avowed racists, anti-Semites, John Birchers, communist conspiracy theorists and "fundamentalist preachers who railed against the forces of humanism, liberalism, and secularism and warned of approaching Armageddon" (Edwards 1999, 107).

In writing the history of their accomplishments, movement leaders claimed to have distanced themselves from their fringe followers.[7] But they also regarded the shift from elite disinterest to disdain as a victory, recognizing that opponents will acknowledge you only if they are feeling threatened. In attempting to marginalize the movement, the mainstream had engaged it, and a long battle for the soul of the Republican Party had begun.

The exact pattern played out 50 years later between Democratic Party elites and movement progressives, whose online discourse prominently featured the dictate attributed to Mahatma Gandhi's battle against British imperialism: "First they ignore you. Then they laugh at you. Then they fight you. Then you win." Like movement conservatives before them, Democratic Party elites generally ignored the early netroots, seeing them largely as a ragtag group of powerless idealists. When they didn't go away, mainstream Democrats started to ridicule them in language reminiscent of how liberal Republicans derided movement conservatives, marginalizing bloggers as inept social outcasts inexperienced in the ways of politics that would hand the country over to radicals if given the opportunity.[8]

While there were radical elements in the netroots, supporters were quick to point out that they didn't define the movement the way some political elites claimed they did. As the blogger Dante Atkins noted of Joe Lieberman during the Ned Lamont primary challenge, in a March 3, 2006 Daily Kos post, "He called us names. 'Radicals.' 'Out of touch.' 'Angry activists.' The list goes on. He did ignore Ned Lamont, though—something he can't afford to do any more." Atkins proceeded to describe how prominent conservative figures were also starting to attack progressives, something he attributed to fear on the right, the product of changes produced "because of us—and we need to keep the pressure on."

Participants in both movements complained bitterly of the way mainstream reporters lined up against them, especially in the beginning when they were struggling to communicate their message to a larger audience. Rusher (1993, 89–91) and Edwards (1999, 105–106) both used the term "echo chamber" to denounce the way elite press opinion attempted to marginalize the right as out of the mainstream before the movement grew too strong. Their claim matches a prominent complaint made by progressives, who felt doubly embittered for having to combat simultaneously the prevailing attitude that the press is in the pocket of liberals—a meme popularized by the right. But both groups took solace in the belief that media pushback brought them attention and gave them an opportunity to enter the debate, even if it was from the sidelines. For groups that started with little ability to disseminate a message and no respect from mainstream journalists and politicians, being marginalized by the media was a mark of progress and far better than being ignored.

Goldwater and Dean

Each movement came of age behind an unvarnished leader who waged a spectacularly unsuccessful presidential campaign devoted unapologetically to movement principles. To their followers, Barry Goldwater and Howard Dean were heroes: politicians unafraid to say in public what their followers said in private. Apart from Goldwater, no major politician in 1964 had the temerity to take the position that Social Security should be a voluntary program. Apart from Dean, no major politician in 2004 was speaking out against the Iraq War and the security policies of the Bush administration.

To the broader public, they were extremists and slightly unhinged. Lyndon Johnson had little difficulty using Goldwater's own words against him in the 1964 campaign to paint him as unstable and trigger-happy, a frightening figure with extreme and dangerous views. Dean's primal scream of solidarity with his supporters following his disappointing finish in the Iowa caucus made him a subject of national mockery and helped underscore the idea that he was an unsteady figure unfit to be president, an image mainstream Democrats were happy to perpetuate.

Dean challenged the Democratic establishment as fully as Goldwater had threatened mainstream Republicans 40 years earlier. In each case, party elites worried that someone identified with outlying elements in their party would spell electoral disaster up and down the ballot, forcing the party to take unpopular positions and damaging relations with voters—a fear that was ultimately realized with Goldwater's drubbing. But, if the short-term fear of party elites was electoral defeat, their long-term concerns were even stronger, because each candidate took aim at elites themselves, promising a revolution in their respective party as a prerequisite to changing the country. Goldwater conservatives were convinced that "mushy moderation" had relegated the Republican Party to permanent second-tier status in the dominant New Deal regime; Dean progressives were convinced that "mushy moderation" had relegated the Democratic Party to permanent second-tier status in the dominant Reagan regime.

Initially, it appeared the elites had little to fear. Goldwater's 1964 nomination began as a draft effort by a small number of movement conservatives who knew each other from their days as college Young Republicans—a small insurgency tilting against the highly funded East Coast establishment led by Nelson Rockefeller, the liberal Republican governor of New York. Howard Dean registered an asterisk in polls of Democratic presidential contenders in early 2003, until he caught fire in the blogosphere and was adopted by the fledgling netroots, who, as we will see in Chapter 3, would provide him with an army of foot soldiers and unprecedented small-dollar contributions (Trippi 2004). Powered by determination born of deep convictions, each group defied expectations. Conservatives were able to exploit divisions in the East Coast establishment and draw on the power of a movement now a decade old to muscle their way to the nomination. Progressives propelled Dean to frontrunner status in the months before the first primaries, out-fundraising and out-hustling better-known mainstream competition. In each case, traditional figures were appalled but could do nothing to stop the movement-backed candidates until they were ultimately rejected at the polls.

Following Goldwater's landslide loss, establishment Republicans and mainstream commentators declared the conservative movement dead, asserted that America remained a center-left nation and reiterated the conventional wisdom that Republicans could only win nationally by imitating Democrats. Following Dean's collapse, establishment Democrats were more than happy to say the same about the progressive movement, while mainstream media ratified the conventional wisdom that America remained a center-right nation where Democrats could win nationally only by imitating Republicans. Neither movement accepted this verdict; although it would be 16 years before conservatives would elect a president, it would become apparent long before Reagan's rise to power that the right was unfazed by defeat, just as it became clear that progressives would dust off Dean's collapse, stand behind him as he became head of the Democratic National Committee and, like conservatives before them, retool and move ahead. Each group would learn from its spectacular failure, and the individual that led them there would become, for group adherents, the movement's defining figure.

Nixon and Obama

Where Goldwater and Dean energized a movement but never reached the Promised Land, Nixon and Obama generated complex reactions from the faithful on their way to, and during their time in, the White House. The relationship between movement conservatives and Richard Nixon parallels the relationship between movement progressives and Barack Obama, driven in no small part by the constraints each president faced as a transitional figure pushing against a decaying but tenacious political regime. Nixon was as much a clear conservative alternative to the New Deal liberalism of Hubert Humphrey and the Johnson administration as Obama was an unambiguous liberal alternative to John McCain and the Bush administration, but neither was a movement figure and neither would govern as the movement would have wished.

Consequently, movement supporters were reserved and at times apprehensive about endorsing Nixon and Obama, as they weren't certain they could trust them to deliver on the promise of moving the country in a new direction. Nixon had support among the group that had promoted Goldwater (including Goldwater himself) despite reservations that he wasn't "conservative enough"—in part because he was more conservative than his challenger for the presidency, Nelson Rockefeller. Some movement conservatives promoted Reagan in 1968, but Nixon was a more strategic choice for pragmatic conservatives because he wasn't widely regarded as being too far to the right. For his part, Nixon ran as a conservative alternative to the liberalism of the Rockefeller wing of his party and to the New Deal, but as a more mainstream alternative than Goldwater.

Deeper animosity with the conservative movement emerged after Nixon was elected. In office, he governed in ways that angered and alienated movement conservatives, particularly his support of wage and price controls, expanding federal regulatory policies and his outreach to China (which, although remembered as a signature accomplishment, was regarded at the time as heresy by anti-communists in the conservative movement). Despite Nixon moving to the right rhetorically in the 1968 campaign by talking about social issues and promising a return of power to the states, movement conservatives felt his governing positions fell far short of his rhetoric and did a lot to reinforce rather than change the status quo. Lee Edwards (1999, 165) recalls that:

> Almost from his first day in office, Nixon offered a pseudo-New Deal at home and an accommodationist policy abroad. And he closed himself off from the conservatives who had nominated and elected him, preferring the counsel of big-government Democrats like former Texas governor John Connally and Harvard professor Daniel Patrick Moynihan, and practitioners of realpolitik like Henry Kissinger.

Substitute liberal for conservative and Obama for Nixon, change the particular issues, and you have an uncanny description of Obama's uneven relationship with movement progressives. Although Obama crafted a gigantic movement to win the White House using some of the same technological innovations propelling the netroots, his organization existed apart from and in parallel to the Internet Left (Kerbel 2012). More than a few pixels on Daily Kos and other community blogs were devoted in 2007 to passionate discussion of who Obama really was and whether the change he was promising would advance or frustrate progressive goals.[9] For his part, Obama positioned himself to the left of Hillary Clinton on the Iraq War, arguably the most animating issue of the 2008 primary campaign, while speaking the language of transformation. And Obama had support among the netroots, including some former Dean enthusiasts, even though he was accurately perceived as having come to prominence outside the movement.

As with Nixon, the real tension between politician and movement erupted after the election, when Obama chose to govern in a manner that failed to advance movement objectives. Where conservatives objected to Nixon's fondness for Moynihan and Kissinger, progressives chafed at Obama's selection of advisers with roots in investment banking, like Treasury Secretary Timothy Geithner, OMB Director Peter Orszag and National Economic Council chief Lawrence Summers, regarding them as anything but the choices of someone bent on changing economic fundamentals. Where conservatives saw Nixon promote policies they regarded as "New Deal light," progressives were perplexed and angered by what they regarded as continuity with the Bush administration on major issues, notably Obama's treatment of the financial sector and domestic surveillance. Although progressives applauded Obama's decision to pursue a universal health care policy, there was disillusionment with his refusal to consider a single-payer system and doubts about his commitment to including a public option (Kerbel 2012). As in the early 1970s, a restless movement sparred with an administration that was nudging American politics in its direction but not addressing its core philosophical concerns.

William Rusher (1993, 198–99) astutely noted—to his dismay—how the tidal pull of the status quo circa 1970 made it impossible to get establishment partisans to pivot too much toward the movement's agenda:

> The Republican Party was forever scolded by its liberal minority for failing to appeal to 'moderate' Democrats and independents [meaning Democrats and independents slightly to the GOP's left], but by that fact it was being successfully pressured not to make a bid for non-Republican conservatives. As far as I could see [in 1976] there would be no end to this stalemate … The GOP would remain locked in its self-defeating posture of appealing only to voters on its left.

This sentiment would sound familiar to movement progressives. Again, substitute "Democrat" for "Republican," "conservative" for "liberal," and "left" for "right," change the year to 2010, and you have a quote right out of many a netroots diary.

Media and advanced mobilization

Following their early organization around the *National Review* and the blogosphere, respectively, it would take mastery of a new medium of communication to enable conservatives and progressives to build a viable independent base to pressure the party closest to its philosophical bent to bend in its direction. For the netroots, the venue would be the Internet, but decades earlier, at a time when Republicans like Nixon were figuring out how to make television work for them, movement conservatives were mastering the art of direct mail. It was a simple but deceptively powerful means of identifying and communicating with potential supporters. Like the Internet for progressives, advances in computer technology facilitated conservatives' direct mail techniques, allowing them to build and maintain databases of potential supporters to enlist in political action and ask for money.

As direct mail techniques proved effective in the 1970s, movement conservatives were able to build an infrastructure apart from the Republican Party to battle elements in the party and in the mainstream media that accommodated the left and accepted New Deal liberalism as the unquestioned status quo ideology. Their strategy was to forge a lasting alliance between economic and social conservatives whose agendas, though different, were noncompetitive. Wealthy conservative donors interested in building a base from which they could counter the left opened their checkbooks and underwrote the costs of direct mail politics. The effort came to fruition with the coalition that promoted and elected Ronald Reagan a short six years after Nixon resigned the presidency in disgrace.

As we will see in Chapter 3, progressive activists use digital media and email to perform comparable functions aimed at achieving parallel objectives to conservatives. Where direct mail gave conservatives the ability to target supporters, email does the same for progressives and digital media gives supporters the ability to self-identify. In the decade since the Dean campaign, progressives have embraced the Internet as a forum for building virtual and real communities—a process mirroring the community ethic of the movement that has provided the means for building infrastructure outside the Democratic Party. Like movement conservatives before them, they aim to move a reluctant political party in their philosophical direction by mobilizing supporters, raising money, shaping media narratives and influencing elections. Although they are hardly alone in their use of the Internet for political ends—the Obama campaign being the obvious example—their success will depend largely on the platform they have built through their understanding and mastery of digital media.

John Mitchell, Nixon's attorney general, once told a reporter, "This country is going to go so far to the right you won't recognize it."[10] If Mitchell was prescient, it was because of events occurring within a conservative movement operating independently of his administration to exploit the deterioration of the New Deal coalition and bring about a rightward shift in American politics. His declaration was premature and without basis in fact, but it captured the general sense that something was changing in America that, if properly addressed, could reshape policy priorities for a long time. And it proved to be correct. It is reasonable to make a symmetrical observation about today's political moment only if we recognize that once again it will require the work of a movement that is savvy about its opportunities to dislodge the entrenched interests of an earlier time and permanently reshape political choices.

Whether America is to venture so far to the left that you won't recognize it, or embark on a second consecutive conservative era, depends in part on how well a group of activists, starting from the political margins, leverage the communication structures of our day to mobilize a movement and dislodge entrenched Democratic Party elites. With the advent of a second-generation, digital media-based Internet Left, they have shown signs of making halting progress toward that objective. We will examine how they have been doing it in Chapter 3.

Notes

1. Skowronek calls Carter a "late regime affiliate" whose administration was undermined by sniping among Democratic factions and the inability to sell the public on liberal solutions to pressing problems such as the energy crisis. Rebuffed by his allies and rejected by the general public, Carter was a prisoner of his place in political time, his personal and administrative shortcomings notwithstanding. In Skowronek's typology, disjunctive leaders like Carter tee things up for their reconstructive successors: Carter before Reagan; Hoover before FDR; Buchanan before Lincoln; John Quincy Adams before Jackson; John Adams before Jefferson.
2. Alternatively, one could argue, with Ladd (1991), that the New Deal realignment was a one-of-a-kind structural transformation that had never before taken place and has not happened since, making it a poor model for understanding other realigning periods. Either way, it contains all the elements scholars point to when describing the birthing of an enduring national coalition.
3. Theodore Lowi (1995) contends that in its embrace of capitalism, the New Deal was a center-right enterprise, and that from a European perspective there is no true left in the United States.
4. Everett Carll Ladd (1976) notes the departure of groups in the economic middle from the New Deal coalition starting in the mid-1960s as a noteworthy element of the coalition's demise. In the mid-1970s he anticipated the alignment of economic interests that would define the Reagan coalition: a curvilinear relationship where Democrats drew support from the top and bottom of the economic scale and Republicans were strongly supported by working-class voters, a pattern consistent with the preferences of workers in a post-industrial economy.
5. This section draws heavily from the biographical accounts of the conservative movement by Edwards (1999) and Rusher (1993).
6. Another blogger, writing June 13, 2007 on the same site, was a bit more indelicate. In a post titled "Bob Schrum is a Hornless Dung Beetle," the blogger chuckles1 compared the consultants' professional behavior with the mating rituals of the dung beetle, where a defeated male will shake off its defeat and reassert itself countless times despite its obvious inferiority.
7. Edwards (1999, 107) acknowledged these marginal groups were "*in* the movement" but claimed they "were not *the* movement."
8. One of the authors of this book was ridiculed by prominent Democrats for his political ignorance in proposing in 2006 that the party run candidates in every House district in order to nationalize the campaign. Party officials called the proposal a waste of money, but an online recruitment effort produced candidates in almost every district the party ignored. One of those was elected to Congress in the 2006 Democratic wave.

9 At Daily Kos there have been more than 100,000 community-generated articles posted about Barack Obama and whether his administration is advancing or frustrating progressive objectives. Over time, two distinct camps formed and were artfully named by readers: the "roxers" (consisting of those who think Obama "rocks") and the "suxers" (those who think he does not).
10 Cited in Mitchell's obituary, as spoken to a reporter. "John N. Mitchell Dies at 75; Major Figure in Watergate." *The New York Times*, November 10, 1988. Retrieved from www.nytimes.com/1988/11/10/obituaries/john-n-mitchell-dies-at-75-major-figure-in-watergate.html?pagewanted=all.

References

Arnold, Peri E. 1995. "Determinism and Contingency in Skowronek's Political Time." *Polity* 27: 497–508.
Brady, David. 1982. "Congressional Party Realignment and Transformation of Public Policy in Three Realignment Eras." *American Journal of Political Science* 26: 333–360.
Edwards, Lee. 1999. *The Conservative Revolution: The Movement that Remade America*. New York: Free Press.
Hoekstra, Douglas J. 1999. "The Politics of Politics: Skowronek and Presidential Research." *Presidential Studies Quarterly* 29: 657–671.
Kerbel, Matthew R. 2012. "The Dog That Didn't Bark: Obama, Netroots Progressives, and Healthcare Reform." In *iPolitics: Citizens, Elections, and Governing in the New Media Age*, edited by Richard Fox and Jennifer Ramos, 233–258. New York: Cambridge University Press.
Ladd, Everett Carll. 1976. "Liberalism Upside Down: The Inversion of the New Deal Order." *Political Science Quarterly* 91: 577–600.
Ladd, Everett Carll. 1988. "The 1988 Elections: Continuation of the Post-New Deal System." *Political Science Quarterly* 104: 1–18.
Ladd, Everett Carll. 1991. "Like Waiting for Godot: The Uselessness of 'Realignment' for Understanding Change in Contemporary American Politics." In *The End of Realignment?: Interpreting American Electoral Eras*, edited by Byron E. Shafer, 24–36. Madison, WI: University of Wisconsin Press.
Lowi, Theodore J. 1979. *The End of Liberalism: The Second Republic of the United States*. New York: W. W. Norton.
Lowi, Theodore J. 1995. *The End of the Republican Era*. Norman, OK: University of Oklahoma Press.
Rusher, William A. 1993. *The Rise of the Right*. New York: The National Review.
Skowronek, Stephen. 2008. *Presidential Leadership in Political Time: Reprise and Reappraisal*. Lawrence, KS: University of Kansas Press.
Smith, Tom W. 1990. "Liberal and Conservative Trends in the United States Since World War II." *Public Opinion Quarterly* 54: 479–507.
Stebenne, David L. 2006. *Arthur Larson and the Eisenhower Years*. Bloomington, IN: Indiana University Press.
Trippi, Joe. 2004. *The Revolution Will Not Be Televised: Democracy, the Internet, and the Overthrow of Everything*. New York: Regan.
Waterman, Richard W. 1990. "Institutional Realignment: The Composition of the U.S. Congress." *Western Political Quarterly* 43: 81–92.

3

NETROOTS RISING

Robert Gibbs was indignant: "I hear [those] people saying [President Obama] is like George Bush," he said in early August 2010. "Those people ought to be drug tested. I mean, it's crazy."[1] By "those people," President Obama's press secretary meant the cluster of activists staffing and supporting the modern progressive movement. Gibbs derisively labeled them "the Professional Left," a term which the activists and staffers took back for themselves. Suggesting they are crazy is nothing new; the netroots have long been treated derisively by establishment Democrats, and for sensible reasons, as they have in their sights anyone in a position of power whom they perceive to stand against their agenda, including would-be allies like President Obama. In the early days of the movement, it was easy for political elites to dismiss them as marginal and ineffectual. That changed in recent years as the netroots began winning policy victories, and they now occupy a crucial role in the push for a progressive realignment. Utilizing low-cost online communication and publishing technologies—email, blogs and social networks—since the turn of the millennium they have steadily built the largest multi-issue, left-of-center political space in the United States.

The netroots developed in two distinct phases. The first iteration was characterized by rapidly growing ad hoc structures operated by political newcomers. Combining the novelty of online politics with resurgent progressive activism, the early netroots generated a lot of media buzz and several "close, but no cigar" results on major electoral and legislative efforts. The second iteration of the netroots expanded and institutionalized many of the early netroots operations. It folded the newcomers into a new class of paid political actors now known (thanks to Robert Gibbs) as the Professional Left, who staff netroots organizations and spread netroots fundraising, mobilization and communication tactics into every corner of the Democratic and progressive political ecosystem.

During President Obama's second term, the netroots and the progressive wing of the Democratic Party began to emerge victorious in several major intra-party fights: Senate filibuster reform, Net Neutrality, diplomacy with Iran and leadership of the Federal Reserve Board (all discussed below), as well as Social Security benefit levels (discussed in Chapter 6). A pattern has emerged from these victories, with netroots organizations, established progressive advocacy operations and a handful of elected progressive Democratic leaders working together in "inside–outside" coalitions that combine large-scale grassroots activism with inside-the-beltway lobbying expertise.

The emergence of these coalitions was made possible by the rise of the Professional Left, a development which brought people with netroots experience into regular contact with the professional class staffing established progressive Washington-based advocacy operations. Two strategic advantages assisted the netroots in these victories. First, rapidly changing national demographics, primarily involving race and religion, are steadily increasing the percentage of Democrats in particular and Americans in general who identify as left-of-center ideologically. Second, the Internet continues to occupy a growing share of American media consumption and in the near future will surpass television in total hours consumed. Both trends give the progressive, digital-native netroots an excellent opportunity to expand the effectiveness of inside–outside coalitions into a progressive realignment of the Democratic Party. In the pages that follow, we will look at the evolution of the progressive movement through the two iterations of the netroots and consider the potential for the Professional Left to leverage its strategic advantages to spearhead a progressive political realignment.

Inside–outside Coalitions: the netroots learn how to win

In the second half of 2013, after more than a decade spent as gadflies, curiosities and election-season ATMs, the netroots regularly began teaming up with established advocacy organizations and winning intra-party fights with the national Democratic Party leadership, thereby fulfilling their early promise as a revitalizing force for the flagging progressive wing of the Democratic Party. On the "inside" of these coalitions are established progressive nonprofits and labor unions with lobbying, policy and media outreach operations that can navigate the inner workings of Washington, D.C., assisted by a handful of Democratic elected officials who function as public champions and behind-the-scenes advocates for progressive causes. On the "outside" are multi-issue netroots organizations such as MoveOn, CREDO and Daily Kos that can apply large-scale grassroots pressure on Washington elites. They can generate petitions, phone calls and emails to elected officials and decision-makers, stage rallies and encampments at high-visibility events and supply a steady stream of supportive content in social media, the progressive blogosphere and Internet Left outlets such as *The Huffington Post*. Each campaign may generate a slightly different coalition of netroots organizations and advocacy operations depending on how the agendas and interests of these groups dovetail with a particular issue, but with the "inside" and "outside" sharing information and coordinating activity through backchannel email listservs, conference calls and in-person Washington meetings, these coalitions regularly emerge victorious whenever there is a divide within the Democratic Party on public policy issues.

In late summer 2013, an inside–outside coalition teamed up to help block the confirmation of Lawrence Summers, President Obama's favored candidate for Federal Reserve Chair. As *The Huffington Post* reported in mid-September of that year after Summers had withdrawn his name from consideration, Obama "faced opposition from a coalition of progressive groups who began to speak out against a Summers nomination once speculation started to gain traction. MoveOn, CREDO, The Other 98%, Democracy For America, UltraViolet, the Campaign for America's Future, Daily Kos, the National Organization for Women, Mike Lux's American Family Voices and Color of Change were among those involved in the coalition."[2]

These (mostly) netroots organizations took the lead in gathering hundreds of thousands of petition signatures opposing Summers. Their efforts focused in particular on generating constant anti-Summers constituent phone calls and emails to members of the Senate Banking Committee, through which any nominee for the Federal Reserve must pass. Meanwhile, influential Democratic–progressive donors from the Women's Donor Network, who opposed Summers both for his Wall Street-friendly economic record and for questionable comments he made about women and science during his tenure as president of Harvard University,[3] made personal calls to Democratic members of the Senate Banking Committee expressing their concerns.[4] Simultaneously, three progressive champions on the committee—Jeff Merkley (D-OR), Elizabeth Warren (D-MA) and Sherrod Brown (D-OH)—lobbied their Democratic colleagues from the inside.[5]

As a result of this inside–outside pressure, Democratic Senators Jon Tester of Montana and Heidi Heitkamp of North Dakota, both of whom sat on the Senate Banking Committee at the time, came around to oppose Summers. In conjunction with the Republican members of the committee, this created a critical mass of opposition to his potential nomination that forced him to withdraw his name from consideration for the job. Afterward, Summers' defeat directly led to the confirmation of Janet Yellen as the first female chair of the Federal Reserve, and the first Democratic nominee to hold that position since Paul Volcker's chairmanship from 1979–1987.

Just before Thanksgiving 2013, progressives won a major victory in a multiyear campaign to break the logjam of unconfirmed Obama judicial nominees brought on by procedural delays from Senate opponents. As CNN reported on the day that Senate Democrats "went nuclear" and ended the filibuster for judicial and executive branch nominations, this effort was started and incubated within the progressive blogosphere:

Daily Kos blogger David Waldman started to drum up support online ... Waldman and his co-conspirators formed a strategy referred to as an inside–outside coalition. The outside consisted of the grassroots, charged with motivating progressives to sign petitions and call their senators. The inside, Waldman said, needed to sway senators. It would need to consist of people senators knew and trusted.[6]

A formal organization called "Fix The Senate Now" was formed to house the inside–outside coalition that eventually led to this victory. Outlines of a campaign were developed at preliminary meetings in July 2010 between Daily Kos, Progressive Congress and Progressive Voices, and better-heeled organizations such as the Communications Workers of America and Alliance for Justice assembled a broad coalition of "labor, civil rights, voting rights, environmental, good government and other like-minded membership organizations"[7] under the Fix the Senate Now umbrella. Working together with progressive Senators Jeff Merkley, Tom Udall (D-NM) and Tom Harkin (D-IA), they began the long, slow work of convincing the Senate Democratic leadership and over 50 of their Democratic colleagues that, for the good of all their shared goals, the time had come to reform Senate rules.

Throughout 2014, the impacts of filibuster reform began piling up as long-vacant positions were filled over Republican objections in agencies such as the National Labor Relations Board and the Consumer Financial Protection Bureau. By the end of the year, it had also allowed President Obama and the outgoing Democratic Senate majority to cement a profound judicial legacy that had previously been blocked by the Republican Senate minority: 305 district and circuit court appointees overall and 89 for the year, twice the confirmation rate as prior to filibuster reform and well ahead of the confirmation rate of Obama's immediate predecessors six years into their terms.[8]

Starting in late 2013, the netroots and the Internet Left came to the aid of President Obama and many congressional Democratic leaders when they helped defeat a largely backbencher-led sanctions bill that was designed to derail the Obama administration's efforts to achieve a diplomatic settlement with Iran over its nuclear program. As the *National Journal* reported in February 2014, with Obama facing a surge of opposition to the agreement that included members of his own party, the president pushed back with the help of a "resurgent progressive movement that capitalized on a war-weary public to push Democrats in Obama's direction. MoveOn, Daily Kos, *The Huffington Post* and other liberal media outlets [successfully] mobilized against Democrats who supported sanctions."[9]

In contrast to Fix the Senate Now, there was little formal coordination between the White House—which in this case functioned as the inside advocacy force in the intra-party fight—and the netroots organizations applying waves of public pressure from the outside. However, the effect was the same: a combination of inside and outside pressure brought enough Democrats over to the progressive side in an intra-party fight to carry the day.

It was also not the only time this coalition defended the Iran talks. In March 2015, at the invitation of Republican Speaker of the House John Boehner, Israeli Prime Minister Benjamin Netanyahu spoke to a joint session of Congress to make the case against the emerging diplomatic deal with Iran. Once again, inside pressure from the White House and outside pressure from MoveOn, CREDO, Daily Kos, RootsAction, Win Without War, Just Foreign Policy, USaction, *The Nation*, Code Pink and other groups helped keep a critical mass of Democrats from opposing the talks. A few weeks after the speech, 151 House Democrats signed a letter supporting the emerging agreement, denying Boehner and pro-sanctions Democrats the veto-proof supermajority required to rein in the diplomatic process.[10]

Perhaps the biggest netroots victory occurred on February 26, 2015, when the Democratic-majority Federal Communications Commission (FCC) ruled 3–2 along party lines to protect Net Neutrality by reclassifying Internet access as a telecommunications service under Title II of the 1934 Telecommunications Act. This was the strongest Net Neutrality move the agency could have taken, and despite sounding wonky and esoteric, achieving full Title II protection was an enormous advocacy triumph. Scholar and activist Marvin Ammori wrote that it was "touted as among the biggest public interest victories in history and arguably the biggest Internet freedom victory ever."[11] Senator Al Franken of Minnesota called Net Neutrality the "free speech issue of our time."[12] Rashad Robinson of ColorOfChange.org wrote that it was "civil rights history in the making."[13]

The FCC ruling precluded cable companies and Internet service providers from blocking content on the Internet as they saw fit, or charging websites and other Internet services to deliver their content to consumers at faster speeds. It was a stunning defeat of the nearly $100,000,000 per year cable and telecommunication lobby[14] that went beyond preventing an unwanted outcome and entered the rarefied realm of achieving political change. To accomplish it, netroots activists had to convince the White House and the FCC to reverse their positions on the issue. Only nine months earlier, FCC Chairman Tom Wheeler had released a proposal that would have destroyed Net Neutrality by allowing cable companies and Internet service providers to divide the Internet into pay-to-play fast and slow lanes.

The Net Neutrality victory was engineered through an inside–outside coalition of netroots and DC-centric advocacy organizations in the vein of the Fix the Senate Now coalition that had succeeded in reshaping the federal courts. Internet freedom groups with full-time lobbying staffs that knew the inner workings of Washington, DC regularly huddled with representatives of virtually every netroots organization. Professional lobbying on Capitol Hill and at the White House and FCC was layered with relentless, multi-faceted grassroots activism. This included public comments to FCC dockets, consistent phone call and email pressure to decision makers, rallies at high-visibility FCC events and even a regular encampment outside FCC offices.

It should be noted that the netroots had business muscle on its side as well. In the words of digital organizer Natasha Chart, Net Neutrality could be regarded as "the victory of one business sector over the other," as large tech companies "like Microsoft, eBay, Facebook, Google and Amazon"[15] all favored Net Neutrality and served as a countervailing business lobby to cable and telecom firms. Even so, on the day of the victory, Craig Aaron of Free Press published a roll call of the advocacy groups involved in pressing for Net Neutrality, and it was impressive:

> The long but probably still incomplete list of key groups that share in the credit for this victory includes 18 Million Rising, Access, the ACLU, the Center for Media Justice, ColorOfChange.org, Common Cause, Consumers Union, CREDO Action, Daily Kos, D.C. Action Lab, Demand Progress, Democracy for America, EFF, Engine Advocacy, Fight for the Future, Free Press, the Future of Music Coalition, the Internet Freedom Business Alliance, the Media Action Grassroots Network, the Media Democracy Fund, the Media Literacy Project, the Media Mobilizing Project, MoveOn, the National Hispanic Media Coalition, Open Media, the Open Technology Institute, PCCC, Popular Resistance, Presente.org, Public Knowledge, Revolutions Per Minute and SumOfUs.[16]

This is a who's who of netroots and Internet freedom organizations, many of whom viewed the fight against pay-to-play Internet fast lanes as an existential matter and correspondingly applied resources to the campaign. Together, they submitted *four million* public comments to the FCC, by far the most public comments ever submitted to the FCC on any issue, and the vast majority of them were in favor of the agency taking the strongest possible action to preserve Net Neutrality (full Title II classification). In so doing, they demonstrated the vast scope of more than a decade of progressive online grassroots organizing, which in this instance turned out to be enough to outmuscle one of the strongest business lobbies in Washington and convince the White House and the FCC to reverse themselves.

Even when the inside–outside coalitions of netroots groups and legacy progressive nonprofits do not win major intra-Democratic party fights, they are still highly competitive. A prominent example of this was the multi-year struggle against the Obama administration's push for Fast Track Trade Authority, which would prevent Congress from filibustering or adding amendments to trade agreements. The primary reason the Obama administration sought this authority was to ease the approval of the controversial Trans-Pacific Partnership (TPP) trade agreement between the United States and a dozen Pacific Rim nations. Fast Track and TPP were opposed by virtually every segment of the progressive advocacy ecosystem, including labor, environmental, civil rights, Internet freedom and netroots organizations. A labor-led coalition of hundreds of progressive organizations, spearheaded by progressive legislators Sherrod Brown, Elizabeth Warren and Rep. Rosa DeLauro (D-CT), managed to block Fast Track during Senator Harry Reid's tenure as Senate Majority Leader. Even when Republicans took full control of Congress following the 2014 midterm elections, the coalition temporarily handed the Obama administration and congressional Republican leaders a stunning defeat of a legislative package that included Fast Track. With *Politico* reporting that "calls and letters into member offices [were] running 10 to 1 against",[17] Fast Track, the measure went down to defeat in the House of Representatives on June 12, 2015, with only 28 of 188 Democratic members voting in favor.[18] While the pro-Fast Track coalition regrouped and managed to pass Fast Track Trade Authority into law for six years, the multi-year fight had been much harder for them than expected.

Left or right, movements exist to pressure nominally sympathetic elected officials into advancing their goals. Movement conservatives understood this and spent years pushing Republican office-holders toward their objectives against the inertia of powerful counter-pressures, as we saw in Chapter 2. Digital-native movement progressives facing comparable pressures are now starting to move the Democratic Party their way. Understanding the role progressives are playing in today's transitional politics requires understanding how the netroots changed since its early days as a largely amateur operation, emerging as a muscular force pushing for a progressive realignment. Derisively ridiculed and ignored only a few years earlier, progressive Internet-based political and media organizations have rapidly gained in reach if not respect, displaying a degree of strength strangely similar to movement conservatism in the waning days of the New Deal coalition.

The first generation: origin of the progressive netroots

The progressive netroots came into its own in late 2002 and early 2003 as Internet-native grassroots outlets for Americans who opposed the impending war in Iraq. While public opinion polls during that time showed a clear majority of Americans favored the use of military force to overthrow Saddam Hussein's regime, a significant minority—between 25% and 40%, depending on the poll—were in opposition. In virtually all polls, the opposition included a majority of self-identified Democrats.

In the political environment that followed the attacks of September 11, 2001, this significant anti-war minority was almost entirely shut out of the nation's most prominent news outlets. The left-leaning media watch group Fairness and Accuracy in Reporting (FAIR) examined 393 on-camera sources appearing on network evening news programs immediately prior to the Iraq invasion and found virtually no grassroots or anti-war voices were provided space in nightly broadcast news programs at that time.[19] The period in question is significant because it was followed a few days later by the February 15, 2003 International Day of Action against war in Iraq which, when it occurred, was the largest coordinated protest event in human history. In the United States alone, over one million Americans are estimated to have attended protests in over 150 cities. There was a tremendous amount of anti-war energy in the United States, but it was not being given a voice in established media.[20]

Americans opposed to war in Iraq were also without representation in the presidential election. In early 2003, the four leading contenders for the 2004 Democratic presidential nomination were Senator John Edwards of North Carolina, former Democratic House Leader Dick Gephardt, Senator John Kerry and former Democratic vice presidential nominee Joe Lieberman. All four supported the Bush administration's military action and, unlike the majority of Democrats in Congress, voted in favor of the 2002 Authorization for the Use of Military Force in Iraq. With a large, engaged left-of-center constituency effectively abandoned by both established media and the leading Democratic presidential contenders, the door was open for new voices, new organizations and new leaders to emerge.

The technological moment of the first years of the new millennium made it possible for an unlikely collection of people to walk through that door and be heard. In the 44 months from May 1998 to January 2002, according to Pew Research, the percentage of Americans using the Internet rose from 36% to 61%.[21] As of 2001, the Census Bureau found that a majority of Americans had Internet access at home, a number that rose to 55% in 2003.[22] For the first time, it was practical to believe that Americans could be reached en masse via the Internet—a medium that had little in the way of established leadership.

The blogosphere, MoveOn and Howard Dean lead the way

During 2002–2003, the confluence of establishment disregard for significant anti-war sentiment and the emergence of the Internet permitted three principal offshoots of the early netroots—the progressive blogosphere, MoveOn and Howard Dean's presidential campaign—to bootstrap themselves into national prominence. As a majority of Americans were discovering a new medium and established journalists and politicians were ignoring a large segment of the American political landscape, low-cost digital publishing and communication technologies were providing the means for soon-to-be-leaders affiliated with these three institutions to connect with and organize the large reservoir of anti-war sentiment.

Most of the key early figures in the first generation of the progressive netroots had little experience in either political journalism or organizing. Instead, they tended to be early adopters of what were then new Internet functions, specifically blogging and email-based political organizing. MoveOn, the fountainhead of email-based political organizing, started in 1998 in reaction to the impeachment of President Clinton.[23] Many of the websites that eventually composed the core of the early progressive blogosphere, such as *Talking Points Memo*, Political Wire, Eschaton, MyDD and Daily Kos, had been in existence for one to three years before the push for war in Iraq ignited their growth. Similarly, Howard Dean had been governor of Vermont for nearly a decade and a presidential candidate for almost a year without attracting much attention. But, once the drumbeat for war began, the modest structures they all had in place were overwhelmed with traffic, forcing them to scale at breakneck speeds.

From the start of the war until mid-2005, combined weekly pageviews from the network of blogs that constituted the progressive blogosphere increased tenfold, from about 1,500,000 per week to 15,000,000 (Bowers and Stoller 2005). This rapid uptick was not merely the result of increasing Internet adoption. Between 2003 and 2005, the progressive blogosphere ballooned from having less than half the traffic of the conservative blogosphere to being nearly double its size. By September 2005, the largest progressive blog, Daily Kos, had nearly as much traffic as the combined total of right-wing blogs constituting the conservative blogosphere.[24] Americans across the political spectrum were swarming to the new medium (conservative blogosphere traffic doubled during the same two years), but progressives were disproportionately inclined to consume new media, possibly because of their lack of representation in established sources.

The progressive blogosphere produced a running, nonstop counter-narrative to the political news reported by the mainstream media. As traditional media outlets portrayed triumphalist images of an American tank pulling down a statue of Saddam Hussein in Baghdad, bloggers focused on the lack of weapons of mass destruction that the Bush administration had used to justify the invasion, as well as stories about American casualties and the escalating cost of the war. In stark contrast to the national media, they argued that the occupation would eventually prove unpopular and that Democrats should not be afraid to challenge President George W. Bush on national security. Markos Moulitsas wrote in a September 2003 blog post, "The sheen is off Bush's War. With ten dead per week and billions frittered away, it's clear the administration is in serious damage control mode."

The blogosphere incubated anti-war sentiment and attracted a growing anti-war readership, playing an important role in eventually turning national opinion against the war. When Democratic officials such as Senator Robert Byrd (D-WV), Governor Howard Dean and, later on, Rep. Jack Murtha (D-PA) publicly opposed the war or advocated for withdrawal from Iraq, they became heroic figures in the blogosphere and were lavished with praise and small donations, thus providing incentive for other Democratic figures to join them.

Progressive bloggers also focused on scandals and wrongdoing by Republican officials that they felt the mainstream media ignored. Bloggers Josh Marshall of *Talking Points Memo* and Duncan Black of Eschaton successfully kept alive a little-reported news item about incoming Senate Majority Leader Trent Lott (R-MS) expressing pride in segregationist Strom Thurmond's 1948 presidential campaign, stating that had Thurmond been elected, "we wouldn't have had all these problems over all these years."[25] Lott spoke those words on the night of December

5, 2002, at Thurmond's 100th birthday party. For four days established media offered little coverage of the comments, but they were extensively discussed within the blogosphere, and after relentless pressure from bloggers, on December 10 the story received widespread coverage in national news outlets, forcing Lott to become the first Senate Majority Leader in history to resign under pressure.

In later years, Jane Hamsher and Marcy Wheeler of FireDogLake won accolades for their coverage of the trial of Vice President Dick Cheney's former Chief of Staff Scooter Libby, who was convicted of five felonies for his role in outing undercover CIA Agent Valerie Plame. Marshall of *Talking Points Memo* was similarly lauded for his coverage of the highly controversial dismissal of seven U.S. attorneys by President George W. Bush's Department of Justice on December 7, 2006.

In the second half of 2002, MoveOn had two petitions opposing the Iraq War that each had multiple hundreds of thousands of signers, and which added well in excess of 100,000 new sign-ups to the organization's email list.[26] In December of that year, MoveOn ran a supporter-funded ad campaign against the war, powered by contributions from individuals who had signed the petitions, that was the subject of over 100 television news stories worldwide. Highly innovative at the time, using petitions to sign people to email lists, then using those lists to solicit funds for campaigns related to the topic of those petitions, remains a staple of netroots organizing to this day.

In early 2003, MoveOn organized a volunteer-led, face-to-face lobbying effort against the Iraq War in hundreds of congressional districts, which "produced 130 signatures on [then-]Congressman Sherrod Brown's Congressional letter calling on the President to respect the UN process and let [weapons] inspections work."[27] On February 26, 2003, the organization made national headlines with a "virtual march" on Washington against the impending war, which resulted in over one million phone calls and faxes being sent to Congress in a single day.[28] This and other anti-war activities were arranged primarily via the organization's email list, allowing MoveOn to pass 750,000 United States email signups in early 2003, and then one million only a few months later. The mainstream media took notice; between 2002 and 2003, news mentions of the organization increased fourteenfold, from 155 to over 2,200.

However, hardly anyone noticed when Howard Dean declared his candidacy for president on May 31, 2002. He barely made a ripple in 12 national polls conducted that year, registering an average of less than 1% support.[29] This changed precipitously in 2003, following widespread blogosphere dissemination of his March speech to the California Democratic convention, where he excoriated his fellow candidates for their support of the war. From that point forward, his support increased dramatically.

Using the website Meetup.com, the Dean campaign signed up 140,000 supporters to attend regular, local, in-person meetings in support of his campaign. At these "Dean Meetups," supporters wrote letters to Democratic voters in Iowa and New Hampshire, organized local door-knocking campaigns, exchanged ideas and increased the social capital of local progressive political networks. By August, Dean's nationwide "Sleepless Summer Tour" of nine rallies in four days generated larger crowds than had been seen in Democratic primaries in several cycles.[30] By September, Dean consistently was either first or second in every national, Iowa and New Hampshire poll. Utilizing an email list with more than half a million members, he also led all of his rivals in fundraising. In the third quarter of 2003, with a thunderous haul of $14.8 million, Dean smashed Bill Clinton's Democratic presidential primary record of $10.3 million for a single fundraising quarter. In November 2003, Dean had raised so much money through small online donations that he became the first Democratic candidate to forgo public matching funds for his campaign so that he would not be bound by spending limits.

Even though Dean's campaign eventually crashed and burned in Iowa, his rapid ascendancy validated the assumption—widely shared among the netroots—that a substantial left-of-center base existed and could be mobilized through the new medium. Dean was the proof of concept for other campaigns to come: Barack Obama's 2008 campaign for the Democratic presidential nomination; Elizabeth Warren's campaign for U.S. Senate in Massachusetts in 2012; and Senator Bernie Sanders' campaign for the 2016 Democratic presidential nomination. The same pattern emerged in each case: large, seemingly spontaneous crowds; massive numbers of small donations online; overflowing volunteer centers; and huge buzz on blogs and social media. This is not coincidental: they were all tapping into the same netroots network that was originally mobilized in 2002–2003.

When progressives who felt ostracized by the political and media environment went online searching for an alternative to what was available over the airwaves and in print, the progressive blogosphere was able to attract and retain them with daily news and commentary, MoveOn.org was able to organize and channel them to action, and Howard Dean provided them with a voice that could be heard nationwide. Subsequently, the progressive blogosphere and MoveOn would become Petri dishes for movement politics, and Dean campaign graduates-turned-political consultants would convert their knowledge of digital technology into a campaign infrastructure serving other progressive candidates (Kreiss 2012). Progressives who had been abandoned by established media and Democratic leaders utilized a new medium to find a way back, and over the next decade would add to those early accomplishments as the structures they were building on the Internet began to mature.

Diaries, search engines, blogrolls and hyperlinks

During a seven-year golden age that concluded with the passage of the Affordable Care Act in 2010, the progressive blogosphere was a close-knit network of do-it-yourself publishing outlets that played a crucial role in the formation and development of the netroots. The blogosphere was led by a group of enterprising progressives who, with no financial backing and little experience in either political journalism or organizing, utilized blogs—newly available, low-cost publishing technologies—to carve out an entirely new media-activist space.

In the beginning there were no barriers to entry, save for access to the Internet (which in the early days of the blogosphere meant having a computer and a modem) and the desire to cast opinions into the vast uncertainty of cyberspace to see what—if anything—came back. Critics (including some with deep experience in journalism or politics) dismissed these early do-it-yourself publishers as uninformed, unqualified and unimportant, the stereotypical dirty hippies in bathrobes pounding away at their keyboards from the security of their parents' basements.

The most common progressive blog structure was a single writer publishing a series of original commentary articles about the news of the day. These short pieces, called "posts" or "diaries," would scroll down a webpage in reverse chronological order. For little or no charge, individuals could easily sign up for a site at one of several available blog platforms such as Blogger or Typepad. In most cases the readership was small, but a few dedicated, passionate writers developed a following even though they had no experience in journalism or politics. Like early radio and television programming, blogs were a novelty and a curiosity but not a viable forum for political action.

When readership expanded with the start of the Iraq War, blogs acquired new readers through two primary means: search engines and hyperlinks from other blogs. A look at Google Analytics data on the top 25 sources of traffic to Daily Kos from November 14, 2005 to January 17, 2006,[31] displayed in Table 3.1, demonstrates the central role of search engines and other blogs in driving traffic to the largest progressive blog.

During these two months, 53.5% of Daily Kos traffic came directly to the website without any referrals, from people accessing the website using bookmarks in their browsers. This large pool of regular readers had previously discovered the blog and decided they liked it enough to return on a regular basis. They formed the backbone of a large, interactive community which every day produced hundreds of user-generated posts and tens of thousands of user-generated comments.

A second line of traffic, constituting almost 9% of visits to *Daily Kos* during the selected timeframe, were people who came to the site through Google keyword searches. While not a large percentage of total traffic, at 36.9% this group represented a disproportionate amount of new eyeballs. Thus search engines, and Google in particular, were a key source of new Daily Kos readers and, more generally, readers of progressive blogs.

Almost all the remaining traffic came from referrals from other progressive blogs who had sent their audience to Daily Kos through a hyperlink referral in either a blog post or a "blogroll"—a list of links to other blogs with related content, typically found in the margins of the blog. This is how sites like those listed in Table 3.1, notably Eschaton, Crooks and Liars, AmericaBlog, FireDogLake, MyDD, *Talking Points Memo* and *Raw Story* could form the nucleus of what would become a vital progressive media nexus, and how *The Huffington*

TABLE 3.1 Top 25 sources of traffic to Daily Kos, November 14, 2005–January 17, 2006

Source	Total sessions Number	Total sessions Percentage	New sessions Number	New sessions Percentage of total
No Referrals	7,206,581	53.5	987,855	13.7
Google	1,205,742	8.9	444,894	36.9
Eschaton	835,091	6.2	32,490	3.9
Daily Kos	296,742	2.2	115,296	38.9
My.Yahoo.com	236,148	1.8	15,871	6.7
The Huffington Post	183,076	1.4	25,796	14.1
Crooks and Liars	138,533	1.0	13,641	9.9
Talking Points Memo	131,141	1.0	10,114	7.7
Buzzflash	113,544	0.8	16,339	14.4
Americablog (blogspot)	95,080	0.7	6,377	6.7
Raw Story	89,192	0.7	8,751	9.9
Democratic Underground	84,134	0.6	12,841	15.3
Google (referral)	82,125	0.6	8,301	10.1
Yahoo	70,418	0.5	11,600	16.5
Political Wire	68,042	0.5	4,617	6.8
Salon	66,624	0.5	13,183	19.8
Haloscan	60,713	0.5	3,296	5.4
MSNBC	60,582	0.5	8,241	13.6
Americablog	53,418	0.4	3,600	6.7
James Wolcott	42,020	0.3	2,385	6.8
Liberal Oasis	39,647	0.3	2,835	6.8
FireDogLake	38,207	0.3	1,689	4.4
MyDD	37,550	0.3	1,894	5.0
National Review	37,473	0.3	14,300	38.2
Bloglines	34,890	0.3	4,832	13.9
Total	**13,482,378**	**100.0**	**2,277,188**	**16.9**

Source: Google Analytics.

Post—part of the Internet Left but not the netroots, and then in its infancy—would expand into one of the largest news and publishing operations in the United States.

In addition to keeping traffic circulating among the blogs within the network, these link exchanges had the crucial effect of increasing the number of people who found blogs in the network through Google keyword searches. At the time, the likelihood of a website appearing near the top of a Google search was closely related to the number of other websites linking to it. In this way, blogrolls and hyperlinks in blog posts and diaries would compound the effect of search engines, and all would serve as force multipliers for a group of amateur political junkies looking to attract and maintain a large audience without any advertising budget, organized publicity or outside funding. The process worked like this:

- Step 1: an individual seeking progressive commentary stumbles upon a progressive blog by doing a Google search.
- Step 2: the reader, if satisfied, bookmarks the blog and returns later, perhaps on a regular basis.
- Step 3: the bookmarked blog, in turn, uses hyperlinks to direct the reader to other blogs in the network, keeping traffic within the blogosphere while increasing the number of new people entering the network through step 1 by boosting the prominence of the linked blogs in Google searches.

This positive feedback loop was necessary for amateurs operating on a shoestring. Traffic and buzz may have been high, but revenue streams were sparse and consisted mainly of low-revenue blog ads, irregular community fundraisers and occasional freelance writing and consulting opportunities. No one was funneling money to bloggers to allow them to operate at a loss; they had to find ways to make ends meet, and some struggled to pay rent or went for years without health insurance.[32]

Despite their relative poverty and against all odds, netroots bloggers began scoring points in their budding power struggle with the Democratic Party, making national political waves during intra-party fights with centrists and conservatives. The heterogeneous Democratic Party had been mired in internal conflict for decades, and thus for many in the traditional media the rise of the blogosphere fit conveniently into a long-running narrative about "Democrats in disarray" dating back to the breakup of the New Deal coalition in the 1960s. Given their progressive bent, bloggers were assigned the role of the fringy left-wing opposition to a set of more conservative and established groups and individuals: the Democratic Leadership Committee, House Blue Dogs, Third Way and, most memorably, Connecticut Senator Joe Lieberman.

Although bloggers may have rejected this characterization, having a place in mainstream news narratives won them mainstream recognition even if it trivialized their objectives. The netroots' uneven record in these early days did little to challenge this dismissive coverage, even as they aimed high in their struggle to reclaim the Democratic Party for progressives. Lieberman in particular was the foil for several major progressive battles during the arc of the first-generation blogosphere and netroots:

- In 2003, as the blogosphere fueled Howard Dean's insurgent candidacy, Lieberman—an early frontrunner for the nomination by virtue of having

been the Democrat's vice presidential nominee in 2000—saw his presidential hopes consumed by the anti-war sentiment Dean channeled into the contest.
- As we noted in Chapter 2, progressive blogs in 2006 drafted Ned Lamont to challenge Lieberman in the Democratic Senate primary.[33] Lamont defeated Lieberman in a netroots-fueled, anti-war campaign that dominated national political headlines in the weeks leading up to the August primary. Although Lieberman was able to win re-election in November as an independent with the de facto support of the Republican Party (the Republican nominee received only 10% of the vote), the contest settled the intra-party fight over whether Democrats should support military withdrawal from Iraq. That fall, Democrats retook Congress on a pledge to begin the process of bringing troops home.
- In late 2009, the blogosphere and netroots were deeply engaged in a major legislative fight over the inclusion of a "public option" or public-sector health insurance plan in President Obama's signature legislation, the Affordable Care Act. Days after an apparent deal had been struck to expand Medicare eligibility to all Americans aged 55 or over—a deal largely welcomed by bloggers—Lieberman blew up the compromise to which he had been a party by declaring his opposition to it, three months after having publicly endorsed the Medicare buy-in and two weeks after privately assuring Senate Majority Leader Harry Reid of his support.[34] Whether or not it was his intent, he achieved a measure of revenge for the Lamont challenge by sinking what would have been the blogosphere's pinnacle legislative achievement.

Social media and the decline of the first-generation netroots

As Lieberman's about-face was undermining the netroots' fight for a public option, the structural underpinnings of the blogosphere were coming undone. For digital publishing, the search engine era was ending and the social media era was at hand. From 2008 to 2009, the percentage of Americans who used social media networks skyrocketed from 33% to 61% (Duggan 2013). This S-curve jump in social media use was highly destructive to the search engine, "front page" and community link-exchange infrastructure of the blogosphere. Instead of people searching for content through sites like Google and then in the future returning to the websites they found through those searches, people began finding content through social networks like Facebook and then returning to Facebook afterward.

This meant publishers needed to attract readers by building up followers within social networks they didn't control, not by maintaining their place in a hyperlink referral community of like-minded activists. Having lots of followers on Facebook and catching those followers' attention by marketing content through attractive images and intrigue-generating headlines (e.g., "Joe Lieberman gets a primary challenger—you won't believe what happens next!") became crucial to maintaining an audience—and thus ad revenue and political relevance. Whereas the search engine-based Internet had led readers to publishers, the social media-based Internet was leading both readers and publishers into sites like Facebook, StumbleUpon, Reddit, Twitter and Digg.

In 2008, Facebook was ranked 89th in sources of referral traffic to Daily Kos, generating only 25,999 total visits for the entire year. In 2009, that total jumped to 1,068,025 visits. StumbleUpon went from 13,015 referrals to Daily Kos in 2008 to 1,017,650 the next year. Reddit skyrocketed from 29,561 to 2,018,070, becoming the fourth highest source of traffic to Daily Kos and passing even Google. Twitter multiplied from 3,442 to 606,652, while Digg went from 50,963 to 1,396,494. Social networks that had been insignificant drivers of digital publisher traffic in 2008 were suddenly essential in 2009, and more so in the years that followed.

This was a crushing blow to the blogosphere. As people moved to social networks, they moved away from finding content through search engines, the "front page" of publisher's websites and referrals from one publisher to another. Starting in late 2009, these three sources of blogosphere traffic slowly began to decline for Daily Kos. As social networks exploded and it became more difficult to drive web traffic by being a member of a community of bloggers sending hyperlink referrals to one another's websites, most progressive blogs faced a steady decline in audience and income that eventually led to their shuttering.

The second generation: social networks

But the netroots survived—and thrived—by redefining themselves in this new age. By all metrics—people reached, revenue generated and political fights won—the netroots are larger than ever. When considered as a single network, the netroots now comprise the largest organizing force of the progressive left of the Democratic Party. Some people involved in the first generation—most of whom were new to the political scene during the anti-war-fueled rise of the progressive netroots—vastly developed their original projects. The paid staffs of first-generation rudimentary blogs MoveOn and the Dean campaign emerged as the prototype for an entirely new class of actor unknown at the dawn of the original netroots: the Professional Left.

While the rise of the social media Internet wreaked havoc on the blogosphere as a network, it provided an unexpected opportunity for a small number of individual blogs and bloggers who were able to adapt to the changing environment. Some first-generation bloggers from the early netroots, such as Arianna Huffington, Nate Silver, Glenn Greenwald and Ezra Klein, were able to translate their cache into true stardom. Some of the larger blogs, most notably Daily Kos, *Raw Story* and *Think Progress* (the latter backed by the well funded Center for

American Progress) were able to adapt to the rapidly changing media environment and not only survive, but scale up by an order of magnitude.

Traffic on these blogs began to take off in the second decade of the twenty-first century and soon could be measured in millions rather than hundreds of thousands. In March 2015, according to the Internet traffic-measuring site Quantcast, Daily Kos, *Raw Story, Think Progress* and *Talking Points Memo* alone combined for 25,000,000 global pageviews per week, roughly two-thirds more than the pageviews generated by the top 50 progressive blogs ten years earlier. During that same month, 5.8 million Americans visited *Think Progress* at least once, 7.2 million visited Daily Kos, and 7.8 million came to *Raw Story*. By way of comparison, the websites of CBS News (4.7 million), ABC News (5.0 million) and CNN (10.2 million) reached roughly the same number of people.[35] By pooling hundreds of millions of people into single locations and giving those people the ability to recommend and share content with each other, large social media networks provide news organizations, publishers and even single activists the ability to reach far more individuals than they ever had in the past.

The primary driver of this trend is Facebook. In December 2014, according to the firm comScore, Facebook accounted for over 80% of all time spent on social networks in the United States, and one-sixth of all time spent consuming all digital media. In January 2015, Shareaholic reported that Facebook drove more than three times as much traffic to publishers as all other social networks combined.[36] The potential reach is so vast that if a publisher can build up enough Facebook followers and optimize their content so that their readers want to share with their own friends or followers on that network, then even once-lowly bloggers have the ability to reach as many people online as the news organizations of broadcast television networks.

Beyond the blogosphere, many other progressive, non-partisan publications of the Internet Left have taken advantage of the social media Internet. These include long-running print publications such as *Mother Jones* (5.5 million monthly unique U.S. visitors in March 2015), and first-generation digital-native publications such as *Salon* (11.3 million) and *Alternet* (5.1 million). It also includes social media-native, venture capital-funded outlets such as *Mic* (13.4 million) and, especially, *Upworthy*. Co-founded by long-time MoveOn Executive Director Eli Pariser, *Upworthy* reached 17.2 million Americans in March 2015, more than any non-digital-native American news organization that month save for NBC News, which reached 27.3 million persons, and Fox News, which reached 23 million.[37]

At the outskirts of the Internet Left are sites featuring non-ideological but "blue state"-oriented content, like Gawker Media, a network of ten blogs dedicated to a variety of cultural and lifestyle topics from celebrity news to science fiction to feminism that collectively reached 64.3 million Americans in March 2015.[38] Like *The Huffington Post*, Gawker Media started out as a single blog and transformed into a vast publishing operation reaching over 50 million Americans a month. The culturally progressive orientation of Gawker, along with *Mic*,

Upworthy and *The Huffington Post*, combined with their lack of partisan activity that distinguishes them from the netroots core of the Internet Left, can appeal to left-of-center Americans who may be less politically engaged than those who frequent the core netroots publishers.

The reliance on Facebook for traffic is not without drawbacks, most notably a drop in individual engagement time. Facebook may allow many publishers to reach vastly more people than they ever did in the past, but on average they are reaching those people less deeply. Readers now primarily start and end their visits to a site by viewing a single article they saw on Facebook or other social media. Previously, most readers started their visit to an online publisher by visiting that publisher's "front page" and would read multiple articles or even post a comment before leaving. As blogger Ezra Klein opined, "we're getting better at serving a huge audience even as we're getting worse at serving a loyal one."[39]

Because of the rise of the social media Internet, the progressive blogosphere is not as central to the netroots as it once was. While many older readers still visit blogs through their front pages and blogrolls, the stranglehold of Facebook and other social media networks on Internet publishing has pushed the old blog network to the margins. It has also pushed many of the old bloggers to find employment elsewhere in political media, or simply to quit.

However, some of the largest progressive blogs survived the transformation into the social media Internet and scaled up in the process. They are now a part of a vast Internet Left offering progressive voices enormous reach on a wide range of topics. Online, the Internet Left has grown large enough to provide a counterpoint to right-wing media, filling a void for the left from the pre-digital world. This is exactly what its originators had found so lacking in the media environment of the first years of the twenty-first century, and which they turned to new media to create.

The emergence of the Professional Left

The rise of large netroots and Internet Left publishers has had a profound economic impact on the progressive digital space by creating scores of salaried, well paying jobs with health insurance and other benefits. Whereas the first-iteration blogosphere was run largely by low-paid activists leading ascetic lives who often struggled—literally—to keep their lights on, the new, larger publishers made it possible for hundreds of people to make a living and build a career within the netroots.

Over the past decade, a wide range of employment opportunities has created an entirely new class of left-of-center political operative colloquially known as the Professional Left. In addition to publishers, the four other major types of employers are: email-based advocacy organizations; digital campaign consultancies; in-house digital campaign and communication departments within Democratic Party committees, progressive nonprofits and unions; and vendors and professional organizations that provide a range of services to the progressive digital organizing world.

E-mail-based advocacy organizations

E-mail is for movement progressives in the twenty-first century what direct mail was for movement conservatives the century prior. Ubiquitous and mundane, it is the engine for fundraising and political action. From 2003 to 2012, MoveOn expanded its email list from 1,000,000 to 8,000,000, employed a staff of more than 30 and raised over $100,000,000 for political advocacy and member-endorsed candidates.[40]

Perhaps more noteworthy than this dramatic growth is MoveOn's work of institution building, encompassing a long list of netroots organizations it incubated directly or which were founded by former MoveOn staffers.[41] With few exceptions, these organizations use the MoveOn operational and funding model. Internet scholar David Karpf (2012) describes the MoveOn model as having four distinct characteristics: a small core staff working out of a virtual office; membership defined by the number of active subscribers to the organization's email list (typically between 500,000 and 3,500,000 U.S. subscribers); advocacy engagement dominated by message-tested email action alerts; and fundraising driven by email alerts crafted around the messages which have sparked the most engagement from email list subscribers. Together with numerous "niche" issue specialists that employ the same operational model, and along with Daily Kos and CREDO action, these organizations provide the collective backbone for "outside" activism in progressive inside–outside coalitions.

Digital campaign consultancies

Democratic officials and committees, progressive nonprofits and labor unions have universally adopted e-mail based organizing and digital campaigning, most commonly by contracting with consulting firms that specialize in the practice. The consulting firm Blue State Digital was founded in 2005 by alumni of Howard Dean's campaign. At the time, Democratic consultants and Washington officials wanted to know how Dean had used the Internet to raise tens of millions of dollars for his campaign. Blue State Digital successfully marketed itself as the firm able to provide the answer, and it found a ready market for its expertise, with clients ranging from Senate Majority Leader Harry Reid to the Democratic National Committee to presidential candidate Barack Obama, for whom it designed the online infrastructure that supported, in the words of its founders, "the biggest nationwide field organization ever created."[42]

Blue State Digital's results with the Obama campaign could hardly have been more immediate or decisive. However, helping to elect Obama president turned out to be just the beginning of the broader impact that email-centric campaigning would have on Democratic Party politics. As the number of people with experience working on the digital side of campaigns continued to grow, consulting firms offering services like Blue State Digital proliferated. Campaign veterans with experience in digital organizing and advertising went on to found or play key roles in companies such as Triology, New Blue Interactive, Bully Pulpit Interactive, Revolution Messaging, Anne Lewis Strategies and Chong & Koster.

These consultancies are now a fixture in the Democratic campaign and progressive advocacy economy, and by 2014 email-based organizing and digital advertising was providing Democratic candidates and committees across the country with a sizable edge in small-dollar donations over Republicans. In September 2014, *National Journal* quantified this advantage with a study showing Democratic candidates in competitive House contests lapping their competition, averaging $179,300 in donations under $200 compared with $78,535 for their Republican challengers. This advantage was evident in red and blue states and for incumbents and challengers.[43]

In-house digital departments

Instead of just contracting with consulting firms, many progressive nonprofits, labor unions and Democratic Party committees have built in-house digital campaign and communication departments. The need for their own operations, according to Karpf (2012), stems from the spread of digital operational norms pioneered by MoveOn in response to a decline in the utility of direct mail as a fundraising source for progressive advocacy groups, and the concurrent rise of the Internet in American life. Consequently, many Democratic Party committees and progressive nonprofits now have email-based campaign and fundraising operations that rival email-based netroots advocacy organizations in size and mimic them in appearance.

In addition to helping these organizations meet fundraising demands in a new communications environment, the rise of in-house digital campaign departments served as a key interface between the netroots and the progressive advocacy infrastructure. It became commonplace for nonprofits, unions and party organizations to hire netroots figures for their experience and skills, creating professional and social bridges between the two worlds.[44] The personal connections created by this intermingling facilitated the rise of progressive inside–outside coalitions.

Vendors

As a sizable economy has developed around digital campaigning, businesses and nonprofits that provide services to that economy have emerged with it. In order to conduct email-based campaigns, organizations need lists of recipients to whom they can send action alerts. This need has spawned companies, most notably Change.org, that specialize in "lead generation," or legally getting people to opt-in to an organization's email list.[45] Once a campaign or an organization has an email list, it needs a means to send emails and host actions for email recipients to take. Several companies have emerged to serve this purpose,[46] with services that test and send email messages, host online petitions, fundraise, contact elected officials and track the behavior of supporters.

Two organizations founded during the Netroots' first generation—the New Organizing Institute (NOI) and Netroots Nation—provide training in a range of digital campaign skills and opportunities to network at large annual gatherings. Founded by MoveOn alumni Zack Exley and Judith Freeman in 2005, NOI offers seminars on the more arcane aspects of digital campaigning, including graphic design, social networking best practices and data analytics, and has its own annual conference in Washington, D.C., called Rootscamp. Netroots Nation, founded in 2006 as Yearly Kos by members of the Daily Kos community who wanted to meet in person, has become the largest progressive professional gathering in America, annually attracting thousands from the Professional Left for training and discussion sessions on topics similar to those covered by NOI. Like the netroots itself, Netroots Nation has evolved from amateur grassroots gathering to professional event.

Strategic advantages: Left rising and Internet rising

Unlike other mass media, the Internet provides for communication from many people to many other people in a web of connections that defined the self-organizing characteristics of the first-generation netroots. But uniquely it provides for one-to-many and many-to-one communication as well, and these relationship patterns have become valuable in the netroots' second iteration as networks of professional progressive organizations have emerged to propel progressive advocacy.

Whereas the first generation of the netroots created new structures run primarily by volunteers or low-paid political newcomers, the second generation boasts a large economy built around progressive, grassroots-oriented digital media and campaigning. Members of the Professional Left who staff these jobs operate a network of progressive publishers, email-based advocacy organizations and digital campaign departments that facilitate activism on a scale that was unimaginable during the netroots' first generation. The emergence of the Professional Left created social and professional bridges between the netroots and the existing progressive advocacy structure, allowing for the rise of inside–outside coalitions that are proving successful at winning intra-party fights with Democratic leadership on major public policy issues. They have spread fundraising tactics pioneered by MoveOn and Howard Dean to every corner of the progressive political world, providing Democratic candidates with a clear, across-the-board small-donor advantage over Republicans.

But the success of the second-generation netroots stems as much from the growing number of like-minded people who are available to be organized online as from mastering the technical wizardry of a new medium. The netroots and Professional Left are propelled by favorable demographic and technological trends that provide them with the opportunity they will need if they are to parlay their growing infrastructure into a lasting progressive realignment.

Whether they see themselves as liberals or progressives, since the end of the previous millennium a steadily increasing number of Americans have been identifying as left of center. According to Gallup, liberal self-identification, which was stuck at 16% the year Bill Clinton was re-elected, rose to 19% of the population the following year and stayed there until 2005, when it began rising into the low twenties. It reached a new peak at 24% in 2014, while self-identifying conservatives remained exactly where they were in 1996, at 38% (Jones 2014). According to the Pew Research Center, liberal self-identification hit a nadir in the two years following the attacks of September 11, 2001, but has been gradually increasing since that time.[47] The trend lines are clear: conservatives, while still the ideological plurality, have flatlined, while liberals are growing in strength as a percentage of the American population.

Just as significantly for the fate of the netroots, in the next few years—likely around 2020 based on present trends—self-identified liberals will become a majority of self-identified Democrats. This is a sweeping change from recent history, with major political implications. Not long ago, self-identified liberals were a small minority of all Democratic self-identifiers. At the start of the previous decade, not only were moderate Democrats a clear plurality within the Democratic coalition, there were almost as many self-identified conservative Democrats as there were self-identified liberal Democrats. According to Gallup, liberals in 2000 constituted a mere 29% of rank-and-file Democrats, barely edging out conservatives (25%) while being swamped by moderates, who made up 44% of the party base. The share of liberals began to rise in 2003 and has been increasing ever since. By 2007, liberals had caught up to moderates, and in 2011 surpassed them. In 2014, fully 44% of Democrats were self-described liberals, while only 36% claimed to be moderates. At 19%, conservative Democrats have become an endangered species (Jones 2014).

If this trend continues, the 2020s will mark the first time in recent history that Americans who self-identify as left-of-center will form the majority of one of the country's two major political parties. And it is likely to continue, given the current generational gap in ideological self-identification. While the ideological identification gap among Americans born in 1945 or earlier (those Gallup calls "Traditionalists") favors conservatives by 31 percentage points, among Baby Boomers (born 1946–1964) conservatives hold only a 23 percentage point advantage, and for Generation X (born 1965–1979) the difference is 12 points. The ideology gap disappears completely among Millennials (born 1980–1996), where liberal identifiers actually hold a narrow two-percentage-point advantage over conservatives. Younger generations are decisively more likely than older generations to self-identify as liberal, and their numbers will only increase compared with older generations both as a relative share of the general population and Democratic self-identifiers.

Life-cycle effects could potentially mitigate this trend toward increasing liberal identification, as Traditionalists, Baby Boomers and Gen Xers have all become more conservative with age. Since 1994, Traditionalists have shifted two percentage points toward conservative identification, Baby Boomers have moved four percentage points, and Gen Xers three percentage points. However, this average shift of three percentage points is small compared with the 33-percentage-point gap between the oldest and youngest generations. The impact of generational replacement greatly outweighs the impact of increasing conservatism with age.

On the demographic side, the leftward shift is being propelled by two identity-based trends: the increasing number and percentage of Americans who identify as non-white; and the increasing number and percentage of Americans who identify as non-Christian. In 2012, Americans who self-identified as either non-white or non-Christian already composed an absolute majority of the population—56%—up from only 34% in 1990.[48] These two populations favored Democrats over Republicans by greater than 2–1 margins in the 2008 and 2012 elections, forming a majority of the winning Democratic coalition.[49] Even at its current size, a Democratic coalition propelled by communities of color and non-Christians has already proven it has the numbers to win national elections. It currently wields enough cultural influence to create popular majorities for ideas such as marriage equality and marijuana legalization that as recently as the turn of the millennium had been considered beyond the left margin of mainstream politics.

And this coalition will continue to grow. Population growth among Americans who identify as either non-white or non-Christian is outstripping overall population growth, and has been for many decades. From 1990 to 2010, while the national population increased by 60,000,000, Americans who identified as either non-white or non-Christian doubled from 85,000,000 to 170,000,000. At the same time, the number of self-identified white Christians declined from 163,000,000 to 138,000,000.[50] That is a net shift of 15,000 people per day, every day for 20 years.

This ideological evolution gives the netroots and progressives a strategic advantage in future intra-party struggles with moderate and conservative Democrats. As liberals approach an absolute majority of Democratic self-identifiers, the strength of the netroots should grow accordingly. A larger pool of progressives promises more readers, social media followers and email signups, which in turn mean more activists, primary voters and monetary resources to sustain growth.

The potential ascendency of progressives in the Democratic Party via the netroots and inside–outside coalitions will also be advanced by the continuing prominence of the Internet in American life. Digital media are following an upward trajectory toward becoming the dominant medium, in parallel with, and more rapidly than, the trend toward majority liberal identification within the Democratic Party.

A comScore report published March 25, 2015 found that total time spent on digital media rose 157% from December 2010 to December 2014. According to The Nielsen Company's 2014 Total Audience Report, Americans went from spending an average of slightly under two hours per day consuming digital media in the third quarter of 2012, to two hours and thirty-nine minutes in the third quarter of 2014. During the same period, time spent listening to the radio declined slightly to two hours, forty-four minutes per day, meaning that the Internet will soon eclipse radio in total engagement. Time spent watching television, whether live or on a time-shifted device, also declined to slightly over five hours per day.[51]

Changes in media-use patterns are particularly pronounced among young people. A look at media consumption by age during the first quarter of 2015, portrayed in Table 3.2, reveals just how dramatically television is associated with older generations, its dominant position being threatened over the long-term. As age declines, so does television usage, from a peak of 249 hours per month for Americans 65 and older to a low of 102.3 hours per month for those aged 18–24. In a pattern reminiscent of generational differences in ideological identification, the television–Internet usage ratio also declines with each age group. While Americans 65 and older watched almost 188 more hours of television per month than they spent online, Americans aged 18–24 spent about five more hours online than in front of a television screen every month during the winter of 2015.

It is still easy to dismiss the netroots because their grand strategic goals remain unfulfilled: public policy remains largely right-of-center and political power remains largely responsive to a wealthy few. At the same time, increased liberal identification coupled with an ever-increasing share of Americans consuming media online give the progressive, digital-native netroots a long-term growth advantage compared with their ideological opponents inside and outside the Democratic Party. A Professional Left media and activist infrastructure emanating directly from the early blogosphere, MoveOn and the Dean campaign now wields far greater reach than the first netroots generation and has begun to score significant victories when acting in concert with established progressive advocacy groups. The left is rising and the Internet is rising at the same time as the Internet Left is rising.

TABLE 3.2 Average monthly television and Internet use by age (hours)

Medium	Age				
	18–24	25–34	35–49	50–64	65+
Television	102.3	136.0	170.5	217.7	249.0
Internet	107.1	104.1	99.8	83.8	61.1
Difference	−4.8	31.9	70.7	133.9	187.9

Source: The Nielsen Company. 2015. "Total Audience Report: Q1, 2015." June 23.

Note: Figures are for the first quarter of 2015.

What this means for national politics is an open question. As we will see in Chapter 6, there are significant limitations to what movement progressives can accomplish, and countervailing forces continue to press for a conservative political alignment. Elected officials and political media remain far more accountable to corporate and conservative interests than to grassroots and progressive ones. Television, though fading in influence, maintains its near-term grip on political media, and a well funded conservative messaging monolith developed and honed over decades remains a formidable force in American political life. In Chapter 4 we explore how the nexus of money and television has long maintained conservative political dominance and how that powerful combination of resources is holding up in the wake of rapid technological change.

Notes

1 Youngman, Sam. 2010. "White House Unloads Anger Over Criticism From 'Professional Left.'" *The Hill*, August 10. Retrieved from http://thehill.com/homenews/administration/113431-white-house-unloads-on-professional-left.
2 Alman, Ashley. 2013. "Larry Summers Withdraws His Name From Fed Chair Job." *The Huffington Post*, September 15. Retrieved from www.huffingtonpost.com/2013/09/15/larry-summers-fed-chair_n_3931476.html.
3 Hemel, Daniel J. 2005. "Summers' Comments on Women and Science Draw Ire." *The Harvard Crimson*, January 14. Retrieved from www.thecrimson.com/article/2005/1/14/summers-comments-on-women-and-science/.
4 Bassett, Laura and Ryan Grim. 2014. "How Women Spiked Larry Summers and Made Janet Yellen the Most Powerful Person in the World." *The Huffington Post*, January 6. Retrieved from www.huffingtonpost.com/2014/01/06/janet-yellen-womens-group_n_4549907.html.
5 Graham, David A. 2013. "How a Small Team of Democrats Defeated Larry Summers – And Obama." *The Atlantic*, September 15. Retrieved from www.theatlantic.com/politics/archive/2013/09/how-a-small-team-of-democrats-defeated-larry-summers-and-obama/279688/.
6 Caldwell, Leigh Ann. 2013. "And the Credit for the Nuclear Option Goes to …" *CNN*, November 22. Retrieved from www.cnn.com/2013/11/22/politics/nuclear-option-background/.
7 See FixTheSenateNow.org, at http://fixthesenatenow.org/pages/who-supports-reform/#.VZ_wOM7s6El.
8 Bendery, Jennifer. 2014. "The Senate Just Cemented Obama's Judicial Legacy." *The Huffington Post*, December 17. Retrieved from www.huffingtonpost.com/2014/12/17/obama-judicial-nominees_n_6328390.html.
9 Kaper, Stacy. 2014. "How Obama Won the War on Iran Sanctions." *National Journal*, February 3. Retrieved from www.nationaljournal.com/defense/2014/02/02/how-obama-won-war-iran-sanctions.
10 Sargent, Greg. 2015. "The Odds of an Iranian Nuclear Deal Just Got Better." *The Washington Post*, May 7. Retrieved from https://www.washingtonpost.com/blogs/plum-line/wp/2015/05/07/the-odds-of-an-iran-nuclear-deal-just-got-higher/.
11 Ammori, Marvin. 2015. "Ten Reasons the Net Neutrality Victory is Bigger Than the SOPA Win." *Forbes*, February 25. Retrieved from www.forbes.com/sites/marvinammori/2015/02/25/ten-reasons-the-net-neutrality-victory-is-bigger-than-the-sopa-win/.

12 Wilhelm, Alex. 2014. "Sen. Franken Calls Net Neutrality the 'Free Speech Issue of Our Time.'" *Techcrunch*, May 7. Retrieved from http://techcrunch.com/2014/05/07/sen-franken-calls-net-neutrality-the-free-speech-issue-of-our-time/.
13 Robinson, Rashad. 2014. "Net Neutrality Victory is Civil Rights History in the Making." *The Hill*, February 25. Retrieved from http://thehill.com/blogs/congress-blog/civil-rights/233700-net-neutrality-victory-is-civil-rights-history-in-the-making.
14 Figures for financial backing of the anti-net neutrality lobby can be found at: https://sunlightfoundation.com/blog/2014/05/16/how-telecoms-and-cable-have-dominated-net-neutrality-lobbying/.
15 Chart, Natasha. 2015. "What the Net Neutrality Victory Should Teach Us About Other Progressive Fights." *RH Reality Check*, March 3. Retrieved from http://rhrealitycheck.org/article/2015/03/03/net-neutrality-victory-teach-us-progressive-fights/.
16 Aaron, Craig. 2015. "How We Won Net Neutrality." *The Huffington Post*, February 26. Retrieved from www.huffingtonpost.com/craig-aaron/how-we-won-net-neutrality_b_6759132.html.
17 Palmer, Anna and Jake Sherman. 2015. "GOP: Business Lobby Blowing It On Trade." *Politico*, May 18. Retrieved from www.politico.com/story/2015/05/gop-business-lobby-blowing-it-on-trade-118039.
18 French, Lauren, Jake Sherman and John Bresnahan. 2015. "Democrats Deal Obama Huge Defeat on Trade." *Politico*, June 12. Retrieved from www.politico.com/story/2015/06/barack-obama-capitol-hill-trade-deal-118927.
19 See Fairness and Accuracy in Reporting at http://fair.org/article/in-iraq-crisis-networks-are-megaphones-for-official-views/.
20 Interestingly, the international press covered the event. See, for instance, "Millions Join Global Anti-War Protests." *BBC News World Edition*, February 17, 2003. Retrieved from http://news.bbc.co.uk/2/hi/europe/2765215.stm.
21 Pew Research Internet Project. 2014. "Internet Use Over Time." Retrieved from www.pewinternet.org/data-trend/internet-use/internet-use-over-time/.
22 U.S. Census Bureau. 2013. "Computer and Internet Use in the United States: Population Characteristics." Retrieved from www.census.gov/prod/2013pubs/p20-569.pdf.
23 The name refers to the group's campaign to censure rather than impeach Clinton and move on.
24 Bowers, Chris. 2005. "Dailykos Is As Large As The Entire Conservative Blogosphere." *Daily Kos*, September 8. Retrieved from www.dailykos.com/story/2005/09/09/147156/-Dailykos-Is-As-Large-As-The-Entire-Conservative-Blogosphere#.
25 Rosen, Jay. 2004. "The Legend of Trent Lott and the Weblogs." *PressThink*, March 15. Retrieved from http://archive.pressthink.org/2004/03/15/lott_case.html.
26 The core function of online petitions, then and now, is as sign-up forms for like-minded political activists.
27 Hazen, Don. 2003. "Moving On: A New Kind of Peace Activism." *Alternet*, February 10. Retrieved from www.alternet.org/story/15163/moving_on%3A_a_new_kind_of_peace_activism.
28 For instance, see CNN. 2003. "Activists Hold 'Virtual March' on Washington." February 28. Retrieved from www.cnn.com/2003/TECH/ptech/02/26/virtual.protest/.
29 See PollingReport.com. 2003. "White House 2004: Democratic Nomination." Retrieved from www.pollingreport.com/wh04dem2.htm.
30 Wolf, Gary. 2003. "How the Internet Invented Howard Dean." *Wired*, December 1. Retrieved from http://archive.wired.com/wired/archive/12.01/dean.html.
31 This period represents the oldest data still available on the topic.
32 This includes one of the authors of this book, whose prominence in the blogosphere did not match his personal situation. On the eve of the 2004 presidential election, traffic on MyDD, then edited by Jerome Armstrong and Chris Bowers, averaged 120,000 daily visits. This outsized total did not impress the electric company, which

turned off power in his apartment for nonpayment. Bowers had not collected a paycheck in two months and had consequently fallen behind on his payments. It took hours before he could convince the electric company to restore the power he needed to continue blogging.

33 Lamont publicly said he wanted 2,000 pledges of volunteer support before running, a goal which bloggers met quickly. Then, through months of volunteer recruitment, small donations and nonstop coverage of the race, the netroots helped Lamont defeat Lieberman in the primary with an anti-war, pro-withdrawal message.

34 Cohn, Jonathan. 2009. "Did Lieberman Double-Cross Reid?" *The New Republic*, December 13. Retrieved from www.newrepublic.com/blog/the-treatment/did-lieberman-double-cross-reid.

35 All traffic figures are from Quantcast. While the blogs may experience more audience crossover than national news organizations, potentially making the combined audience reached by news outlets larger, the fact that the audiences for the two groups are of the same magnitude is evidence of the transformation of the media landscape by the explosion of social networks.

36 Wong, Danny. 2015. "In Q4, Social Media Drove 31.24% of Overall Traffic to Sites." *Shareaholic*, January 26. Retrieved from https://blog.shareaholic.com/social-media-traffic-trends-01-2015/.

37 Data are from Quantcast. The NBC News figure includes all affiliated NBC sites including MSNBC and CNBC.

38 Data are from Quantcast.

39 Klein, Ezra. 2015. "What Andrew Sullivan's Exit Says About the Future of Blogging." *Vox*, January 30. Retrieved from www.vox.com/2015/1/30/7948091/andrew-sullivan-leaving-blogging.

40 See OpenSecrets.org, at https://www.opensecrets.org/pacs/lookup2.php?strID=C00341396.

41 The list includes Avaaz, ColorofChange.org, MomsRising, Progressive Change Campaign Committee (PCCC), The Other 98%, Rebuild the Dream, Ultraviolet and Win Without War. Other large netroots email-based advocacy groups that function using MoveOn's organizational model, but which were not directly built by MoveOn, include the Courage Campaign, CREDO (a wireless company with a large progressive advocacy operation), Democracy for America (the organizational descendent of Howard Dean's presidential campaign), Demand Progress, Presente, Progressives United, RootsAction and SumOfUs.

42 Talbot, David. 2009. "The Geeks Behind Obama's Web Strategy." *Boston.com*, January 8. Retrieved from www.boston.com/news/politics/2008/articles/2009/01/08/the_geeks_behind_obamas_web_strategy/?page=full.

43 Goldmacher, Shane. 2014. "Democratic House Candidates Are Walloping Republicans in the Small-Money Game." *National Journal*, September 28. Retrieved from www.nationaljournal.com/politics/2014/09/28/Democratic-House-Candidates-Are-Walloping-Republicans-Small-Money-Game?ref=nj_toolboxbullets_for_your_briefings.

44 Perhaps the most dramatic example of this was when one-time MoveOn staffer Ilyse Hogue became President of NARAL Pro-Choice America in January 2013.

45 Change.org has over 100 employees and, as of 2015, 86 million emails in its database. While Change.org originally began as a progressive, American-oriented organization, it has since become a non-ideological international platform where anyone can start a petition campaign. Other lead generation vendors include Care2, LeftAction, Democrats.org and Daily Kos.

46 Prominent examples include Salsa, Blue State Digital, We Also Walk Dogs, Action Network and NGP Van.

47 Pew Research Center. 2014. "Political Ideology." Retrieved from www.pewresearch.org/data-trend/political-attitudes/political-ideology/.

48 Data are from the General Social Survey (GSS) on religious identification and 1990 and 2012 census figures on race and ethnicity.
49 See CNN 2008 and 2012 exit polls, at www.cnn.com/ELECTION/2008/results/polls/ and www.cnn.com/election/2012/results/race/president.
50 Data are from the General Social Survey (GSS).
51 See Nielsen Company. 2015. "The Total Audience Report: Q4 2014." March 11. Retrieved from www.nielsen.com/us/en/insights/reports/2015/the-total-audience-report-q4-2014.html.

References

Bowers, Christopher J. and Matthew Stoller. 2005. *The Emergence of the Progressive Blogosphere: A New Force in American Politics*. Research Report. Washington, DC: New Politics Institute.

Duggan, Maeve. 2013. *It's a Woman's (Social Media) World*. Research Report. Washington, DC: Pew Research Center. Retrieved from www.pewresearch.org/fact-tank/2013/09/12/its-a-womans-social-media-world.

Jones, Jeffrey. 2014. "Liberal Self-Identification Edges Up To New High in 2013." *Gallup.com*. Retrieved from www.gallup.com/poll/166787/liberal-self-identification-edges-new-high-2013.aspx.

Karpf, David. 2012. *The MoveOn Effect: The Unexpected Transformation of American Political Advocacy*. New York: Oxford University Press.

Kreiss, Daniel. 2012. *Taking our Country Back: The Crafting of Networked Politics from Howard Dean to Barack Obama*. New York: Oxford University Press.

4

TELEVISION, MESSAGE CONTROL, MONEY AND REPUBLICAN DOMINANCE

On February 4, 2014, in the run-up to that year's midterm elections, national Republicans were handed a "gift" in the form of a Congressional Budget Office report that undermined one of their biggest arguments about the Affordable Care Act (ACA). More accurately, national reporters handed them a gift by repeating a misinterpretation of the report in a manner that bolstered the claims they had been making about Obamacare's detrimental impacts.

That day, the CBO reported that Americans in large numbers would choose to work fewer hours as a result of the law, resulting in a decline in the labor force as people are less dependent on their jobs for health care. The report makes clear that the decline, equivalent to 2.5 million jobs by 2024, does not equal an increase in unemployment:

> CBO estimates that the ACA will reduce the total number of hours worked, on net, by about 1.5 percent to 2.0 percent during the period from 2017 to 2024, almost entirely because workers will choose to supply less labor—given the new taxes and other incentives they will face and the financial benefits some will receive ... The estimated reduction stems almost entirely from a net decline in the amount of labor that workers choose to supply, rather than from a net drop in businesses' demand for labor, so it will appear almost entirely as a reduction in labor force participation and in hours worked relative to what would have occurred otherwise rather than as an increase in unemployment (that is, more workers seeking but not finding jobs) or underemployment (such as part-time workers who would prefer to work more hours per week).[1]

On the face of it, the CBO report validates a key argument *for* the Affordable Care Act by quantifying the value of having health coverage regardless of employment status. That's not how leading Republicans spun the news. It didn't take long for South Carolina Senator Lindsey Graham to tweet, "Obamacare will cost our nation about 2.5 million jobs." Conservative news outlets followed suit, pushing a simple if inaccurate message in harmony. A Fox News banner read, "Cost of Obamacare: 2.3 million jobs," while a headline in *The Daily Caller* proclaimed, "CBO Triples Estimate of Obamacare Work Force Cuts to 2.3 million."[2]

Within no time, the "two million jobs" spin worked its way into the national media, with reporters who understood the misrepresentation repeating it because of their interest in covering the horserace ramifications of Republicans having such a simple and potent angle of political attack. As in the beginning of the Republican era, when Richard Nixon reinvented himself without changing anything but his image, television proved an ideal medium for communicating a simple but misleading message. Chuck Todd tweeted: "CBO essentially reaffirms GOP talking points on health care." His NBC colleague Luke Russert agreed: "New report from the non-partisan Congressional Budget Office is an election year killer for Affordable Care Act/Obamacare."[3] To these reporters, the story wasn't about the policy ramifications of the report, or even whether what Republicans were saying was truthful; it was about the right's political bounty of having an easy hook to advance a campaign attack—a hook made significantly easier to use when reporters refused to swat it down as false. The White House fought back, but its reply was wordy and sounded defensive. A *Politico* story summed up the thinking of Washington reporters, acknowledging but dismissing the true interpretation of the CBO report by saying, "what matters politically is how the numbers look in attack ads."[4]

This, in microcosm, is how Republicans maintained their dominance in national politics for decades. It is a strategy built around media, message control and money, the components of which include a mature, well funded media infrastructure capable of churning out simple talking points repeated by disciplined elected Republicans and conservative opinion leaders in national news stories and paid political ads, and a national press corps more interested in politics than policy that views its role as reporting political disputes rather than deconstructing them. Notably, it is a strategy built around television, or more precisely the national reach television has provided for decades, for the strategy works best when the message can be repeated unchallenged to a broad audience until it becomes accepted truth.

The conservative movement spent decades investing in and refining a media infrastructure designed to turn its version of events into conventional wisdom, encompassing think tanks to generate policy ideas, pollsters to test and craft political messages, elected Republican officials and conservative pundits on television and talk radio to repeat them and deep-pocketed benefactors to fund the entire operation. Rush Limbaugh, *The Wall Street Journal*'s editorial page and Fox News are the visible tip of this communication iceberg, while coordinated message development and dissemination occurs below the surface. Their messaging appears in campaign ads and through repetition to reporters in mainstream news coverage (Jamieson and Cappella 2010; Clark and Van Slyke 2010).

Initially, this apparatus was designed around and for television, a medium built for the top-down communication of easily articulated ideas to a mass audience. For decades, television and center-right governance have been a perfect fit, with conservatives mastering the medium and the medium providing a platform for the mass dissemination of simple messages. Over time, the right successfully expanded its communication infrastructure, adding talk radio, cable and eventually the Internet to its centralized communication model (Jamieson and Cappella 2010). In each instance, they did so without making alterations to accommodate the new medium.

At the time, it was sensible for conservatives to co-opt the Internet to echo ideas expressed in other media because it gave them a new way to enhance the range of their megaphone. It was not particularly apparent in the first years of the twenty-first century that these efforts would come at a long-term cost. When the Internet came into its own years later as a viable political tool built around decentralized, bottom-up engagement, failing to have an organically developed online presence confounded efforts by the right to use the medium as the left was doing to motivate and mobilize supporters through grassroots action.

It did not have to be this way. As with primitive television and radio, conservatives were among the first movers who understood the Internet's networking potential. During the early days of the political Internet, the right was ahead of the left in traffic, and the top weblogs were conservative.[5] But, the right blogosphere was not left alone to thrive. In 2005, a group of conservative blogs united to form Pajamas Media, a well funded mainstream consortium with a pipeline to the right's media infrastructure. Mainstream figures such as Michelle Malkin, a conservative media fixture, began building online empires. The right blogosphere soon resembled every other chamber of the conservative media conglomerate, communicating the same messages from the same individuals, and remains dominated by the likes of Glenn Beck (via *The Blaze*) and Tucker Carlson (*The Daily Caller*), ubiquitous figures on conservative radio and television. Even the digital-native Drudge Report, one of the original blogs, remains a top-down clearinghouse of news items for dissemination elsewhere in the conservative media space.

Integration of the Internet into the right's centralized messaging model was particularly destructive to its community blogs. Although conservatives maintained a strong online profile with a tremendous amount of traffic, they lacked the community presence that was the engine for the first-generation progressive blogosphere and that best exploits the Internet's potential for bottom-up political organizing by permitting ordinary users to initiate discussions, debate freely and engage in collective action. This permitted the left to create a movement around the architecture of the Internet while the right used the Internet to amplify an established and effective messaging machine. Multiple times over several years, *Politico* trumpeted stories about how conservatives were going to build, or had just launched, their own version of MoveOn; it never happened.[6] RedState.com, the closest conservative counterpart to the community blog Daily Kos—where individuals are free to post and comment on diaries, disagree with one another and drive political discussions—is tiny in comparison. During every month of 2014, RedState consistently had one-tenth as many pageviews and less than 15% as many unique visitors as Daily Kos,[7] which continues to thrive as a progressive community site and an important bridge between the first-generation netroots and its newer and larger social media-centered offspring.

As user-generated content shifted to social media at the expense of community blogs, overall traffic on conservative websites rebounded relative to the left; as in the early days of the Internet, conservatives once again have surpassed progressives. However, this has not changed the character of the right side of the blogosphere, which is still dominated by the same messaging found in other conservative media. Where the left side of the political blogosphere emerged from—and, in the form of Daily Kos, continues to support—networked communities of many-to-many, one-to-many and many-to-one political activities built from a decentralized, bottom-up foundation, its conservative counterpart remains more vertically organized and dominated by a few voices. In other words, even in the second generation of online activism, in structure and appearance, conservative digital media looks and acts like television.

Evidence of this may be found in how the left and right use Facebook, the dominant social networking site. Facebook produces a publicly available metric of interactivity called "Talking About This," measuring how many people are actively engaged with the status updates posted by a given page beyond just reading—specifically, by recording how many different people comment on, share or "like" the status updates posted on a given site over the course of a week.[8] A comparison of leading conservative and progressive news and activism Facebook pages illustrates how online communities of the left are appreciably more interactive than their counterparts on the right. Table 4.1 displays "Talking About This" statistics for the Facebook pages of some of the largest conservative and progressive media and activist operations from the third week of November 2014, covering the period immediately after that year's midterm elections.

The top conservative sites are unquestionably larger, with more combined traffic than the progressive sites, making them ideal vehicles for driving messages like the Republican response to the CBO report. Additionally, with the notable exception of *Upworthy*, conservative sites have more people "liking" their Facebook pages, giving them a more sizable pool of followers than the left for potential interaction. But that interaction isn't happening. Conservative sites have appreciably lower absolute rates of active engagement than their progressive counterparts.

TABLE 4.1 Traffic, "Likes" and "Talking About This" figures for leading conservative and progressive Facebook pages, November 2014

	"Talking About This" Mentions	"Likes"	Traffic
Conservative Sites			
The Blaze	368,200	1,600,000	20,100,000
Heritage Foundation	357,000	1,800,000	2,900,00
ijreview	98,400	324,000	17,900,000
Daily Caller	73,100	427,200	6,200,000
Drudge Report	44,700	680,200	10,100,000
Newsmax	27,800	452,600	6,700,000
Progressive Sites			
Think Progress	1,200,000	1,400,000	6,100,000
MoveOn	688,800	640,800	1,400,000
Upworthy	664,900	7,400,000	21,300,000
Daily Kos	569,600	646,900	4,800,000
Salon	202,600	679,200	11,000,000
Raw Story	181,800	321,000	7,300,000

Source: Quantcast.

Note: ijreview also has an app with over 100,000 users that the authors believe are not included in these statistics.

The one glaring exception to this is Fox News (not depicted in Table 4.1). With 1,800,000 people "Talking About This" on Facebook, Fox News has a Facebook following worthy of its presence on cable television. But it is a cable entity—a centralized, top-down television news operation. That a cable news channel is the dominant conservative presence on Facebook speaks to how the right has not developed the grassroots, interactive online communities that for years have been the hallmark of netroots activism. In the age of social media, conservatives continue to co-opt the Internet as an arm of an existing, television-centered messaging machine.

Progressives, as we noted in Chapter 2, did not create a vital Internet presence by design; rather, it emerged from a position of weakness because there were no organized, well funded liberal institutions to stand in the way of its development. Without a movement or message-dissemination mechanism like the right had fine-tuned over many years, progressive online communities emerged organically as a result of an Internet architecture that rewards bottom-up expression, person-to-person organizing and decentralized interactions. These "open-source" communication patterns are ideal for the development of new relationships and participatory communities of individuals who self-select for membership on the basis of their political leanings and their interest in political action.

None of this mattered much until the first-generation netroots started achieving results and a movement emerged around collective bottom-up mobilization. Well into the George W. Bush years, as the Internet was trying to prove itself to be commercially viable, the right was arguably well served by having an additional vehicle for vertical messaging. With television still dominant in politics and culture, horizontal political action—what the Internet does best—was still mostly a theoretical construct, and bloggers were easily dismissed as angry social outcasts typing into the abyss.

Over time, as a professionalized progressive movement emerged from an Internet model of bottom-up political activism, the left and the right have moved in divergent directions with respect to political organizing, with the right still largely dependent on a television-based message-dissemination strategy. The once substantial return on this investment is diminishing as television's unchallenged influence yields to a rise in political engagement consistent with Internet-driven grassroots activism, structural changes in television itself that are turning it into a more decentralized on-demand medium and the fragmentation of a once unified national audience at the hands of the Internet. The question for conservatives is how effectively they can use their greatest asset—money—to counteract the gradual but inexorable shift to a post-television world.

Engagement

After the rupture of the Dean campaign in 2004, some of the harshest criticism of the Internet Left came from establishment Democrats. Marshall Wittmann, who served as Communications Director for former Democratic Senator Joe Lieberman in 2006, wrote that the candidate's online supporters, who called themselves "Deaniacs," were "clearly in no position to speak for the 'heart and soul' of the [Democratic] party."[9] It would take the events of a decade for those same Democrats to stop rejecting, then appreciate, then ultimately embrace new digital media techniques designed to identify and mobilize otherwise disengaged voters, moving away from the persuasion efforts of massive television ad buys that defined two generations of political consultancy. In part, this strategic shift came in reaction to the effectiveness of field experiments that confirmed precise ways to target and mobilize voters, and to Barack Obama's success with a combination of new and old media strategies (Issenberg 2012; Green and Gerber 2008). In part, it reflected a simple numbers game: changing demographics meant Democrats had more supporters than Republicans, but they were less likely to vote, particularly in non-presidential years, and the Internet provided an effective way to reach them. The promise of increased fundraising through small donors was undoubtedly another factor. However, it is also a tacit acknowledgment of the declining power of television to decide national elections.

In 2014, national Democrats poured money into field efforts to identify and mobilize uninvolved base voters—money that would have paid for television ads in previous cycles. As Democratic Senatorial Campaign Committee executive director Guy Cecil told *The New York Times*, "We're making a fundamentally different choice [on campaign strategy] ... Yes, we have to be on TV, and yes, we have to help close the gap between Democrats and Republicans on the air, but we're not willing to sacrifice the turnout operation or the field operation to do that."[10] This type of strategic adjustment would have been unthinkable ten, six, perhaps even two years earlier, and indicates how the political media environment is shifting.

Fundamental to the Democrats' mobilization strategy is the assumption that people *can* be mobilized to take political action. During television's long era of cultural dominance, this assumption would have been suspect. This is because a steady and precipitous decline in civic engagement is one of the hallmarks of the television age. Among those who have written about this decline, perhaps the most noteworthy is Harvard political scientist Robert D. Putnam (2001), who documented the deterioration in the social networks people form with one another for reasons often unrelated to civic activities—things like peer groups, church and community organizations—and the concurrent decline in social capital lost when people spend more time in isolated enterprises like commuting to work or watching television. Social capital refers to the benefits derived from communal engagement, which can include heightened trust, reciprocity with others and improved communication, all of which are fundamental to a sound civic society.

The television era witnessed a profound decline in numerous measures of social capital. At the start of the Kennedy administration, nearly four in five Americans trusted government officials to do the right thing. Today, nearly four in five distrust the government. As images of the Vietnam War and Watergate flashed across our television screens, our faith in government evaporated and failed to recover over the following decades.[11] During that period, we became far less likely to say government officials will do the right thing and our confidence in public and private institutions dramatically decreased. Federal agencies like the Food and Drug Administration and the Department of Education have seen their favorability plummet since the turn of the century. Banks and large corporations are viewed as negatively as Congress and the federal government, with only one quarter of Americans regarding them positively. The national news media fare only slightly better.[12] Even the venerable Supreme Court, for years the most revered federal institution, has seen its public support eroded to record lows.[13]

In Putnam's view, as we became a more disgruntled society, we were less inclined toward civic involvement and less able to draw on the resources we need to engage effectively in social and political action. He is careful not to place the blame for the decline of social capital at television's feet, or at least not to blame television exclusively, although he does suggest more than a correlation between the heightened use of television and civic decline. Acknowledging that a host of factors likely contributed to diminished social capital, including the rise in two-career families and migration to the suburbs, he puts television at the head of the list of things that reshaped social interaction. Television, he notes, has a particularly strong tendency to alienate people from civic involvement, and almost exclusively soaked up our additional leisure time from the 1960s through the turn of the century (Putnam 2001). It's a circumstantial case, to be sure, but a case with compelling evidence nonetheless.

If you wanted to drive political outcomes with a mass communication strategy, high levels of disengagement would be a feature of your plans rather than a negative byproduct. Television politics operates on a saturation basis: repeatedly expose as many people as possible to the same simple message. Anything that contradicts that message undermines its effectiveness, including a politically engaged electorate or face-to-face communication of the sort that diminished along with the decline in formal and informal associating. Television is also a passive medium, capable of communicating messages to people without their active involvement. From a messaging perspective, it is an asset to have passive and disengaged viewers who will not feel particularly motivated to think about or question the messages washing over them, especially to the degree that television messages are misleading or lack context.

And so it was for decades, when television ruled the media landscape and conservatives ruled television. So dominant a force is television that, even with the explosion of online activity, it remains possible to run a mass-messaging strategy to great effect. But it is no longer possible to do so unchallenged. With a multitude of social networking possibilities available for pushing back against televised messaging, there are ways for motivated individuals to be heard who may not have the resources for expensive ad buys or access to mainstream reporters. It took little time for the Internet Left to challenge the CBO story and begin a counter-narrative, castigating conservatives as liars and mainstream reporters who accepted their spin as enablers.

The key to a successful social networking strategy, of course, is motivation. Unlike television, the Internet is designed for active participation and can be a natural source of civic engagement (Blumler and Coleman 2001; Shane 2004), but there will be no engagement without individual willingness. Finding like-minded people online can be the incentive that provides the initiative to participate, making the community-building quality of the Internet essential to its ability to challenge the supremacy of television.[14] This is why the early development of large and thriving online communities on the left is noteworthy, and why the development of the modern progressive movement would not have been possible without a medium that enabled people to seek and find like-minded others.

Equally noteworthy as a sign of the fading influence of television are reversals in apathy and social disengagement among the Millennial Generation. Eschewing conventional institutions such as organized religion, marriage and political parties (while espousing liberal views and voting overwhelmingly for Democrats),[15]

Millennials are upbeat about the future and highly connected through social networks[16] that correlate with a string of socially affirming attitudes. Among social network users, figures on social engagement are striking. The Pew Research Center's Internet and American Life project finds 46% of Internet users believe most people can be trusted, 19 points higher than individuals who are not connected online, a difference that's even greater for frequent users of Facebook. Controlling for demographic factors, social network users are better able than the population as a whole to appreciate multiple points of view, an element of empathy (Hampton et al. 2011).

Social media users are also more likely than the population at large to take political action. Two-thirds of social media users, representing four in ten Americans in 2012, report having used social media to perform at least one significant civic act, including encouraging people to vote or take action on a social issue, sharing political materials with their network or posting their thoughts on political or social issues (Rainie 2012; Rainie et al. 2012). Millennials are more likely than older social media users to engage in these civic behaviors, and the propensity for online civic engagement has grown dramatically since the 2008 election. Perhaps more noteworthy is the tendency for online civic action to spill over into in-person action; better than eight in ten social network users report engaging in social or political action in the non-virtual world (Smith 2013).

This re-engagement is a hallmark of virtual communities on the left—communities that at times spill over to the three-dimensional world.[17] These communities had no counterpart during the television era, and independently of whatever success they may have achieved to date in advancing their political goals, their robustness is a sign that the media environment as we knew it is morphing into something new, and with it the promise or threat of a different kind of politics built around collective engagement and the creation of social capital.

Convergence

Complementing the trend toward online civic involvement and further threatening the right's long-dominant political strategy is a dramatic evolution in the nature of television into an on-demand vehicle for personalized viewing and two-way interaction whose architecture resembles the Internet far more than the top-down, centralized device of the twentieth century. As television sets become less distinguishable from computers, they become less suited to top-down information dissemination and more easily adapted to bottom-up networking strategies.

Television has been moving in this direction for years. During its first three decades as a commercially viable product, television offered a limited selection of programs predominantly on three private networks. Television's second three decades, in contrast, witnessed the gradual increase of user control over viewing patterns. The introduction of cable increased the volume and variety of content but viewers remained beholden to schedules created by somebody else. That changed with the mass-market success of the VCR in the 1980s, lending versatility to television viewing although content was still controlled by programmers. DVD and Blu-Ray technology would eventually surpass the VCR, and cable and satellite providers began offering on-demand services early in the twenty-first century.

Then came the Internet. As streaming video and social networking sites became readily available on home computers and personal devices, it was a logical next step for television to find a way to support them, too. Likewise, it was perhaps inevitable that television programming would find its way online for users to search for and view at their leisure, and comment on through interactive features on program websites and networking sites like Facebook and Twitter. Getting people to purchase devices that would allow them to watch Internet video on their televisions was more difficult, as manufacturers confronted familiar difficulties with the introduction of new technology. Consumers balked at buying additional boxes and found them to be too expensive and too slow.[18] Eventually, technological development and market forces resolved these issues, as the faster, simpler device for viewing Internet content on TV became the television itself. Over time, it also became possible to employ devices like smartphones and tablets to watch television without having a television, or to watch television with others in virtual communities. Television, which began life as a highly structured, vertically organized medium of one-to-many communication, was acquiring the bottom-up, decentralized, many-to-many characteristics of the web.

This phenomenon is a form of convergence, a term invoking the idea that distinct forms of electronic communication will inevitably merge, bringing with it cultural changes as people find new ways to communicate, share and—for the first time—produce their own media content (Jenkins, Ford and Green 2013; Jenkins 2004). Political scientist Ithiel de Sola Pool once observed:

> The key technological change, at the root of [other] social changes, is that communication, other than conversation face to face, is becoming overwhelmingly electronic. Not only is electronic communication growing faster than traditional media of publishing, but also the convergence of modes of delivery is bringing the press, journals, and books into the electronic world ... The technological constraints on electronic communication are now becoming less confining. Alternative transmission systems such as the telephone network, cable systems, and microwaves can all be used in a great variety of ways. They can be used at low cost with low fidelity if that is sufficient to the need, or at higher cost for higher fidelity. They can be used point-to-point or broadcast. They can be encrypted for privacy or transmitted in the clear. The design of communication systems today need not follow a cookbook recipe for each purpose to be served but is more a matter

of optimizing among the several alternatives for which a multipurpose system may be used in a mix of markets.

(Pool 1983, 6, 26)

These words may seem obvious today, but they were clairvoyant when they were written in 1983, before the emergence of the contemporary Internet, when two-way interactive visual communication of the sort we use every day through services like Skype or FaceTime was a fantasy feature of the hypothetical year 2015 depicted in the film *Back to the Future*. In the decades following, Pool's concept of convergence can be applied to the delivery of digital content to multiple platforms such as personal devices, computers and television, and the development of television into a device with the key attributes of computers (Gordon 2003).

"Internet television" is a natural outcome of this evolution, and while it may not represent the final stage of convergence, it is a big step toward eliminating the distinction between the two devices. It is now possible to purchase at a declining price point a television that can access the Internet, receive and store digital content from online services like Netflix, Hulu and YouTube, wirelessly accept pictures from handheld devices and permit web surfing while simultaneously showing traditional television programs, allowing complete user control over the television experience. It redefines watching television in online terms as individualized, customized and bottom-up.

Convergence may be a source of convenience and versatility to end users, but it is also socially destabilizing because it alters the relationships among individuals and between individuals and technology (Jenkins 2008). As electronic communication media become ubiquitous and functionally interchangeable, it is increasingly difficult to disconnect from technology or to discern the boundary between virtual and real. New social patterns emerge, facilitated by a dizzying array of increasingly interchangeable technological options. Two friends walking together while simultaneously texting two other friends may be sharing time with each other or separately engaged in virtual relationships. Web-based collectives like the progressive netroots produce social capital for their members and in the process blur the line between real and virtual communities. Conventional distinctions do not easily apply.

With new social communities forming around new means of communication, political strategies designed around outdated modes of mass communication are becoming increasingly tenuous. Convergence is squeezing the right's communication strategy from two directions. From above, as television morphs into a decentralized, bottom-up, on-demand medium, message-saturation strategies become more complicated to implement and promise diminished returns from the day when you could guarantee that a large television ad buy would be viewed multiple times by every eyeball residing in a given media market and challenged only by opposing ad buys with opposing messages. Advertisers from all walks of life, including politics, have been forced to catch up with shifting audience preferences and react to declining television audiences.[19] From below, newly empowered activists with technological savvy like those of the Internet Left, who understand how to operate in an environment of convergent technology, are shifting the locus of media power to the grassroots. As the sands shift beneath a communication network that reliably served the conservative movement and Republican politicians for decades, the right finds itself less well positioned than the left to capitalize on the atomized media politics of the post-television era. But it is not without significant resources to fight back.

Money Again

By the start of the second month of 2014, with *nine months* remaining before Election Day, a group calling itself Americans for Prosperity had already spent $8.2 million primarily on television ads in North Carolina in an effort to defeat Democratic Senator Kay Hagan. According to *Politico*, that was more money than the combined spending of every affiliated group promoting Democratic senators in every race in the country.[20] Democratic groups responded with an ad campaign of their own, but with a fraction of the reach of what conservative groups could manage.

Americans for Prosperity, co-founded by conservative billionaires Charles and David Koch, can spend at will in a post-*Citizens United* world, and according to *Politico* they had a "seemingly bottomless pot of cash" to invest in producing a Republican Senate majority. "The staggering figures," they concluded, "make North Carolina ground zero in the unprecedented TV war expected to define the 2014 midterm elections."[21] Conservatives have money in abundance and have taken advantage of unrestricted spending opportunities to counteract the effects of the changing media landscape. That they are using it in support of a traditional television advertising strategy is not surprising. That Democrats reacted with concern and felt the need to fight back on television is instructive. Unable to hold off the withering attacks against her, Hagan lost re-election in the Republican wave of 2014, albeit by a narrow margin.

The character of television is changing but has not disappeared. For all the advantages realized by the netroots and the Internet Left through mastery of grassroots online engagement, it has not been enough to date to dislodge the hold of television on our politics, and especially on those segments of the population that, for reasons of economics or habit, have not migrated with the technology. Warning signs for television's future abound: The audience for news at the three legacy networks (CBS, NBC and ABC) was a combined 15.6 million in 2012, deeply diminished from over 42 million in 1980 (Guskin, Jurkowitz and Mitchell 2013). Ratings also declined for the three major cable news channels, with CNN, Fox News and MSNBC all experiencing a loss in viewership between 2009 and 2013.[22] These figures are portentous for network executives and practitioners of the old media, but television was the dominant medium for so long that it continues to exert tremendous gravitational pull on the tides of information dissemination. Despite the rapid growth of the Internet as a source of political news, as recently as 2012 it was outpaced by cable and local television coverage as a regular source of campaign information and only surpassed network news broadcasts that same year.[23] For the time being, this leaves practitioners of conventional media strategies with a sufficient platform for reaching voters, particularly older, Republican-leaning voters who lag behind in their Internet use but not in turnout on Election Day. These strategies are expensive, and the right has the means to implement them.

They also have the means to take advantage of micro-targeting possibilities in the post-television landscape, which, unlike online community building or bottom-up activism, can be accomplished with good political consultants who can identify the media consumption patterns of targeted groups. In fact, a portion of the Americans for Prosperity ad buy went to Internet advertisements. Micro-targeting does not capitalize on the potential of the Internet realized through online community building and mobilization, but it gives the right an opening to expand its centralized messaging operation to more decentralized media and reinforce televised messages through other technological outlets. This may not be an optimal use of the Internet, but it is not without relevance.

To this end, it is significant that convergence has coincided with consolidation of media ownership, which, along with money, gives the right an opening to fight back. The reach of media conglomerates has accelerated over time, aided by a favorable deregulatory environment carved out during 40 years of center-right governance. It has produced a centralized locus of elite power that we will explore more fully in Chapter 6, competing directly with the growing power of individuals who engage in community action using new media. These competing centers of media power mirror the two poles of political debate: top-down versus bottom-up; elite-based versus mass-based; money-driven versus labor-driven; old versus new.

As the left looks to the new world to percolate a politics of many, the top-down politics of the right benefits from centralized control at the apex of the media food chain. For a strategy threatened by audience fragmentation, it is helpful that media corporations have fanned out across industries and platforms in an attempt to protect against the erosion of their markets and adjust to rapid technological changes (Jenkins 2004). Countless media tributaries lead back to the same few headwaters. The cable channel MSNBC, which for years has featured progressive programming, is owned by NBCUniversal, whose parent company is Comcast, which counts among its nearly 200 individual holdings a television network, film studio, cable channels, digital media, theme parks and sports teams.[24] The end-users may drown in a sea of choices; things look quite different at the top.

Past the headwaters and the tributaries is the mainstream, and it is not surprising that something called conventional wisdom remains a force to be reckoned with, at least among traditional political elites. While the netroots and Internet Left have succeeded in building and mobilizing communities, they have struggled with agenda setting in the wake of the enduring messaging muscle of a political class long oriented to television and which still defines and drives narratives, as with the case of the CBO report. When the Internet Left find themselves complaining about mainstream journalists and politicians, they unwittingly acknowledge their defensive position through their inability to define the agenda. The crucial question for the formation of the next political regime is how quickly this dynamic will change. Television as a top-down medium is on the way out. Are the conveyers of conventional wisdom on the way out with it? We consider this question more fully in Chapter 5.

Like our red/blue political alignment, the current media environment is not dynamically stable. If this is not yet the Internet era, it is no longer fully the television age. The technological landscape is changing in still unpredictable ways and the growth curve has yet to flatten. One thing is clear: the more rapidly television converges with the Internet, the more quickly the participatory, interactive community structure of the netroots and Internet Left will give it an advantage in political competition. Financial heft has helped the right maintain political stalemate in the wake of the left's rebirth through bottom-up activism, but in the past their centralized strategy guaranteed the right political hegemony. The era of big media strategies is over, even if the era of big media is not; the technological playing field is tilting, and as is the case with changing demography, those who stand to inherit the conservative movement find themselves committed to a medium that's disappearing.

Notes

1 See "The Budget and Economic Outlook: 2014–2024." 2014. Congressional Budget Office, February 4, 117–18. Retrieved from www.cbo.gov/publication/45010.
2 Cited in Scott, Dylan. 2014. "The GOP Has It Wrong: Obamacare Won't 'Cost' 2 Million Jobs." *Talking Points Memo*, February 4. Retrieved from http://talkingpointsmemo.com/dc/obamacare-cbo-report-jobs.
3 Ibid.
4 Nather, David and Jason Millman. 2014. "Obamacare and Jobs: CBO Fuels Fire." *Politico*, February 4. Retrieved from www.politico.com/story/2014/02/obamacare-first-year-enrollment-numbers-103098. To be fair, not every major national outlet promoted the job-loss spin. Notably, *The New York Times* editorial board characterized the employment estimates as "liberating" and excoriated Republicans for misrepresenting them. However, by the time their editorial was published on February 5, 2014, the job-loss meme had already been established in the mainstream press.
5 In early 2003, the conservative blogosphere had more than twice the traffic of the progressive blogosphere. See Bowers and Stoller (2005).
6 See, for instance, Allen, Mike. 2007. "Move Over MoveOn: GOP's A-comin'." *Politico*, June 29. Retrieved from www.politico.com/story/2007/06/move-over-moveon-gops-a-comin-004712; Zenilman, Avi. 2008. "Drill Now As the Conservative MoveOn?" *Politico*, July 1. Retrieved from www.politico.com/story/2008/07/drill-now-as-the-

conservative-moveon-011436; and Catanese, David. 2010. "MoveOn Unfazed By New Group." *Politico*, August 20. Retrieved from www.politico.com/story/2010/08/moveon-unfazed-by-new-group-041291.

7 Traffic figures from Quantcast at www.quantcast.com/dailykos.com?country=US and www.quantcast.com/redstate.com.

8 For an explanation of Facebook "Talking About This" and "Likes" metrics, see www.facebook.com/notes/art-jonak/facebook-likes-vs-talking-about-this-numbers-talking-about-is-the-number-that-ma/10151465281555517.

9 See "Another Take On the Pew Research Poll On Dean Supporters." *Democratic Underground*. Archives. Retrieved from http://election.democraticunderground.com/discuss/duboard.php?az=view_all&address=132x1711410.

10 Parker, Ashley. 2014. "Democrats Aim for a 2014 More Like 2012 and 2008." *The New York Times*, February 6. Retrieved from www.nytimes.com/2014/02/07/us/politics/democrats-aim-to-make-2014-more-like-2012-and-2008.html?_r=0.

11 The greatest drop-off in trust occurred during the Vietnam and Watergate years and, despite some recovery during the Reagan and Clinton administrations, trust levels never came close to returning to their post-war highs. See "Public Trust in Government, 1958–2013." 2013. Pew Research Center. Retrieved from www.people-press.org/2014/11/13/public-trust-in-government/.

12 For an overview of levels of distrust in public institutions, see "Distrust, Discontent, Anger and Partisan Rancor: The People and their Government." 2010. Pew Research Center. Retrieved from www.people-press.org/2010/04/18/distrust-discontent-anger-and-partisan-rancor/.

13 See "Supreme Court's Favorable Rating Still at Historic Low." 2013. Pew Research Center. Retrieved from www.people-press.org/2013/03/25/supreme-courts-favorable-rating-still-at-historic-low/.

14 Putnam, wrestling with the question of whether the Internet promotes or retards social capital, recognized the potential for both and pointed to the community-building elements of online communication as having the greatest ability to reverse generations-old social trends.

15 "Millennials In Adulthood." 2014. Pew Research Center. Retrieved from www.pewsocialtrends.org/2014/03/07/millennials-in-adulthood/.

16 "Millennials: Confident. Connected. Open to Change." 2010. Pew Research Center. Retrieved from www.pewsocialtrends.org/2010/02/24/millennials-confident-connected-open-to-change/.

17 The most notable crossover effort is the Yearly Kos conference, now Netroots Nation, which began as an effort by Daily Kos readers to find a way to meet in person after having established online relationships. As far back as the Dean campaign, people who engaged in online political action through Dean's Blog for America expressed interest in meeting one another in the everyday world.

18 Wingfield, Nick. 2007. "The Internet. The TV. Here's How to Finally Bring Them Together." *The Wall Street Journal*, December 11. Retrieved from www.wsj.com/articles/SB119706406734417529.

19 Taube, Aaron. 2013. "Facebook and Google Are About To Overtake All of TV In Audience Size." *Business Insider*, November 25. Retrieved from www.businessinsider.com/facebook-and-google-to-overtake-tv-in-reach-2013-11.

20 Raju, Manu and Anna Palmer. 2014. "Koch Brothers Bombard Vulnerable Senate Democrat Kay Hagan." *Politico*, February 12. Retrieved from www.politico.com/story/2014/02/koch-brothers-kay-hagan-103406.

21 Ibid.

22 "Key Indicators in Media and News." 2014. Pew Research Center. Retrieved from www.journalism.org/2014/03/26/state-of-the-news-media-2014-key-indicators-in-media-and-news/.

23 The figures for October 2012 are: cable news, 41%; local television news, 38%; Internet, 36%; network news, 31%. See "Politics+Internet/Tech: Our Research." 2012. Pew Research Center. Retrieved from www.pewinternet.org/2012/11/29/politics-internettech-our-research/.
24 *The Columbia Journalism Review* maintains a database of major corporate holdings. See "Resources: Comcast Corporation." Retrieved from www.cjr.org/resources/index.php?c=comcast.

References

Blumler, Jay G. and Stephen Coleman. 2001. *Realising Democracy Online: A Civic Commons in Cyberspace*. London: Institute for Public Policy Research.

Bowers, Christopher J. and Matthew Stoller. 2005. *The Emergence of the Progressive Blogosphere: A New Force in American Politics*. Research Report. New Politics Institute.

Clark, Jessica and Tracy Van Slyke. 2010. *Beyond the Echo Chamber: How a Networked Progressive Media Can Reshape American Politics*. New York: New Press.

Gordon, Rich. 2003. "The Meanings and Implications of Convergence." In *Digital Journalism: Emerging Media and the Changing Horizons of Journalism*, edited by Kevin Kawamoto, 57–74. Lanham, MD: Rowman & Littlefield.

Green, Donald P. and Alan S. Gerber. 2008. *Get Out The Vote: How To Increase Voter Turnout*. Washington, DC: Brookings.

Guskin, Emily, Mark Jurkowitz and May Mitchell. 2013. *The State of the News Media in 2013*. Washington, DC: Pew Research Center. Retrieved from www.stateofthemedia.org/2013/network-news-a-year-of-change-and-challenge-at-nbc.

Hampton, Keith, Lauren Sessions Goulet, Lee Rainie and Kristen Purcell. 2011. *Social Networking Sites and Our Lives*. Washington, DC: Pew Research Center. Retrieved from www.pewinternet.org/2011/06/16/social-networking-sites-and-our-lives.

Issenberg, Sasha. 2012. *The Victory Lab*. New York: Crown.

Jamieson, Kathleen Hall and Joseph N. Cappella. 2010. *Echo Chamber*. New York: Oxford University Press.

Jenkins, Henry. 2004. "The Cultural Logic of Media Convergence." *International Journal of Cultural Studies* 7: 33–43.

Jenkins, Henry. 2008. *Convergence Culture: Where Old and New Media Collide*. New York: New York University Press.

Jenkins, Henry, Sam Ford and Joshua Green. 2013. *Spreadable Media: Creating Value and Meaning in a Networked Culture*. New York: New York University Press.

Pool, Ithiel de Sola. 1983. *Technologies of Freedom*. Cambridge, MA: Harvard University Press.

Putnam, Robert D. 2001. *Bowling Alone: The Collapse and Revival of American Community*. New York: Simon & Schuster.

Rainie, Lee. 2012. *Social Media and Voting*. Washington, DC: Pew Research Center. Retrieved from www.pewinternet.org/2012/11/06/social-media-and-voting.

Rainie, Lee, Aaron Smith, Kay Lehman Schlozman, Henry Brady and Sidney Verba. 2012. *Social Media and Political Engagement*. Washington, DC: Pew Research Center. Retrieved from www.pewinternet.org/2012/10/19/social-media-and-political-engagement.

Shane, Peter, ed. 2004. *Democracy Online: The Prospects for Political Renewal Through the Internet*. New York: Routledge.

Smith, Aaron. 2013. *Civic Engagement in the Digital Age*. Washington, DC: Pew Research Center. Retrieved from www.pewinternet.org/2013/04/25/civic-engagement-in-the-digital-age.

5

OBJECTIVITY AND TRANSPARENCY

For decades, journalists have made their living and validated their professionalism through what is termed "objective" reporting. And while pure objectivity may be a challenging and aspirational benchmark for any subset of human beings, for decades the method worked effectively, or at least effectively enough to ward off significant critiques of press practices. Not so today. Consider what happened when the mainstream press repeated erroneous Republican claims that the February 2014 Congressional Budget Office report, discussed in Chapter 4, predicted the Affordable Care Act would cost millions of jobs. Instantaneously, the Internet Left was all over the story, condemning Republican misinformation efforts alongside mainstream media reports enabling them. "The traditional media, under the direction of the Republican talking-points machine, immediately misrepresented the [CBO] report," wrote a front page Daily Kos blogger on February 9, 2014 in one of a volley of posts pushing back against Republican claims. Another blogger added the following day: "This was a textbook case of reading incomprehension, preconceived assumptions, susceptibility to spin and inability to admit an error, spread out over the airwaves, the Internet, and blowing up in real time." Not only did prominent members of the mainstream press let the story slide by without a fact check, given their stubborn determination to adhere to a model of objective reporting, it was predictable they would.

How can this be? Steve Benen, blogging for the television/Internet outlet MSNBC on February 5, 2014, suggested the possibility that reporters understood the difference between freeing two million people to leave the labor force (the CBO claim) and the loss of two million jobs (the Republican claim), but didn't choose to draw the distinction because these details were less newsworthy to them than the political advantage to Republicans of getting people to believe Obamacare would devastate employment. He cited *New York Times* reporter

Jackie Calmes' recognition of the false Republican interpretation, which she nonetheless saw as a problem for Democrats because they were left in the politically disadvantageous position of having to explain why Republicans are wrong. Truth, Benen concluded, was no longer a function of what was empirically valid, but what reporters perceived people might believe: "The Obama administration isn't closing the U.S. embassy to the Vatican; ACORN doesn't actually exist; there is no IRS scandal; there was no Benghazi cover-up; the government isn't stockpiling ammunition to be used against civilians; and the Arms Trade Treaty wouldn't undermine the Second Amendment. And while all of these truths are very nice, [to quote Calmes,] 'what matters politically is how they'll look in attack ads.'"

It is possible that reporters aren't as feckless as Benen suggests, but are instead trapped inside a reporting model that makes no sense in a world where the political center has disappeared. Regardless of what journalists may or may not say, a percentage of Americans believe as a factual matter that the Obama administration is closing the American embassy to the Vatican; ACORN exists and is stealing elections; the IRS is targeting conservative political organizations and ignoring progressive ones; Benghazi is a bigger cover-up than Watergate; the government is preparing an all-out armed assault against civilians; and the Arms Trade Treaty would mean ordinary citizens have to surrender their guns. Objectivity was difficult to achieve when there was widespread factual agreement on the terms of public discourse. It is a near impossibility now that consensus has broken down.

The inability of mainstream journalists to report objectively in an era when objectivity itself is in question is of a piece with the decline of traditional media, which in turn is part of the larger picture of political realignment and the likelihood that the emerging era will be defined by a coalition capable of driving news narratives through non-traditional means. As newspaper owners fight a losing battle to redefine themselves in an age of open-source information while traditional print and television journalists struggle to justify reporting practices that can unintentionally mislead, a new group of self-appointed writers, reporters and editors has emerged online, on the left and right, to report the news with a blatantly partisan cast more in sync with the political moment. For the time being the traditionalists continue to hold sway, but they can find themselves in noisy clashes with their younger and more opinionated cousins.

Traditional Journalism: objectivity as balance

On the surface, the traditional reporting model is simple. Journalists are professionals trained in distinguishing everyday events with news value from everyday events not worthy of coverage, and in assessing the proper factual information about newsworthy events to convey their content to readers or viewers without bias or prejudice. For contested or controversial stories such as political news, journalists are trained to rely on balance, to juxtapose the position of one side against the position of the other without drawing conclusions about the validity of either. The result is supposed to be news without a point of view, what political scientist Edward Jay Epstein (1973) ironically called "news from nowhere" and press critic Jay Rosen, channeling the philosopher Thomas Nagel, dubbed a "view from nowhere."[1] If pressed, journalists can defend their work by invoking their professionalism. They write objectively because they are trained to write objectively (Wein 2005).

A sizable media sociology literature deconstructs these claims. Far from existing in a vacuum, factual information makes sense only in a context provided by the reporter. From this perspective, Jackie Calmes' decision to cast the CBO report in terms of Republicans spinning it to their political advantage represents a framing choice. It may be—and was—the same choice other political reporters made, but it was a choice nonetheless. A shift in frame to how Republicans were *disingenuously* spinning the report to their political advantage would have couched the same factual material in a different context and resulted in a dramatically different story.

Because reporters determine the frames that organize the facts, and because they do this in conjunction with other reporters, editors and sources, news stories are socially constructed entities (Goffman 1974). All news comes from somewhere, and that place is shaped by a set of professional, social and economic forces. Private occurrences become public events through the interplay of those who seek news coverage, such as politicians and elected officials, with those who construct news reports—reporters and editors or producers (Molotch and Lester 1974). Parties with an interest in the shape of news stories are constantly negotiating the terms of their content, which will by definition reflect the purposes of those who create and market it, even if the process by which this occurs remains invisible to the reporter (Peterson 2001; Molotch and Lester 1974). At a broader level, news framing reflects the cultural values of the political and social elites who constitute the vast majority of news sources (Kennamer 1992; Gans 1979). This gives news reporting a conservative quality (in a non-ideological and, some would argue, ideological sense) by legitimizing and reinforcing the values of existing political and social institutions (Salmon and Moh 1992), and explains why reporters continue to give deference to center-right politicians just as they deferred to center-left assumptions about American politics even as the New Deal coalition was crumbling as a national political force.

These dynamics are deeply at odds with the idea of objective reporting, which media sociologists like Gaye Tuchman (1972) regard as a strategic ritual employed as a defense against criticism of their work. In practice, if news is a social construct it is impossible for objectivity to exist in any meaningful form, as the rules journalists apply to distance their work from personal opinion are themselves socially constructed (Johnson-Cartee 2005).[2] Reliance on balance as a means to achieve objectivity is a product of choices made by journalists and, as such, is fraught with subjectivity. Presenting both sides of a story presumes there are no more or less than two sides worth reporting, that each side is of equal merit to the other and, considering the sources employed by mainstream journalists, that the two perspectives worth repeating come from elites representing official institutions. These are contestable propositions, as bloggers of the right and left will loudly proclaim.

They are also propositions with their roots in twentieth-century journalism. What passed for reporting for the better part of the republic's first century more closely resembled the partisan blogosphere of the twenty-first century, with political parties publishing newspapers and editors serving as partisan agents. Profound political, social and economic changes brought about by industrialization and reactions to it converged in the late nineteenth century to undermine the party press, create large markets for advertiser-driven commercial newspapers and propel journalism from a trade to a profession (Campbell 2006). By the end of the century, newspapers had become accessible to a wide swath of the population (Campbell 2003; Leonard 1986), making them magnets for advertisers pushing a burgeoning number of products to expanding markets. The concurrent decline of political parties during a long period of progressive reform saw the transformation of journalism from a stenographic trade to a profession steeped in a new set of values (Schudson 1978; 2001).

In the political world of the middle and late nineteenth century, journalism reflected the open partisanship of strong political parties locked in intense debate. However, as Progressive Era reforms weakened the parties, a new set of values based on reason and the scientific method took hold. In the relatively new profession of journalism, objectivity arose in tandem with the ideal of politics as a reasoned debate about the public good (Kaplan 2002). The sociologist Michael Schudson (2001) regards objectivity as a "moral code" developed by journalists looking for social cohesion amidst the shifting values of the early twentieth century, as much a product of the scientific revolution designed to distance the budding profession of journalism from the budding profession of public relations, whose practitioners sought to use journalists to get their clients' names in the news. In this regard, objectivity was about separating journalists from the sensational reporting of the partisan press and the self-promotion of sources while creating a professional identity built on reason and rationality. But it was not about establishing neutrality in reporting (Strekfuss 1990).

Failure of the traditional model

Early advocates of objectivity were liberals like Walter Lippmann, who hoped objective journalism would lead to social change rather than passively validate the status quo. Only later in the twentieth century did objectivity become a means for reporters to keep their opinions out of their stories—a practical model for everyday reporting rather than a methodology for finding truth and preserving democracy (Strekfuss 1990). However, as objectivity morphed into a strategic ritual, in the name of balance the journalist had to find and report two sides of each story without passing judgment on the veracity of the competing facts, ensuring only that each side holds to a particular set of facts while leaving journalists unable to weigh in on which side's facts are grounded in empirical reality (Wein 2005).

This wasn't a particularly big problem for reporters or their craft through the latter part of the twentieth century, as an enduring news consensus among elites rendered these judgments largely irrelevant to political discourse.[3] The breakdown of that consensus, however, presented reporters with an enormous burden. Their response—to defend their reporting as reliable accounts of the facts as told to them without regard to accuracy or partisan content—looks remarkably like what Schudson (2001) calls "stenographic fairness," the reportorial norm in place when journalism was still a trade, before objectivity was a professional value. The irony is that objectivity, which began as a liberal reform to anchor journalism in scientific principles, now prevents journalists from making empirical judgments about competing fact claims in an age without factual consensus, often to the detriment of liberals.

This dilemma tracks with the breakdown of traditional media audiences, with implications for the sustainability of classical models of journalism not unlike the political ramifications foretold by the demise of television as a centralizing medium. Although talk radio and cable television audiences have long been able to choose their preferred messages, the steady decline of broadcast television means the loss of a centripetal force capable of providing a consensus alternative to the ideological poles. The objective model, at least so far as it applies to television reporting, first fell victim to the collapse of a consensus understanding of reality, then experienced further distress by the precipitous decline of traditional patterns of media use. As we have noted, broadcast and cable television ratings are deteriorating as audiences dwindle, even for previously collective national events such as the World Series. Millions of broadband customers are electing to eschew television subscriptions entirely as mobile viewing—by far the largest growth medium—replaces television viewing, and as tablets emerge as the prime-time device of choice.[4] Balanced coverage struggles to find a place in this atomized environment, where people get to customize their information sources and, if they wish, plug into their own reality.

The situation is even more disastrous for newspaper reporters, where the business model is collapsing along with the reporting model. Newspapers have long suffered from declining readership and ad revenues, a problem dating back to the era of broadcast television that reached a tipping point once people could reliably Google their way to the information of their choice. Newspapers depend on the willingness of people to pay for information they don't need and won't use in order to get the information they want. National and local news, sports, arts, entertainment and features are bundled together and sold at a fixed price. This model makes no sense in a world where anyone can download an app to a portable device to get movie listings and buy tickets, check the weather or find baseball scores in real time (Ryfe 2007). Subscriptions, once a necessity for many people, are now a luxury—or an anomaly. But newspapers are weighed down by high production costs paid for by subscriptions and ad revenues, neither of which can be easily recouped online, where users are reluctant to pay for content and advertisers are reluctant to pay for ads when anyone can advertise on sites like Craig's List for free.[5]

Publishers have been hard pressed to defend a centralized publication model in an age of decentralized media. Solutions typically center on ways to monetize content through digital delivery, usually by restricting prime online material to subscription customers, assuming people will pay for information when free options are available.[6] This means superimposing the logic of centralized control on an open-source medium.

The hashtag world of social media and self-publication therefore threatens an antiquated top-down publication model along with the objective news reporting model upon which it has long depended.[7] Where the Internet draws readers to partisan writing with an edge, traditional journalists favor and defend a balanced approach to reporting as best approximating a truthful account of political and social events, holding themselves up as honest observers in contrast to the defective commentators of the right and left. Given the value structure of their trade, it should be clear why the simple presence of a point of view would lead traditional reporters to disqualify the accounts of partisan bloggers and other self-publishing online writers as amateurs not trained to view the world objectively. But this approach is increasingly out of step with the changing media culture, where reporters occupy an imagined neutral zone in an era of zero-sum politics and writing with a point of view. Not surprisingly, bloggers across the ideological spectrum take issue with the idea that truth claims must originate in a hypothetical center, and can be quite caustic in their criticism of traditional journalism as misleading and detrimental to political discourse. And they have a point.

Consequences

If newspapers were buggy whips, they could continue to exhaust their relevance without much consequence for the general public, who simply bought automobiles in increasing numbers until horse-drawn carriages quietly disappeared. The same applies to network television news programs. But as a source of information with continued influence and relevance, mainstream media confound political discourse through narratives, built around the pretext of objectivity, that fail to present an accurate picture of the fundamental elements of the political moment, and complicate the ability of mainstream news consumers to understand the asymmetric elements of contemporary politics. Traditional media may be struggling for relevance but they are neither gone nor forgotten, leaving the public poorly served by their determination to report the news from a non-existent center.

Specifically, traditional media fail to grasp the ideological struggle on the right or the power struggle on the left; reduce meaningful political debate to game playing; and dismiss the validity of media practitioners who attempt to point this out, all to the detriment of a public badly in need of substantive and meaningful political information.

Inability to cover political asymmetries

Balanced coverage precludes mainstream reporters from considering how intramural conflict on the right may be substantively and structurally different from intramural conflict on the left, just as it prevents reporters from addressing the possibility that right and left have not contributed equally to political polarization. Nonequivalent political conditions inhabit a journalistic blind spot. Balance requires a pox on both houses else reporters will be forced to side with one set of truth claims, forever tagging them as partisans—to their professional detriment.

Political scientists Thomas Mann and Norman Ornstein, authors of the 2012 volume about Washington dysfunction disturbingly titled *It's Even Worse Than It Looks*, are perhaps the most high-profile figures to make the case for political asymmetry, complete with data demonstrating that congressional conservatives have moved to the extreme right while liberals have essentially marched in place. Mann and Ornstein had amassed decades of credibility among Washington reporters through their expertise on the ways of Congress and their respective affiliation with Brookings and the American Enterprise Institute, two of Washington's most respected think tanks. For years they had been staples on political talk programs and go-to sources for mainstream political news, and they always had a welcome platform on television to discuss their published work. Not this time. Apparently, calling the Republican Party an "insurgent outlier" driven by "tribal hubris" turns out to be the wrong way to get airtime, even for scholars with deep connections to establishment Washington (Mann and Ornstein 2012). As Ornstein recounted to liberal blogger Greg Sargent in May 2012, "Not a single one of the Sunday [political talk] shows has indicated an interest [in booking him]," despite 200,000 Facebook recommendations for his work, which Ornstein described as "a level of attention for a book that we haven't received before."[8] Progressive media enthusiastically received their work,[9] including Sargent's *Washington Post* Plum Line blog, no doubt reinforcing the mainstream belief that unbalanced news is inherently partisan. From conventional news outlets there was radio silence.

If the mainstream press are unwilling to consider empirical claims about political asymmetry, they will be incapable of understanding differences within the coalitions that make up the right and left and drive partisan polarization. For the right, this means incorrectly portraying factional battles as nothing more than different shades of conservatism. For the left, it means the failure to understand the goals of the progressive movement as a struggle with economic elites for power in the Democratic Party rather than as a battle for ideological purity akin to the Tea Party. For mainstream news consumers, it means having an impoverished basis for understanding the key dynamics of the political moment.

Traditional news framing of right-wing factionalism portrays a struggle for control of the Republican Party between mainstream conservative elites and Tea Party insurgents. The struggle has an inside–outside dynamic, especially when reporters focus on legislative action and political campaigns, and turns on questions of who is driving the party, and whether internal conflict is undermining Republican prospects as a governing and political entity. Narratives of this nature abound: Is the Tea Party faction preventing House leaders from moving ahead on immigration reform at the expense of the Republican Party's national prospects? Are Republican House and Senate incumbents moving to the right to inoculate themselves from Tea Party primary challengers? Did Republicans prevent themselves from claiming a Senate majority in 2010 and 2012 by nominating Tea Party-backed candidates who were "too far to the right" of their states' electorates, and did they correct the situation by nominating more moderate candidates in 2014?

The problem with this framing, apart from reflecting the simplistic tendency of political reporters to reduce politics to a horserace, is the odd way the players are categorized. Individuals with strong conservative bona fides are presented as being "not conservative enough" for the Republican electorate, or portrayed as moderates. Take the prominent example of former House Majority Leader Eric Cantor's unexpected 2014 primary defeat at the hands of an underfinanced and relatively unknown primary challenger. *The New York Times* characterized Cantor's loss as coming at the hands of "a Tea Party-backed economics professor who had hammered him for being insufficiently conservative."[10] *The Washington Post* proclaimed that Tea Party supporters in the Republican Party had concluded that Cantor "was not conservative enough for them."[11] This interpretation may accurately reflect the language used in Tea Party circles to describe Republicans who do not share their views, but it makes no sense to describe someone with an 83.5% conservative ranking from the *National Journal* as insufficiently conservative.[12] Likewise, it makes no sense to describe former Defense Secretary Chuck Hagel (a onetime Republican senator from Nebraska with a lifetime 83.7% rating from the American Conservative Union[13]) as a moderate because he opposed the Iraq War, or former Republican presidential candidate Jon Huntsman as a moderate because he supports immigration reform and has been open to the possibility that global warming is a human-made phenomenon.

What is clear is none of these individuals is an ideologue, or sufficiently ideological to adhere to an agenda that allows no room for deviation. More precise terms for those who demand fealty to an unwavering rejectionist agenda would be radical or reactionary. Employ these terms and the internal struggles of the Republican Party make sense. Cantor is a conservative politician affiliated with a House Republican establishment viewed by reactionary elements as too willing to thwart the wishes of those seeking to undo the welfare state and return to a pre-New Deal society. Hagel is a right-wing politician willing to accept an important role in an administration viewed by reactionaries as an enemy combatant in an existential battle over the direction of the country. Huntsman is a center-right politician with traditionally conservative economic and social views who opposes reactionary politics.

Mainstream reporters cannot frame the conflict this way without marginalizing the Tea Party, even if the Tea Party represents the margins of public opinion (and opinion polls consistently suggest that it does). The term reactionary is both descriptive and pejorative. It connotes an agenda well out of the mainstream and detrimental to the functioning of a complex, advanced nation. But the Tea Party is so influential in Republican politics, as the horserace version of their influence attests, that to marginalize them as reactionary is to marginalize the Republican Party, forcing reporters to make a value judgment at odds with their understanding of objectivity. So terminology that might bring the political moment into focus remains out of bounds, to the great detriment of those seeking to understand the political convulsions of the right. Properly naming something is the first step toward understanding it, and meaning is obscured when appropriate labels are elusive.

For similar reasons, traditional journalists are unable to portray conflict on the left as a struggle for power between progressive elements represented by the netroots and entrenched Wall Street-backed Democratic elites who returned the party to relevance in the 1990s by embracing business interests, at times to the detriment of traditional Democratic Party alliances with organized labor and the middle class. Instead, to achieve symmetry with their account of the conservative ideological struggle, they frame progressives as ideological insurgents out of step with mainstream party thinking and American public opinion who, if successful, would undermine Democrats' ability to appeal to "centrist" or "mainstream" voters and return the party to pre-Clinton-era irrelevance. Not coincidentally, this framing aligns with the perspective of neoliberal elites who still run the Democratic Party and serve as sources for mainstream reporters.

As we will see in Chapter 7, there is an important ideological distinction between progressives and self-described "New Democrats" just as there is a crucial power dynamic between conservative and Tea Party elites. But where the Tea Party is best understood through its ideological positioning because it is animated by an ideological agenda, the netroots fashion themselves in the mold of progressive political thought with a long, mainstream bipartisan history. Closer intellectually to the progressive movement of a century ago than to the New Deal coalition but compatible with center-left thought throughout much of the twentieth century, it represents a break with the strategy and tactics of the Clinton era in order to bring about progressive change. It does, however, threaten to upend party elites with ties to financial and corporate interests by reinventing the party as a bottom-up vehicle for broad-based, small-d democratic participation utilizing the community structure of the Internet.

This dynamic eludes balanced reporting. The netroots operate outside establishment Washington, where elite sources with regular access to journalists and an interest in diminishing the influence of their opponents can marginalize progressives as out of touch and politically inexperienced. For their part, progressives employ the range of grassroots mobilizing and messaging tactics discussed in

Chapter 3 and, as noted there, have begun to claim a number of victories in skirmishes with Democratic Party leaders, but their methods lack the splash (and big-money backing) of Tea Party primary challenges to Republican incumbents, which in their own right have been successful. Because of this, and to their detriment, progressives are readily portrayed as politically hapless.

As outsiders who pose a threat to the status quo and who are not secretive about their disdain for mainstream reporting, progressives are not natural sources for journalists and therefore lack the clout to challenge sticky narratives about their political naivety. Nonetheless, because they are positioned to the left of elite Democrats the way the Tea Party is positioned to the right of elite Republicans, the need for balanced reporting provides journalists a natural narrative counterpoint: The progressive movement is pulling the Democratic Party to the left the same way the Tea Party movement is pulling the Republican Party to the right, albeit with less efficacy.

With accurate language to categorize the Tea Party, it would be more difficult for journalists to assert symmetry with progressives. In an asymmetrical framing of events, the Tea Party would be portrayed as posing a challenge to a century of established politics and policies, whereas progressives would be viewed as posing a risk to the power of economic elites at the helm of the Democratic Party. This understanding arguably does more justice to contemporary political narratives than the right–left dichotomy of mainstream political reporting, but it does not exist in an objectively balanced world.

Diminished political understanding

The simplest way for political reporters to overlook asymmetries is to cram political events into a horserace structure, where two teams of combatants compete for electoral or policy "victories" in a never-ending series of contests. In this telling of events, "team blue" faces off against "team red" for the right to control the House, set the rules of the Senate, hand President Obama a legislative "win" or thwart his agenda or, if the contest is intramural, demonstrate the ascendency or limits of Tea Party influence or see if Democrats acquiesce to the wishes of the left in what would be characterized as a "win" or a "loss" for progressives.

A framework that portrays politics as feats of strength, scrimmages and playoff games offers several benefits to journalists faced with covering complicated political terrain. It comes naturally to reporters drawn to the competitive aspects of politics, who are inclined to regard candidates and officials as motivated to seek political advantage, and can be rationalized by the *prima facie* assertion that only a bad politician or an ex-politician would do otherwise. This makes horserace framing easy for mainstream reporters to justify; at a basic level, all political activity can be reduced to winning and losing. And focusing on wins and losses provides a safe way for reporters to avoid making value judgments about the structure and meaning of political agendas. Whether a politician holds conservative or radical views is irrelevant to a storyline about whether he or she succeeds in blocking President Obama's judicial appointments (a "loss" for the president) or beats back a Tea Party primary challenge (a "win" for the Republican establishment). Ironically, reporting politics as competition is the easiest way for reporters to avoid conflict.

It is, however, a sterile and one-dimensional understanding of political events devoid of any sense of *why* politicians compete, save for the self-evident and empty observation that everybody wants to win because winning is how you attain or preserve power. The resulting narrative is innocuous, highlighting the least controversial elements of the process. At the same time, it is detrimental to our political intelligence for what it fails to address. *What* is to be accomplished with power escapes mention. Reducing politics to its lowest common denominator deprives mainstream news consumers of a way to comprehend the complex asymmetries driving political competition.

Transparency

More complex political narratives are available from partisan sources that are not hamstrung by the professional demands of objectivity. Without the requirements of balanced coverage to prevent them from seeing the imbalances in political debate, bloggers who are this generation's journalists are free to relate a richer political discourse at once more partisan and more illuminating than conventional mainstream fare. Traditional reporters may dismiss what bloggers do as defective *because* they are partisans, but this critique assumes the sanctity of a methodology tied to a particular moment in journalistic history. Step outside the confines of objectivity, recognize it as a value structure suited to a particular set of professional conditions rather than as the last word on how to report news, and the partisan argument falls away. True, bloggers have agendas. So do reporters. The difference is that bloggers are transparent about theirs.

Over the past several years, prominent bloggers have contributed to the national political discourse, at times significantly, by virtue of their transparency, most notably as follows:

- In 2008, while being transparent about his support for Barack Obama, Nate Silver revolutionized electoral horserace journalism through his blog fivethirtyeight.com by introducing a rigorous, data-driven methodology for understanding election polls that challenged the more simplistic, ad hoc approach long employed by political reporters.
- In 2013, blogger-turned-journalist Glenn Greenwald ignited an international political debate by releasing documents provided to him by Edward Snowden that detailed the breadth and depth of the surveillance operations conducted by the National Security Agency. Greenwald's transparency about his opposition to such surveillance actually helped him break the story, because Snowden

otherwise would not have approached Greenwald with what he knew. As Columbia professor Jay Rosen blogged at the time, "That is the lesson that Glenn Greenwald has been teaching the profession of journalism for the last week. Edward Snowden went to him because of his commitments."[14]

- Through a long series of community diaries on Daily Kos and his blog ACASignups.net, Charles Gabba played a crucial role in changing the national media narrative about the number of previously uninsured Americans who acquired health care coverage as a result of the Affordable Care Act in 2013 and 2014. Weeding through mountains of data from government and insurance company websites, Gabba kept a running count of the number of people covered that was so meticulous it was widely cited by the mainstream media,[15] despite Gabba's transparent support for Obamacare.

The failure of reporters to acknowledge that objectivity is a value choice speaks to the opaque quality of an approach theoretically superior by virtue of its claim to represent all perspectives. Transparency is also a value choice, and there is no obvious reason to believe it is any more or less suited to serve as the guiding principle for journalism. It did for years during the early decades of the republic. With the writer's political affiliation unmasked, bloggers are unburdened by the need to temper their analysis to appeal to all perspectives and can address political asymmetries without apology. There is no obligation to appeal to imaginary moderates, offering bloggers the advantage of not having to write from the center at a time when the center does not exist.

Professional journalists might respond that relaxing the objectivity requirement reduces reporting to screeching and news to an unfathomable mix of partisan rants, conspiracy theories, fabricated claims, half-truths and non-truths. In other words, journalism starts to look like the Internet. Progressive analysis of the politics of conservative reaction sits a click away from reactionary assertions about the Obama administration's socialist agenda. The cost of transparency is using the partisan or philosophical bent of the writer as a point of departure for deciding if his or her claims make sense. This shifts the burden of discovery to the reader.

Journalists may further contend that most readers are uninterested in, or ill equipped to engage in, this kind of reasoning. They may be correct. Giving otherwise ordinary voices access to mediated political discourse creates a loud and confusing media environment. But that is the media environment of the twenty-first century. That marginally engaged readers may not be able to navigate this environment effectively without being sidetracked by groundless claims or fabricated evidence is in its own right a weak reason to ignore the potential benefits of journalistic transparency, at least to the degree that its benefits address the weaknesses of objective reporting. Strong, evidence-based arguments have long shelf lives. They can be the online equivalent of the enduring narratives preferred by mainstream journalists in that, over time, if news developments bear them out, they can become the default assumptions that structure political discussion. The

Internet is a flowing river of ideas as well as a stagnant pool of conspiracy theories, and moving water has a cleansing effect.

Implications for Realignment

The failures of the professional reporting model in an era of zero-sum partisanship and the concurrent rise of bottom-up, open-source journalism which is transparent about ideology have the potential to shape the coming political era. Dramatic changes in political communication evident during the past decade are most reminiscent of the Jackson realignment, with the Internet playing the role of local newspapers joined in a makeshift network that formed the backbone of Jackson's insurgent campaign to upend a presidential nominating process controlled by Washington congressional elites. In Jackson's time, partisan reporting was the norm, and Jackson understood how to work it to his benefit during a period of mass expansion of the franchise.

Today's Internet Left shares that understanding and is pushing back against mainstream reporting modalities to leverage the benefits of partisan journalism during a partisan era. Thus far, the endurance of television and newspapers and the objective reporting methods they support has worked against replacing objectivity with transparency as the prevailing journalistic value. Objectivity still has tremendous institutional support. But as journalism continues to move online, the logic of Internet communication will pose a challenge to generations of journalistic practices.

In the meantime, the Internet Left has been successful in using new media to build a movement. Without a vehicle for grassroots communication, the breakdown of political consensus would have left alternative voices without a means for expression, and limited the universe of political information to whatever was provided by the twentieth-century news model. With the Internet, the left has a medium for bottom-up communication, message dissemination and political mobilization. As much as they would also like their narratives to displace the objective framing of the mainstream press, their brand of partisan reporting has served to communicate with, motivate and develop a progressive base.

If there is to be a realignment of the left, transparent, partisan digital journalism will continue to be an irreplaceable resource. The struggle between progressives and mainstream journalists over the content of news narratives runs concurrently with the power struggle between progressives and neoliberal Democrats and is instrumental to how that struggle is communicated. The leadership of the Democratic Party may still pose the greatest obstacle to a progressive realignment, as we will see in Chapter 6. But, as a matter of values as well as practical politics, an era dominated by progressive governance aligns most naturally with a media environment where objectivity is replaced with transparency.

Notes

1 Rosen faults journalism, not journalists, for promulgating professional rules that require practitioners to defend not having a point of view in order to maintain their authority. See Rosen, Jay. 2010. "The View From Nowhere: Questions and Answers." *PressThink*, November 10. Retrieved from http://pressthink.org/2010/11/the-view-from-nowhere-questions-and-answers/.
2 Johnson-Cartee applies the same critique to use of the scientific method by social scientists to distance themselves from subjective assessment of data, contending that no amount of training can overcome inherently subjective human tendencies.
3 It did, however, have detrimental consequences for those outside elite opinion who sought coverage of alternative perspectives and viewpoints. See, for instance, Parenti (1993).
4 Edwards, Jim. 2013. "TV Is Dying, and Here Are the Stats That Prove It." *Business Insider*, November 24. Retrieved from www.businessinsider.com/cord-cutters-and-the-death-of-tv-2013-11.
5 For views on the problem from bloggers, see "Voodoo Newspaper Economics." 2008. Newsosaur, October 24. Retrieved from http://newsosaur.blogspot.com/2008/10/voodoo-newspaper-economics.html; and Heath, Robert T. 2009. "The Unraveling of Newspaper Economics." *SeekingAlpha*, July 5. Retrieved from http://seekingalpha.com/article/146934-the-unraveling-of-newspaper-economics.
6 "Newspaper Economic Action Plan." 2009. American Press Institute. Retrieved from www.niemanlab.org/pdfs/apireportmay09.pdf. One newspaper, the Newport, R.I. *Daily News*, even tried charging a steep premium *not* to get the physical newspaper in the hope that it would steer people to purchase a print-and-online bundle, the middle choice in a three-tiered pricing structure with print-only as the least expensive—but from the publisher's perspective, least desirable—option. See "Can Behavioral Economics Save Newspapers?" 2009. *The Economist*, June 23. Retrieved from www.economist.com/blogs/freeexchange/2009/06/can_behavioural_economics_save.
7 For a perspective on the challenges to the reporting model of journalists as autonomous actors serving a unitary public, see Anderson (2013).
8 Sargent, Greg. 2012. "Only One Party's To Blame? Don't Tell the Sunday Shows." *The Washington Post*, May 14. Retrieved from www.washingtonpost.com/blogs/plum-line/post/only-one-partys-to-blame-dont-tell-the-sunday-shows/2012/05/14/gIQAXOcPPU_blog.html.
9 It was a frequent topic of conversation on Daily Kos diaries during and immediately after the 2012 election.
10 Martin, Jonathan. 2014. "Eric Cantor Defeated by David Brat, Tea Party Challenger, in G.O.P. Primary Upset." *The New York Times*, June 10. Retrieved from www.nytimes.com/2014/06/11/us/politics/eric-cantor-loses-gop-primary.html?_r=0.
11 Fahrenthold, David, Rosalind S. Helderman and Jenna Portnoy. 2014. "What Went Wrong for Eric Cantor?" *The Washington Post*, June 11. Retrieved from www.washingtonpost.com/politics/what-went-wrong-for-eric-cantor/2014/06/11/0be7c02c-f180-11e3-914c-1fbd0614e2d4_story.html.
12 The ranking placed Cantor as the 66th most conservative member of the 435-member House.
13 See http://acuratings.conservative.org/acu-federal-legislative-ratings/?year1=2008&chamber=13&state1=40&sortable=1.
14 Rosen, Jay. 2013. "Politics: Some/Politics: None. Two Ways To Excel In Political Journalism. Neither Dominates." *PressThink*, June 13. Retrieved from http://pressthink.org/2013/06/politics-some-politics-none-two-ways-to-excel-in-political-journalism-neither-dominates/.
15 See ACASignups.net, at http://acasignups.net/in-the-news.

References

Anderson, C. W. 2013. *Rebuilding the News: Metropolitan Journalism in the Digital Age.* Philadelphia, PA: Temple University Press.
Campbell, W. Joseph. 2003. *Yellow Journalism: Puncturing the Myths, Defining the Legacies.* New York: Praeger.
Campbell, W. Joseph. 2006. *The Year That Defined American Journalism: 1897 and the Clash of Paradigms.* New York: Routledge.
Epstein, Edward Jay. 1973. *News from Nowhere: Television and the News.* New York: Random House.
Gans, Herbert. 1979. *Deciding What's News: A Study of CBS Evening News, NBC Nightly News, Newsweek, and Time.* Evanston, IL: Northwestern University Press.
Goffman, Erving. 1974. *Frame Analysis: An Essay on the Organization of Experience.* Cambridge, MA: Harvard University Press.
Johnson-Cartee, Karen S. 2005. *News Narratives and News Framing.* Lanham, MD: Rowman & Littlefield.
Kaplan, Richard L. 2002. *Politics and the American Press: The Rise of Objectivity, 1865–1920.* New York: Cambridge University Press.
Kennamer, J. David. 1992. "Public Opinion, the Press and Public Policy: An Introduction." In *Public Opinion, the Press and Public Policy*, edited by J. David Kennamer, 1–18. Westport, CT: Praeger.
Leonard, Thomas C. 1986. *The Power of the Press: The Birth of American Political Reporting.* New York: Oxford University Press.
Mann, Thomas E. and Norman J. Ornstein. 2012. *It's Even Worse Than It Looks: How the American Constitutional System Collided With the New Politics of Extremism.* New York: Basic Books.
Molotch, Harvey and Marilyn Lester. 1974. "News as Purposive Behavior: On the Strategic Use of Routine Events, Accidents, and Scandals." *American Sociological Review* 39: 101–112.
Parenti, Michael. 1993. *Inventing Reality: The Politics of News Media.* New York: St. Martin's Press.
Peterson, Mark Allen. 2001. "Getting to the Story: Unwriteable Discourse and Interpretive Practice in American Journalism." *Anthropological Quarterly* 74: 201–211.
Ryfe, David. 2007. "The Future of Media Politics." *Rhetoric & Public Affairs* 10: 723–738.
Salmon, Charles and Chi-Yung Moh. 1992. "The Spiral of Silence: Linking Individuals and Society Through Communication." In *Public Opinion, the Press and Public Policy*, edited by J. David Kennamer, 145–161. Westport, CT: Praeger.
Schudson, Michael. 1978. *Discovering the News.* New York: Basic Books.
Schudson, Michael. 2001. "The Objectivity Norm in American Journalism." *Journalism* 2: 149–170.
Strekfuss, Richard. 1990. "Objectivity in Journalism: A Search and a Reassessment." *Journalism Quarterly* 67: 973–983.
Tuchman, Gaye. 1972. "Objectivity as Strategic Ritual: An Examination of Newsmen's Notions of Objectivity." *American Journal of Sociology* 77: 660–679.
Wein, Charlotte. 2005. "Defining Objectivity within Journalism." *NORDICOM Review* 26: 3–15.

6

THE LIMITS OF NETROOTS INFLUENCE

In the spring of 2014 something highly unusual happened in the field of political science: an academic paper went viral and was read by millions of people across the country. It was a study that appeared to validate some of the core principles of the progressive movement, while at once illustrating why the netroots may have far to go in its effort to claim power from a Democratic Party elite supported by an influx of money from the flush side of the growing national economic divide.

The study in question was "Testing Theories of American Politics: Elites, Interest Groups and Average Citizens," by Martin Gilens of Princeton University and Benjamin Page of Northwestern University. It was widely perceived to document how the United States had become an oligarchy, even though the authors never actually used that term, and that perception made it something of an Internet phenomenon. In November of that year, a Google search for "Martin Gilens Benjamin Page Oligarchy" returned over 5,000 results, many of them linking to articles discussing the study that were in turn shared thousands, tens of thousands or even hundreds of thousands of times on social media.[1]

Given the subject matter, the authors themselves became a source of interest in the progressive blogosphere. In an April 2014 interview with *Talking Points Memo*, Gilens summarized his work by saying that "contrary to what decades of political science research might lead you to believe, ordinary citizens have virtually no influence over what their government does in the United States. And economic elites and interest groups, especially those representing business, have a substantial degree of influence. Government policy-making over the last few decades reflects the preferences of those groups—of economic elites and of organized interests."[2]

The study provided an academic stamp of approval to the belief that politicians work primarily for the rich and powerful, an animating sentiment for the netroots

116 The Limits of Netroots Influence

as well as a widely held public belief. Opinion surveys consistently show that large majorities of Americans believe the income gap is widening, that the wealthy have more opportunity to influence the political process than average citizens, and that the government is focused mainly on helping the rich, as shown by the following examples:

- In June 2014 a poll conducted for Bloomberg News by Selzer & Company found that 67% of Americans thought "the gap between the rich and everyone else is getting bigger," versus only 29% who did not.[3]
- In May 2014 a CBS News poll found that 75% of Americans thought "wealthy Americans have more of a chance to influence the elections process than other Americans," versus only 23% who thought all Americans have an equal chance.[4]
- In September 2013 a poll by YouGov for *The Huffington Post* found that 53% of Americans thought the government was focused mainly on helping the rich, versus 18% who said it focused on helping the poor, and 8% the middle class.[5]

It is easy to find the source of these popular beliefs. Income inequality has skyrocketed in the United States for several decades. The wealthiest have seen their income dramatically increase, while those at the bottom have fallen behind.[6] Figure 6.1 presents a striking overview of these trends.

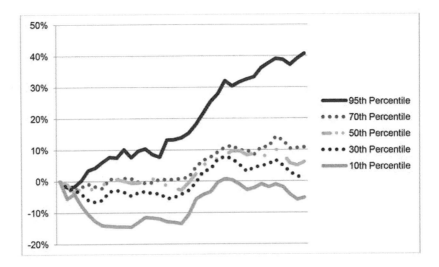

FIGURE 6.1 Cumulative change in real hourly wages of all workers, by wage percentile, 1979–2013

Source: Gould (2014).

As wealth has become increasingly concentrated in the hands of a smaller percentage of the American population, so has political power. For the first time ever, in 2014 the median net worth of members of Congress surpassed $1,000,000, according to a study released in January of that year by the Center for Responsive Politics.[7] This placed the majority of all lawmakers well within the top 1% of the United States, and more than 15 times greater than the median household net worth of $66,740.[8] It is hardly surprising that Americans on the other side of the economic divide would feel that public policy enacted by members of Congress most closely reflects the interests of their own economic class.

The same can be said for donations to federal campaigns. While the email-based organizing conducted by the Professional Left has significantly increased the number of small donors and donations to political campaigns, large donations have nearly kept pace. Between 2004 and 2012, small donations (under $200) to House candidates increased by one-quarter, to 10% of contributions, but were still dwarfed by large donations (over $1,000) from big contributors and PACs, which accounted for 71% of the political money donated in 2012—an increase from 2004.[9] These figures do not include undisclosed "dark money" and unlimited Super PAC donations, which have played an increasingly central role in independent campaign expenditures since the 2010 electoral cycle.

In fact, while the 2014 campaign saw a record-breaking number of small donations for Democratic political candidates, mainly due to the work of the Professional Left, a handful of uber-wealthy donors easily matched their efforts. Following the 2014 election, digital strategist Melissa Ryan summed up the imbalance between small and large contributors by noting that "[G]rassroots donors gave more often and in larger numbers than ever before. By Election Day, ActBlue had processed a fundraising-cycle record: 6,925,384 contributions under $250 from 1,396,074 unique donors ... [But] shortly before Election Day, USA Today reported that super PACs have raised $615 million this cycle—a full $200 million of that from just 42 individual donors."[10]

As the rich get richer, they continue to dominate political spending and occupy the majority of seats in Congress. It should be clear why Americans believe public policy reflects primarily the interests of economic elites and organized business groups. And while these beliefs may align the public with the objectives of the progressive movement and give the netroots a claim to speak for the broader electorate, the conditions underpinning these beliefs illustrate why the movement faces steep challenges in its quest for power in the Democratic Party.

The Resilience of the DLC

As Gilens or any member of the netroots would argue, while the Democratic Party is somewhat more responsive than the Republicans to middle- and working-class opinion, the influence of large dollar contributions is a bipartisan phenomenon. *Talking Points Memo* asked Gilens whether his research found both Democrats and

Republicans to be responsive to wealthy interests. He responded that other research he had conducted suggested they are:

> There are a set of economic issues on which the Democratic Party is more consistently supportive of the needs of the poor and middle class. But it's by no means a strong relationship. Both parties have to a large degree embraced a set of policies that reflect the needs, preferences and interests of the well to do.[11]

Since its inception, the netroots has raged against what its supporters widely view as the capture of the Democratic Party by elite, wealthy financial interests. Howard Dean's rise to prominence in the progressive blogosphere was rhetorically framed around this idea. In the March 2003 speech he gave to the California Democratic Party Convention that ignited his presidential campaign, he included a line borrowed from the late left-wing champion Senator Paul Wellstone: "I'm Howard Dean, and I'm here to represent the Democratic wing of the Democratic Party."[12] The speech was widely shared within the progressive blogosphere (Markos Moulitsas of Daily Kos and Jerome Armstrong of the progressive blog MyDD, who were in attendance as credentialed media, blogged first-hand reports about the event) and was crucial to Dean's ascendency as the favorite Democratic presidential candidate of the netroots in 2004. The "Democratic wing of the Democratic Party" has been a popular rallying cry for the netroots ever since.

Dean's framing was a clear shot at the ascendant, neoliberal, pro-business wing of the Democratic Party, which at the time was best represented by the Democratic Leadership Council (DLC). Bill Clinton, Al Gore and Missouri Rep. Richard A. Gephardt, among others, founded the DLC and other "New Democratic" institutions such as the House Democratic Caucus' Committee on Party Effectiveness in the 1980s in order to remake the Democratic Party in a more centrist, competitive mold following the landslide losses of Jimmy Carter and Walter Mondale to Ronald Reagan. Their aim was to wrest the party from the grip of organized labor and left-leaning advocacy groups, and reorient it toward economic policies that would meet with less opposition from wealthy financial and business interests. Nine months after his speech in California, Dean made his anti-DLC framing explicit when, as the then-frontrunner for the Democratic presidential nomination, he responded to criticism from rival candidates by calling the DLC "the Republican wing of the Democratic Party."[13]

For their part, the DLC did not merely sit idly by in the face of Dean's rise. During 2003, DLC founders Al From and Bruce Reed attacked Dean's candidacy in multiple memos and op-eds, including his "Democratic wing of the Democratic Party" phrase, using terminology that could have been mistaken for talking points from Republican opposition research:

> The fact is, "the Democratic wing of the Democratic Party," as former Vermont Gov. Howard Dean likes to call it, is an aberration, a modern-day

version of the old McGovern wing of the party, defined principally by weakness abroad and elitist interest-group liberalism at home. That wing lost the party 49 states in two elections and turned a powerful national organization into a much weaker, regional one.[14]

From and Reed's opposition to Dean was not merely for show, as they privately fumed about his candidacy as well. In 2006, Moulitsas and Armstrong wrote about this in their book, *Crashing the Gate*:

> In one of the DLC's monthly staff meetings, From explained his fears of a Dean candidacy—his angry tone, his borrowing of the Wellstone rhetoric, his "weakness" on national security issues and his opposition to the brewing Iraq War. From believed that Dean's use of Wellstone's "Democratic wing of the Democratic Party" line was directly aimed at Clinton's centrist policies and therefore at the DLC. From took it as a personal affront, saying that "Dean would undo everything that Clinton had stood for" and put the Democratic Party permanently back into minority status.
> (Moulitsas and Armstrong 2006, 142–3)

Even after Dean's presidential campaign ended, the conflict between the netroots and the DLC/centrist wing of the Democratic Party continued unabated, most notably in the netroots scrums with Senator Joe Lieberman. Different sources of funding for the two factions played a significant role in their ongoing, unresolved dispute. As we saw in Chapter 3, the first-generation netroots was funded primarily through small donations from readers, ad revenue from a small boutique operation called BlogAds, and the occasional opportunity to freelance as a political consultant or op-ed writer. On the other hand, large corporations funded the DLC—the same organized, elite economic interests identified by Martin Gilens and Benjamin Page as dominating public policy.

Following DLC co-founder Al Gore's addition of then-DLC Chairman Joe Lieberman to the 2000 Democratic presidential ticket, *Newsweek* provided a rare glimpse into the DLC's donor base. It reads like a Who's Who of corporate America:

> If Gore ... hopes to score populist points by bashing Big Oil and pharmaceutical companies that oppose his plan to add a prescription-drug entitlement to Medicare, he may have some explaining to do. Among the DLC's biggest benefactors last year (contributions of between $50,000 and $100,000) were ARCO, Chevron and the drug giant Merck. Other big underwriters include Du Pont, Microsoft and Philip Morris (which has kicked in $500,000 since Lieberman became DLC chairman). There is no evidence that the DLC has trimmed policies to accommodate its patrons, but some contributors say the money has helped ensure an open door to Lieberman. "We've been able to have a dialogue with the senator and his staff,"

said Jay Rosser, spokesman for another DLC benefactor, Koch Industries, an oil-pipeline firm that is also a big GOP donor.[15]

The open door to Koch Industries is particularly noteworthy. In 2014, the Koch network spent over $100 million on the midterm elections, entirely to defeat Democratic candidates.[16]

Nearly bankrupt, the DLC folded in early 2011.[17] The reasons for its demise were mundane and largely organizational. Its chairman, Bruce Reed, left the organization in 2010 to become Vice President Joe Biden's Chief of Staff, and the DLC was unable to recruit a new chair with similar fundraising prowess. As such, while the end of the DLC was greeted with glee in netroots circles, it did not signal a shift in power within the Democratic Party. It also did not end the dispute between the netroots and the institutional progeny of the DLC.

In December 2013, two of the co-founders of Third Way—a think tank with effectively the same mission as the DLC—penned an op-ed in *The Wall Street Journal* attacking netroots favorite Senator Elizabeth Warren over her anti-Wall Street message and support for increasing Social Security benefits. It read much like From and Reed's anti-Dean op-eds had a decade earlier, describing a "fantasy-based populism" that would be "disastrous" for the Democratic Party.[18]

The op-ed was well received by some Washington journalists—*National Journal*'s Ron Fournier tweeted that it was a "thorough Third Way Takedown" of the "professional Left's magical thinking"[19]—but it met with outrage in netroots circles. Democracy for America, the Progressive Change Campaign Committee and Progressive United, an organization founded in the aftermath of Senator Russ Feingold's failed 2010 re-election campaign, demanded that Third Way co-chair Rep. Allyson Schwartz (who at the time was running for the Democratic nomination for Pennsylvania Governor) resign her position from the organization in response. Schwartz obliged, calling the op-ed "outrageous" and promptly co-sponsoring a bill to expand Social Security benefits.[20] Daily Kos revised its candidate endorsement criteria to exclude anyone who was a member of Third Way.[21] It also produced a graphic, reproduced in Figure 6.2, pointing out that Third Way's Board of Trustees was composed almost entirely of investment bankers with a few CEOs sprinkled in, implying their arguments against economic populism were self-interested and suspect. In March 2015, 42 of 44 Democrats in the U.S. Senate voted for a bill to increase Social Security benefits,[22] thus settling the specific cause of the December 2013 dust-up with Third Way in favor of the netroots, making Social Security expansion the de facto position of the Democratic Party.

Despite occasional victories such as this, New Democrats and their offspring remain entrenched in the Democratic Party, and the netroots will not be a political force to reckon with until they are able to mount consistent challenges to this power. As blogger Ezra Klein noted following the demise of the DLC, "the major policy initiatives Democrats have pushed in recent years—the Affordable

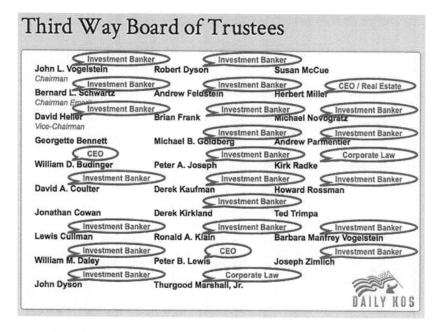

FIGURE 6.2 Third Way Board of Trustees
Source: *Daily Kos*.

Care Act and cap-and-trade—both hew closely to the 'liberal means through market ends' formula that the DLC favored."[23]

In a November 2014 review of DLC co-founder Al From's memoirs, progressive blogger Matt Stoller described From's (and thus the DLC's) remarkable legacy:

> Bill Clinton chaired From's organization, the Democratic Leadership Council (DLC) and used it as a platform to ascend to the Presidency in 1992. His wife Hillary is a DLC proponent. Al Gore and Joe Biden were DLCers. Barack Obama is quietly an adherent to the "New Democrat" philosophy crafted by From, so are most of the people in his cabinet, and the bulk of the Senate Democrats and House Democratic leaders. From 2007–2011, the New Democrats were the swing bloc in the U.S. House of Representatives, authoring legislation on bailouts and financial regulation of derivatives.[24]

This is indeed a sprawling legacy, and despite the successful intra-party policy fights waged by the Internet Left, described above and in Chapter 3, movement progressives continue to find themselves frustrated by a party infrastructure as tenacious in its own right as the institutional advantages still enjoyed by the remains of the Reagan coalition.

The Limits of Netroots Organizing

Compounding the issue of entrenched power in the Democratic Party elite is the inability of the Internet Left to reach large portions of the Democratic coalition. One year after progressives regularly began to prove decisive in high-level intramural Democratic Party policy fights, and more than a decade after the netroots first rose to prominence in opposition to the Iraq War, an obscure primary election in New York State provided the clearest snapshot yet into the obstacles facing progressives as a rank-and-file movement.

The date was September 9, 2014, and the primary in question was the Democratic gubernatorial contest featuring incumbent Governor Andrew Cuomo, perhaps the epitome of the Wall Street-friendly, Third Way "new" Democrat that has occupied the lion's share of party leadership positions over the past 25 years. In order to pursue corporate-friendly economic policies in a deep blue state, Cuomo went so far as to coordinate with a group of Democrats in the State Senate known as the "Independent Democratic Caucus," who broke from their party and handed control of the chamber back to Republicans after Democrats had won a majority of seats in the 2012 election.[25]

Cuomo's challenger was Zephyr Rain Teachout, a Vermont-raised, Yale-educated Fordham law professor with a hippy name. Her main—really her only—claim to fame was serving as the Director of Internet Organizing on Howard Dean's 2004 presidential campaign. Teachout had never previously run for office. She raised a few hundred thousand dollars for the campaign, and her only endorsements were a smattering of netroots organizations such as MoveOn and the Progressive Change Campaign Committee, as well as left-wing media outlets such as *The Nation*.[26]

In stark contrast, Cuomo had nearly 100% name recognition, both as the current governor and as the son of former three-term Democratic governor Mario Cuomo. He raised $5 million a month every month in the six months before the election, and spent that money freely.[27] Virtually every elected Democratic official in the state had endorsed him, out of loyalty or fear; at least one official complained anonymously that Democrats thought to be considering a Teachout endorsement received phone calls telling them that their pet projects might be endangered if they followed through with their subversion.[28] Finally, and just for good measure, Cuomo pursued a failed legal effort to get Teachout kicked off the primary ballot.[29]

Given this situation, the outcome was never in doubt. Cuomo won 62–34%, with a 3% remainder going to a third candidate. This was a clear victory for Cuomo, but to some observers and participants a surprisingly strong showing under the circumstances for Teachout.[30] As for movement progressives, the lessons to be learned were alternately sweet and bitter:

- Teachout—surprisingly—threatened Cuomo because of her strength in the progressive movement. The netroots and Internet Left are significant political

- players because they have organized the largest left-wing media and activist network in the country, which operates independently of established media channels and Democratic Party leaders. It is equal in size to roughly 20–30% of the nationwide Democratic vote for Congress in midterm elections, giving it an estimated size of between seven and ten million in 2014.
- However, the network is demographically unrepresentative of the Democratic Party base writ large, and thus faces significant challenges in achieving further growth. Whereas the Democratic Party tends to be disproportionately female, non-white and working class compared with the country as a whole, the netroots are disproportionately male, white and well educated.[31] As a result, the netroots do not yet have a wide enough reach to take over the reins of the party. Furthermore, since the populations where the netroots must increase their reach are demographically quite different from the populations they have organized, they are further away from majority status in the Democratic Party than the electrifying reactions to candidates like Howard Dean and Bernie Sanders would suggest. Unless the netroots can break out of this demographic cul-de-sac, they will have difficulty becoming the dominant force in the Democratic Party.

Evidence of these lessons can be found in the wide variance in Teachout's support across counties and state assembly districts. Despite her great disadvantages in money, endorsements and name recognition, Teachout managed to win large swaths of the state in whiter, more rural and higher-income areas, often by wide margins. At the same time, she was defeated in areas with sizable urban working-class and/or minority populations by margins that resembled the vast general election gulfs between Democrats and Republicans within these communities.

Surprisingly, Teachout won the same number of counties as Cuomo—31 apiece. Her victories were concentrated in the eastern portion of Upstate New York, around the Hudson Valley and Albany capital region. However, Cuomo dominated the urban centers—especially New York City and Buffalo—where most of the voters live. Both candidates won several counties with more than 70% of the vote, but Teachout's high was 77.5% of the vote in rural, sparsely populated Columbia County; Cuomo carried The Bronx by a similar margin.

There was also enormous variation across New York City districts. Teachout won several of the wealthier, whiter state assembly districts in the city, including a gentrified portion of Brooklyn with 67% of the vote. However, she lost by 9–1 margins in heavily minority, working-class, immigrant and ethnic white areas. Even though Teachout ran a populist, progressive campaign squarely to Cuomo's left, she lost because she failed to attract enough support among the very communities to whom the netroots have often assumed such a message would be the most appealing.

The geography and demography of Teachout's support closely tracked with the maximum reach of the Internet Left and the netroots at the time. Evidence of this may be found in Table 6.1, which portrays rates of New York state traffic to

TABLE 6.1 New York State traffic to Daily Kos during the 2014 New York State Gubernatorial Primary

City	Population	Number of visits
1. New York City	8,491,079	723,493
2. Ithaca	30,720	18,535
3. Syracuse	144,263	16,997
4. Rochester	209,983	15,932
5. Buffalo	258,703	15,671
6. Albany	98,566	12,307

Sources: Google Analytics and United States Census Bureau.

Daily Kos in the 30 days leading up to the gubernatorial primary.[32] Not surprisingly, Daily Kos received most of its New York State traffic from New York City. However, the second best source of traffic in that timeframe came from the small university town of Ithaca, which at 30,000 residents is much smaller than the cities just behind it in visits to Daily Kos: Syracuse (144,000); Rochester (210,000); Buffalo (259,000); and Albany (99,000). Daily Kos readership was seven times as dense in Ithaca—the seat of Tompkins County, where Teachout won 69% of the vote—as in the Cuomo strongholds of New York City (8,500,000) and Buffalo.

Like Teachout's supporters, Daily Kos readership demographics skew heavily toward well educated white liberals when compared with Democratic voters as a whole.[33] Within New York State, its readership density overlaps areas where Teachout won her highest percentage of the vote. She was able to win 34% of the vote with virtually no money because she won populations where the Internet Left is well represented, but she was able to win only 34% of the vote because she lost badly where it is not.

A comparison of Democratic voters in the 2014 midterm election with the readership of the largest Internet Left websites further illuminates the progressive movement's demographic problem. In that election, a total of 35,626,309 votes were cast for Democratic candidates for the U.S. House of Representatives.[34] According to exit polling, 61.2%—21.8 million—were white. Additionally, 43.6% of those voters—roughly 15.5 million—were male. A comparable 43.5% identified as liberal.[35] By contrast, according to Quantcast, in April 2015 the audience for Daily Kos, *Think Progress, Raw Story* and *Salon*—the four largest politically focused, progressive news websites for which demographic data are available—ranged from 74% to 83% white and 64% to 66% male.

In 2014, roughly 4.1 million Democratic U.S. House voters were white, male and liberal,[36] while the four largest progressive political news websites averaged approximately 3.8 million white male readers each month.[37] Although not every white American male visiting Daily Kos, *Raw Story, Think Progress* and *Salon* is a

Democratic voter and/or self-identified liberal, it is reasonable to assume that the vast majority of them are. The political blogosphere has cornered the market on white, male liberal Democrats, and has very little growth potential with this group.

However, these four websites have attracted a comparatively smaller percentage of liberal Democrats from other demographic groups. Roughly 11.8 million liberals who are not white males voted Democratic in 2014, but an average of only 3.7 million non-white males visited Daily Kos, *Raw Story*, *Think Progress* and *Salon* in the nine months examined. So while the Internet Left has reached a saturation point with white, male liberal Democrats, it reaches at best one-third of the non-white and/or female Democratic base.

The netroots have faced this demographic challenge since the Dean campaign. In 2005, Pew found that early supporters of Howard Dean were overwhelmingly highly educated liberals.[38] In early 2015, Quantcast found the audiences for Daily Kos, *Raw Story*, *Think Progress* and *Salon* were disproportionately college-educated, and even more disproportionately in possession of graduate degrees. In fact, possession of a graduate degree is the most distinct characteristic of the *Salon* and *Think Progress* readership, the second most distinct for Daily Kos and the fourth most distinct for *Raw Story*.

The netroots have organized a large constituency of Democrats around an independent media and activist nexus that is entirely free from the control of the existing Democratic Party machinery. Netroots-based campaigns that charge aggressively at the Democratic establishment can, with few resources and little institutional buy-in, do well enough to give their supporters the illusion that they are close to seizing control of the Democratic Party in a grand, populist digital epiphany. At the same time, the progressive movement faces a significant demographic challenge to future growth, as the remaining 20–25% of the Democratic base that these campaigns need in order to form a majority consistently proves to be beyond their grasp. The primary reason for this continued frustration is that the grassroots networks which form the backbone of netroots media and activist organizations are not connected on a day-to-day basis to working-class and minority communities that make up the rest of the party rank-and-file. Until the grassroots superstructure of the netroots overcomes gender, racial and class divides, the netroots and Internet Left will have difficulty forming a progressive coalition of sufficient size to topple the incumbent New Democrats.[39]

The Left's Midterm Problem

Beyond intra-party Democratic struggles, the autumn of 2014 also revealed the current limitations of netroots organizing in interparty conflicts with Republicans. Once again, the failure of the netroots to connect broadly with non-white and working-class portions of the Democratic base was the primary source of this limitation.

As a general approach to politics, netroots activists are more excited about the idea of achieving electoral victory through increased voter turnout than through clever messaging and slick advertising campaigns. It is a longstanding progressive belief that increased participation in the democratic process would be enough in-and-of-itself to result in the victory of left-of-center candidates and the enactment of left-of-center public policy. It is also a natural manifestation of the community model of democracy that birthed the online progressive movement. Since the Professional Left who staff netroots organizations are well aware that the grassroots activists with whom they connect—and from whom they receive their funding—are more enthusiastic about get-out-the-vote (GOTV) operations than advertisements, they direct more energy and resources toward GOTV with every passing electoral cycle.

Recent electoral dynamics make this direction of resources seem strategically sound. Because the young, non-white and low-income voters who are most likely to support Democratic candidates tend to have the lowest participation rates in non-presidential elections, making every effort to reach "drop-off" Democratic voters—people who cast a ballot for the Democratic presidential nominee every four years but who tend to not vote at all in other elections—and get them to the polls would appear to be an optimal strategic move.

As such, in 2014, the netroots made its strongest push to date to increase Democratic voter turnout by targeting Democratic drop-off voters in key races with a historic number of voting contacts. Using the same type of methodology as was employed by Barack Obama's 2012 re-election campaign, a coalition of groups led by MoveOn and Daily Kos made 6.74 million phone calls into seven Senate battleground states.[40] CREDO, which after MoveOn boasts the largest netroots email list in the country at 3.5 million, simultaneously opened offices in five states with key Senate races and organized local volunteers to make two million phone calls and knock on over 65,000 doors.[41] The Progressive Change Campaign Committee added four million phone calls for its slate of endorsed candidates.[42] These combined efforts from the largest netroots organizations surpassed their GOTV operations in the 2012 presidential election. It was the largest netroots voter contact effort in history.

But turnout in the 2014 election was dismal. According to the United States Election Project, overall voter turnout was only 36.4% of the eligible population, the lowest since the midterm elections of 1942 when millions of Americans were deployed in overseas military service.[43] Predictably, turnout was especially poor among the Democratic-leaning groups where disproportionate numbers of Democratic drop-off voters are historically found:

- in 2012 voters under the age of 30 made up 19% of all voters, versus 13% in 2014;
- in 2012 non-white voters made up 28% of all voters, compared with 25% in 2014; and
- in 2012 voters making less than $50,000 annually composed 41% of the electorate, as opposed to 36% in 2014.[44]

Although turnout among these three strongly Democratic groups might have been even lower without the vast netroots effort, the overall goal of closing, much less ending, the drop-off gap was not achieved.

Greater distance from the 2014 election may yield a more complete understanding of turnout patterns, but it is not unreasonable to assume that the netroots could not generate the desired response from these groups because of a weak cultural and demographic connection with them. If progressive groups are unable to build strong connections to communities of color and the working class between electoral cycles, they will also have trouble reaching them during the height of election season, especially when an African-American presidential candidate is not at the top of the ballot.

The netroots' problem in forming a majority coalition within the Democratic Party is thus closely intertwined with the Democratic Party's difficulty turning out the vote in midterm elections. Given the crucial role they now play in left-of-center voter-turnout operations, if the netroots and the Internet Left are unable to connect with drop-off voters and get them consistently involved in the political process, then it is difficult to imagine how establishment Democrats with far fewer grassroots activists will fare any better. Not only are the netroots doomed to remain a minority within the Democratic Party unless and until they can reach new constituencies, their failure might doom the Democratic Party to the same fate in midterm elections.

Democrats—and progressives—may reap the advantages of changing demography by default and go into presidential years with a strong built-in voter edge. However, losses in the midterm years undermine their ability to emerge as the predominant partners in a stable new political regime and prolong the period in which the right continues to enjoy institutional advantages in the political process. Through the creation of new barriers to voting, the elimination of fundraising and campaign spending restrictions, and the drawing of legislative maps to favor Republican victories, the right can continue to hold power as the left struggles to figure out how to mobilize the broader Democratic base that is their strongest potential asset. Whether the left can solve this problem before the right cements its institutional advantages will go a long way toward determining the shape of the next political alignment. We consider the possibilities in Chapter 7.

Notes

1 See James, Brendan. 2014. "Princeton Study: U.S. No Longer An Actual Democracy." *Talking Points Memo*, April 18. Retrieved from http://talkingpointsmemo.com/livewire/princeton-experts-say-us-no-longer-democracy.
2 Kapur, Sahil. 2014. "Scholar Behind Viral 'Oligarchy' Study Tells You What It Means." *Talking Points Memo*, April 22. Retrieved from http://talkingpointsmemo.com/dc/princeton-scholar-demise-of-democracy-america-tpm-interview.
3 PollingReport.com. Retrieved from www.pollingreport.com/budget.htm.
4 PollingReport.com. Retrieved from www.pollingreport.com/politics.htm.

5 Swanson, Emily. 2013. "Most Americans Think Government Is Focused On Helping The Rich." *The Huffington Post*, September 27. Retrieved from www.huffingtonpost.com/2013/09/27/government-helping-the-rich_n_3998409.html.
6 Thompson, Derek. 2012. "A Giant Statistical Round-Up of the Income Inequality Crisis in 16 Charts." *The Atlantic*, December 12. Retrieved from www.theatlantic.com/business/archive/2012/12/a-giant-statistical-round-up-of-the-income-inequality-crisis-in-16-charts/266074/.
7 Choma, Russ. 2014. "Millionaire's Club: For the First Time, Most Lawmakers Are Worth $1 Million-Plus." *OpenSecrets.org*, January 9. Retrieved from www.opensecrets.org/news/2014/01/millionaires-club-for-first-time-most-lawmakers-are-worth-1-million-plus/.
8 Gottschalck, Alfred and Marina Vornovytskyy. 2012. "Changes in Household Net Worth from 2005 to 2010." Random Samplings: The Official Blog of the U.S. Census Bureau, June 18. Retrieved from http://blogs.census.gov/2012/06/18/changes-in-household-net-worth-from-2005-to-2010/.
9 Sifrey, Micah. 2014. "Great for the Tea Party, Bad for the People: How the 1 Percent Conquered Internet Activism." *Salon*, August 3. Retrieved from www.salon.com/2014/08/03/great_for_the_tea_party_bad_for_the_people_how_the_1_percent_conquered_internet_activism/.
10 Ryan, Melissa. 2014. "Begging for Dollars." *Campaigns and Elections*, November 10. Retrieved from www.campaignsandelections.com/magazine/2357/begging-for-dollars.
11 Kapur (2014).
12 Howard Dean, Address to California State Democratic Convention, Sacramento, March 15, 2003. Retrieved from www.gwu.edu/~action/2004/cdp0303/dean031503spt.html.
13 Gold, Matea. 2003. "Dean, Centrist Branch Spar." *Los Angeles Times*, December 23. Retrieved from http://articles.latimes.com/2003/dec/23/nation/na-dean23.
14 From, Al and Bruce Reed. 2003. "Activists Are Out of Step." *Los Angeles Times*, July 3. Retrieved from http://articles.latimes.com/2003/jul/03/opinion/oe-reed3.
15 Turque, Bill. 2000. "The Soul and the Steel." *Newsweek*, August 20. Retrieved from www.newsweek.com/soul-and-steel-158731.
16 Roarty, Alex. 2014. "The Koch Network Spent $100 Million This Election Cycle." *National Journal*, November 4. Retrieved from www.nationaljournal.com/politics/2014/11/04/Koch-Network-Spent-100-Million-This-Election-Cycle.
17 For an account of the demise of the DLC, see Smith, Ben. 2011. "The End of the Democratic Leadership Council Era." *Politico*, February 7. Retrieved from www.politico.com/story/2011/02/the-end-of-the-dlc-era-049041.
18 Cowan, Jon and Jim Kessler. 2013. "Economic Populism Is a Dead End for Democrats." *The Wall Street Journal*, December 2. Retrieved from www.wsj.com/articles/SB10001424052702304337404579213923151169790.
19 @ron_fournier. Retrieved from https://twitter.com/ron_fournier/status/407909020704727040. *Politico* also telegraphed its approval of the sentiment in the op-ed.
20 See Clawson, Laura. 2014. "Allyson Schwartz Leaves Third Way." *Daily Kos*, January 23. Retrieved from www.dailykos.com/story/2014/01/23/1271925/-Allyson-Schwartz-leaves-Third-Way.
21 Kos. 2013. "Daily Kos Will Not Enable Those Who Enable Third Way." *Daily Kos*, December 5. Retrieved from www.dailykos.com/story/2013/12/05/1260388/-Third-Way-s-congressional-enablers.
22 Rosenfeld, Steven. 2015. "In Vote to Expand Social Security, 42 Democratic Senators Vote Yes While Every Republican Votes No." *Alternet*, March 27. Retrieved from www.alternet.org/news-amp-politics/vote-expand-social-security-42-democratic-senators-vote-yes-while-every-republican.
23 Klein, Ezra. 2011. "The Death of the DLC?" *The Washington Post*, February 7. Retrieved from http://voices.washingtonpost.com/ezra-klein/2011/02/the_death_of_the_dlc.html.

24 Stoller, Matt. 2014. "Why the Democratic Party Acts the Way It Does." *Nakedcapitalism*, November 9. Retrieved from www.nakedcapitalism.com/2014/11/matt-stoller-democratic-party-acts-way.html.
25 Zeff, Blake. 2014. "Another Cuomo Noninterference Story Falls Apart." *Capitalnewyork*, September 2. Retrieved from www.capitalnewyork.com/article/albany/2014/09/8551681/another-cuomo-noninterference-story-falls-apart.
26 Additionally, none of these groups went particularly all-in for Teachout, doing little more than notify their supporters or readers that she was on the ballot as a progressive alternative to Cuomo.
27 Cuomo spent over $60 for each vote he received, including spending dating from 2011, to Teachout's $1.57. See Bump, Philip. 2014. "Andrew Cuomo Spent Almost 40 Times As Much For His Votes As Zephyr Teachout." *The Washington Post*, September 10. Retrieved from www.washingtonpost.com/news/the-fix/wp/2014/09/10/andrew-cuomo-spent-almost-40-times-as-much-for-his-votes-as-zephyr-teachout/.
28 Kos. 2014. "Wu Has Freaked Out Cuomo and He's Cracking Skulls Over It." *Daily Kos*, September 8. Retrieved from www.dailykos.com/story/2014/09/08/1328040/-Wu-has-freaked-out-Cuomo-he-s-cracking-skulls-over-it.
29 Hamilton, Matthew. 2014. "Teachout Still On the Ballot, But Numbers Are Low." *Albany Times Union*, August 20. Retrieved from www.timesunion.com/local/article/Teachout-still-on-ballot-but-numbers-are-low-5702046.php.
30 Karni, Annie. 2014. "Zephyr Teachout's Primary Election Loss Has Air of a Victory Party." *New York Daily News*, September 10. Retrieved from www.nydailynews.com/new-york/zephyr-teachout-primary-loss-air-victory-party-article-1.1934371.
31 One interesting exception is that females constitute the majority email list membership for MoveOn, Democracy for America and Daily Kos, although it is not clear that women are more engaged in political action through these sites.
32 It should be noted that Daily Kos did not endorse Teachout, but did endorse Teachout's running mate, Tim Wu, and conducted a last-minute get-out-the-vote blitz on his behalf. Daily Kos also published voluminous amounts of negative content on Cuomo for several months—and even years—before the primary took place.
33 Reader demographics are publicly available on Quantcast at www.quantcast.com/dailykos.com?country=US.
34 The Green Papers, General Election, 114th U.S. House Popular Vote and FEC Total Receipts by Party. Retrieved from www.thegreenpapers.com/G14/HouseVoteByParty.phtml.
35 CNN Exit Polls. Retrieved from www.cnn.com/election/2014/results/exit-polls.
36 This estimate expresses the product of the exit poll figure for each demographic category as a percentage of the total vote.
37 This estimate expresses the product of the midpoint of the Quantcast average monthly demographics and readership figures.
38 Pew Research Center. 2005. "The Dean Activists: Their Profile and Prospects; An InDepth Look." Retrieved from www.people-press.org/2005/04/06/the-dean-activists-their-profile-and-prospects/.
39 We observe in Chapter 7 that this may have started happening in a tentative fashion among African-American supporters during the months following Teachout's primary loss.
40 See MoveOn.org at http://pol.moveon.org/2014calls/home_shift_signup.html.
41 See CREDO SuperPAC at http://credosuperpac.com/national/while-others-wasted-millions-we-found-a-model-that-works/.
42 See Progressive Change Campaign Committee at www.facebook.com/boldprogressives/photos/a.441707488366.241042.94047978366/10152502228078367/.
43 DelReal, Jose A. 2014. "Voter Turnout in 2014 Was the Lowest Since WWII." *The Washington Post*, November 10. Retrieved from www.washingtonpost.com/news/post-politics/wp/2014/11/10/voter-turnout-in-2014-was-the-lowest-since-wwii/.

44 See CNN exit poll and final election results at www.cnn.com/election/2012/results/race/president and www.cnn.com/election/2014/results/race/house#exit-polls.

References

Gilens, Martin and Benjamin I. Page. 2014. "Testing Theories of American Politics: Elites, Interest Groups, and Average Citizens." *Perspectives on Politics* 12: 564–581.

Gould, Elise. 2014. *Why America's Workers Need Faster Wage Growth—And What We Can Do About It*. Washington, DC: Economic Policy Institute.

Moulitsas, Markos and Jerome Armstrong. 2006. *Crashing the Gate: Netroots, Grassroots, and the Rise of People Powered Politics*. White River Junction, VT: Chelsea Green.

7
RESOLUTION

Dismayed by the Democratic Party's second landslide midterm election loss in four years, Daily Kos founder and publisher Markos Moulitsas lamented what he called the "boom–bust" election cycle that handed the Senate and most governorships to Republicans in 2014. He predicted Democrats would again see victory in the next presidential year, only to squander it in 2018 in an indefinite repeat of a well established pattern built on a rapidly growing but easily disengaged electorate:

> We have two separate Americas voting every two years. We have one that is more representative, that includes about 60 percent of voting age adults. Then we have one where we can barely get a third of voting age adults to turn out, and is much whiter and older than the country. And Democrats can win easily with the one, and Republicans can win easily with the other. And that cycle won't be broken until 1) the Democrats figure out how to inspire their voters to the polls on off years, or 2) Republicans figure out how to appeal to the nation's changing electorate. And given that each party is validated every two years after a blowout loss, the odds of either happening anytime soon? Bleak.[1]

As tempting as it may be to see the future in current patterns, it is likely unsustainable to have two mutually exclusive electorates supporting two mutually exclusive sets of representatives in a political environment without a center. If Republicans continue to lose presidential elections, conservatives will inevitably lose their grip on the courts, undermining the strategic lynchpin of movement conservatism and the right's strongest ally in protecting big-dollar corporate campaign spending, the most important institutional advantage enjoyed by

Republicans. Or if Democrats continue to be absentee players in midterm elections, the commitment and durability of the coalition Barack Obama assembled could be permanently hobbled by Republican governors and legislators elected in midterm years with a record of making it more difficult to vote and, through gerrymandering, for votes to matter as much. It is not hard to see outcomes that look quite different from the status quo.

Although Moulitsas' prediction of endless gridlock may have reflected frustration with Democrats in the aftermath of a loss of unexpected magnitude, it also rests on an assumption at the core of the progressive movement's power struggle with the party establishment: Democratic partisans did not vote in 2014 because Democratic leaders did not give them reason to turn out. And Democratic leadership cannot convincingly promise to work for the rank-and-file until they divorce themselves from their dependence on moneyed interests whose concerns are at odds with addressing the wealth imbalance that in their view is at the heart of public unease about the future. It is a widely expressed refrain among movement progressives and it drives their efforts to take control of the Democratic Party, as fiercely and with as much focus and determination as the desire to erase New Deal liberalism motivates the takeover of the Republican Party by the Tea Party right.

On the Left: a power struggle

To read about the history of the Democratic Party from the vantage point of the netroots, an infrastructure that became dominant because of the electoral success of Clinton-era triangulation continued through the Bush years to keep the party wedded to an agenda that served corporate interests over the concerns of the poor and working class, historically the backbone of the Democratic Party. In their view, terms like "centrist" and "pragmatic" are code for doing the bidding of hedge fund managers who oppose Wall Street regulation and tax increases on the wealthy, and who were behind the years-long push for a bipartisan deficit-reduction effort that would have changed the terms of Social Security policy. The netroots see organizations such as the former Democratic Leadership Council and Third Way, along with their affiliated representatives in government, feeding entrenched mainstream media narratives about the necessity for Democrats to compromise their more liberal instincts in order to maintain electoral viability. They reject that narrative while leaving no doubt about their feelings toward those they see enabling it.

Writing in 2005, one of the authors of this book identified the budding online activism of the left as driven by an emerging class of activists not unlike the individuals who propelled the progressive movement of the previous century (Bowers and Stoller 2005), which in the second iteration of the Internet Left has grown to include the Professional Left. Middle-class reformers who sought to combat the political corruption of the first Gilded Age spearheaded the

Progressive Era by implementing good-government correctives to a political system constructed by and for wealthy interests and party bosses. A second progressive era would be spearheaded by reformers of the Professional Left, those who earn a comfortable living as Internet activists and who seek to combat the political corruption of the second Gilded Age by reforming the role of money in politics and creating a more participatory democracy in which elected officials would be broadly responsive to the needs of all socioeconomic groups. Where nineteenth-century progressives found a voice in both political parties, contemporary progressives have gravitated to the Democratic Party as the only fertile ground for their plans. They feel both parties have been corrupted by big money, but only Democrats provide the philosophical proximity to offer them a political home.

Like their counterparts from the previous century, they are focused on the democratic process, taking aim at what they regard as undemocratic money and power relationships that define contemporary Washington. They are opposed to an entrenched power structure that favors an established set of elite voices and ideas, opposed to the influence of concentrated wealth over the political agenda, and opposed to a revolving door between the public and private sectors that favors the interests of those with access. A decade of online activism provided them with a model for mitigating these conditions. Grassroots politics using the horizontal structure of the Internet would replace the vertical politics of traditional political elites, opening the system to the greater public. Small-dollar Internet-based fundraising or publicly financed campaigns would supersede big-dollar contributions, rendering economic elites less influential and freeing the party to pursue economic policies in line with its rhetoric and its historic support of the working class. The Professional Left would supplant or share power with the party establishment.

These reforms would come at the expense of Clinton-era triangulators, deficit hawks and Wall Street. Like the original progressives, they would push the Democratic Party and American politics in a leftward direction programmatically because, like that century-old movement with its focus on process changes such as referenda, primary elections, increased suffrage and the Australian ballot, the means to a progressive politics is viewed as structural and small-d democratic. Their twenty-first-century agenda: to get money out of politics, increase voter participation, end gerrymandering, reform Senate procedures and maintain a participatory Internet through net neutrality. As the Internet Left and netroots see it, if you democratize the rules of the game and get more people playing it, you will bring about a more progressive politics reflecting the interests of the new participants. Outcomes will continue to follow influence, but influence patterns will be reshaped by changes to the political process.

This is why the netroots have not gone to war with the Obama administration despite its resistance to progressive policies. President Obama, who as we noted earlier did not emerge from the progressive movement and who is hamstrung by the residual strengths of the center-right political order, has on numerous occasions aggravated and even angered the netroots by—for rational political reasons—governing from the center of the Democratic coalition as currently constituted. As we noted earlier, they battled over the administration's unwillingness to entertain a single-payer health care option and its abandonment of a public option in the final health care law. They pushed back against the politics of a team of financial advisors plucked from Wall Street, and against the president's failure to hold anyone accountable for the 2008 economic collapse. They fought hard to get the administration to support Net Neutrality. They have also criticized Obama for his failure to close the detention camp at Guantanamo Bay, for his use of unmanned drones and for undermining civil liberties in the name of maintaining security.

Still, they did not break with the president. The netroots actively worked for his re-election, and despite spirited discussions about how best and how much to offer their support, there was never serious talk of a political challenge that might undermine their long-term objective to remake the process so that a future president with progressive impulses might have the latitude to govern where the small money is.

This is also why, as the 2016 presidential landscape came into focus, the netroots did not emerge as a significant obstacle to Hillary Clinton's campaign for the Democratic presidential nomination, despite her Democratic Leadership Council and Wall Street ties and the Clintonian history of triangulation. As an ideological matter, many among the netroots were animated more by the prospect of a presidential campaign by Senator Elizabeth Warren of Massachusetts, a product and favorite of the movement, or by the actual movement campaign of Vermont Senator Bernie Sanders, a self-styled democratic socialist and progressive luminary. A Professional Left-organized draft effort called "Ready for Warren" urged the senator to run, as did MoveOn following a vote of its members. When she declined, Sanders filled the space she would have occupied by drawing enormous crowds, raising millions of dollars from small online donors and lighting up Daily Kos with enthusiastic support from progressive diarists for his call to a political revolution.

Although passionate about their candidates, for the most part the Sanders and Clinton camps remained civil toward one another. Among Sanders supporters, the question of whether to support Clinton if she ultimately prevailed was more strategic than ideological. While a Warren or Sanders nomination would represent an accomplishment akin to what the Reagan nomination meant to movement conservatives, as of this writing a Clinton nomination was not widely viewed as a cause for dividing the movement; the former secretary of state even received some high-profile progressive support, including an endorsement from Howard Dean in late 2014.[2] Writing in Daily Kos, Moulitsas explained why it would be counterproductive for progressives to engage in a divisive, anti-Hillary primary fight. His reasoning is strategic:

With Clinton's commanding general election trial heats, not to mention demographic shifts shoring up our electoral picture, we'll have the luxury to look beyond the presidential [election] and take a more holistic approach to the cycle. And we've got a lot of work ahead of us ... I won't ignore Hillary, but I won't worry about her either ... Instead, I'll focus down ballot, on those Senate, House and state-level races that will determine the partisan composition of our government [in] the coming decade. My approach is constructive, rather than destructive. The more people adopt that approach, the more success we will have as a movement.[3]

In other words, work on supporting candidates at all levels of government who are committed to reforming the party and the political process. This is not to suggest that progressives refrained from a vibrant discussion of the meaning of a potential Clinton candidacy to their movement or from pressing Clinton closer to progressive positions. As with President Obama, there were substantive disagreements with the candidate. But ideological warfare is not raging among Democratic Party factions. While the netroots and Internet Left may pose a long-term threat to party elites, they have no intention of leaving the tent or burning it down if they do not get their way in any given short-term campaign. Their objective remains achieving political power in order to reform the process and realize progressive change.

On the Right: an ideological struggle

On this score, the contrast with the right could not be more striking. During the 40-year arc of conservative governance, parties to the Republican coalition could agree on a limited government agenda defined by tax cuts, deregulation and the theoretical value of balanced budgets; a loosely connected set of traditional "family values" featuring opposition to drug use, legalized abortion and same-sex marriage; a muscular profile for America abroad; and a tough-on-crime posture at home. As with any coalition, these positions at times were more useful for their rhetorical value than as governing guidelines, but in any event the coalition was flexible enough to endure compromise with Democrats (George H. W. Bush's violation of his "read my lips" tax promise being a notable exception). Spending would increase, deficits would climb, abortion would remain legal and social programs would stay in place, but the coalition held together as a governing entity.

No longer. During the period of center-right dominance, older Americans, whites, men and evangelicals contributed many of the votes needed to sustain Republicans in power. As the regime entered twilight, some members of these groups became radicalized in response to the social and economic upheavals of the twenty-first century brought on by the demographic changes discussed in Chapter 1 that culminated in Obama's election. What came to be called the Tea

Party revolution was an important Republican demographic stepping outside the longstanding partisan consensus and saying, essentially, no. No to the welfare state. No to a positive role for government. No to the rejection of mid-twentieth-century morality. No to a reordering of the power structure. No to the new demography. Facing paradigm-shaping immigration and generational changes that came to fruition with the Obama coalition, they decided they could take no more, and sought redress from the political process within the confines of the Republican Party.

The decision by these groups to stand apart from the decades-old political consensus that powered the Republican regime occurred while the broader party coalition was experiencing the effects of regime decay discussed in Chapter 2. The Tea Party revolt is noteworthy here because, as the Reagan coalition started winding down, Tea Party groups were positioned to have outsized power in a party lacking significant centripetal forces. Mainstream business elites once could rely on rank-and-file conservatives to support their distinct but aligned agenda. Now some of these foot soldiers, in an alliance of convenience with conservative advocacy groups and some wealthy pro-market backers, were making demands of their own.[4]

Facing an existential crisis, the radicals began drawing bright DayGlo lines around the policies they would permit their party to accept. New spending would have to be offset with budget cuts. Social programs benefiting the poor should be slashed or eliminated entirely.[5] People should not be reliant on the government for unemployment benefits, a minimum wage or health coverage. Undocumented immigrants should be returned to their country of origin. Rather than representing a new conservatism, or even a new shade of conservatism, these dictates stem from a libertarian-tinged anti-government sentiment representing the radicalized remainder of movement conservatism, at odds with non-radicalized Republicans, Democrats and, increasingly, the rest of the country. As the Republican coalition faced end-regime circumstances, an animated Tea Party base could impose this agenda on its former coalition partners and a weakened party establishment. The result is an ideological struggle for the carcass of the Reagan-era Republican Party that in the immediate term has been won by the reactionaries.

Nowhere is this more evident than in the almost comical attempt of 2012 Republican presidential nominee Mitt Romney to convince a radical base that he was one of them while simultaneously trying to convince unaffiliated voters that he was a pragmatic moderate. For base voters participating in the presidential primary process, it wasn't enough that the one-time moderate governor of a deep blue New England state had systematically rolled back his support for abortion rights, gays serving in the military and, most emphatically, the universal health care law that was the crowning achievement of his term as Massachusetts governor.[6] He found himself defending his conservative bona fides to base voters during and after his grueling march to the nomination against a field of less serious and unserious candidates whose reactionary impulses appealed to primary voters enough to postpone what should have been an easy nomination victory.

Because the base was united against all things Obama, Romney was constrained from embracing anything the president had done. Rather than claim partial credit for a national health care law, built on conservative free-market principles, that he had long espoused, Romney spent the campaign distancing himself from his signal accomplishment as Massachusetts governor because Obamacare had been effectively demonized on the far right as a socialist plot to let the government choose your doctor. One survey taken late in the president's first term found a majority of Republicans believed Obama to be a socialist.[7] The same applied to Republican elites: a confidential survey of 75 GOP leaders taken for *Esquire* at around the same time found four-fifths of them considered Obama a socialist.[8] Georgia Rep. Paul Broun, in a fundraising letter to supporters, claimed credit for being the first member of Congress to openly call Obama a socialist "who embraces Marxist–Leninist policies like government control of health care and redistribution of wealth."[9] He was in good company: former Republican vice presidential nominee Sarah Palin, Texas governor and former Republican presidential candidate Rick Perry, and former congresswoman and Republican presidential candidate Michelle Bachmann all prominently made the socialist claim. Among those to be put off by the label: genuine socialists, who believed Obama's policies were so far from socialism as to be offended by the comparison.[10]

Because of his past dalliance with moderation, Romney had to pour it on. In an attempt to shore up base support, Romney described himself as a "severely conservative" governor to a gathering of the Conservative Political Action Conference (CPAC), an unfortunate characterization that inadvertently betrayed his sense that anything less than a punishing conservatism would be unacceptable to the radical base. "CPAC 'Severely' Conflicted Over Mitt Romney," read the headline in *Politico*'s coverage of the event.[11] The claim was out of sync with Romney's contention, made ten years earlier, that he was "someone who is moderate, and … my views are progressive."[12] But that was another time and a different electorate.

Unfortunately, Romney would need the votes of a portion of the general electorate who found "severe conservatism" unattractive. This presented the Romney campaign with a general election challenge: Having secured the nomination by outlasting candidates with more natural appeal to base voters, Romney would need to broaden his attractiveness without demotivating a base that hadn't fallen in line behind him. Typically at this point in a campaign, the nominee could assume the base would have no place else to turn, and pivot toward moderation. Instead, Romney was squeezed on one side by core supporters who were not willing to give him latitude and on the other by the absence of a political center. There was no way to align the promises he had made to his base with the rest of the electorate.

But he tried. During the early months of his general election campaign, Romney employed a conventional challenger's strategy, attempting to tie poor economic conditions to the incumbent and make the election a referendum on the Obama record in the hope that the promises he had made to his base wouldn't matter. Weak monthly jobs reports were flogged by the campaign as evidence of the need to make a change at the top. It wasn't enough; although the race was tantalizingly close, Romney was unable to break through and move ahead of Obama in national polling and in most swing states.[13]

By late summer 2012, it became apparent that Romney was at a disadvantage in a retrospective campaign. Although two in three Americans felt the country was going in the wrong direction,[14] a stubbornly large percentage of voters were more likely to blame Congress or George W. Bush for creating the unfavorable economic climate.[15] To win, Romney would need to juice up his base in a way he had failed to do during the primaries, while simultaneously keeping a distance from them so as not to alienate voters who could embrace conservatives but not the Tea Party. This choice left him to fight on two contradictory fronts simultaneously: He would deepen his "severely conservative" base credentials while maintaining a temperate posture for everyone else. Performing this task entailed a large degree of moral flexibility, something the candidate proved remarkably adept at displaying.

For the base, Romney offered to turn the election into an ideological choice. He selected Tea Party favorite Rep. Paul Ryan as his running mate, thereby welding himself to the harsh and broadly unpopular budget blueprint for which his electoral partner was known.[16] His move was the antithesis of the classic moderate pivot commonly executed by candidates in a close contest. Romney had decided he could not win without a huge turnout from white working-class voters who did not live in Judis and Teixeira's "Ideopolises" and who might be reached through appeals to social and racial anxieties.

Concurrently, Romney chose to embrace a view of Barack Obama that resonated with the base but did not always survive scrutiny, building his campaign on a web of factual assertions about the president accepted as reality by the right. Obama had weakened the work requirements of the welfare law. He stole over $700 billion from Medicare to pay for health care reform. He believed that business owners didn't build their own businesses. His policies shuttered a General Motors factory in Paul Ryan's Wisconsin district, even though it had closed several months before Obama took the oath of office.[17] Whether taken out of context or simply fabricated, these accusations were designed to play to those who were predisposed to believe Obama hated American free enterprise and had usurped his power in an effort to assist his multicultural base at the expense of all others.

For the rest of the electorate, Romney offered a far gentler version of himself that was more in line with the moderate Massachusetts governor he insisted to primary voters he had never been. In a debate with President Obama, widely credited by the press with briefly breathing life into his moribund campaign, Romney brazenly cast aside well trodden campaign positions on salient issues such as health care and immigration as though he had never held them in a play to appeal to general election voters who hadn't been paying attention. "Romney's brazen chutzpah knows no bounds," wrote Mark Halperin in *Time* magazine.[18] Romney temporarily closed the gap with the president, and he might have been competitive had he really been the candidate he claimed to be on debate night.[19] But the Republican primary electorate never would have nominated that candidate.

Romney made a calculated decision that the objective reporting model of the mainstream press would preclude journalists from calling out his contradictions for fear of looking prejudicial, even when the extent and prominence of the campaign's factual deviance strained their ability to look the other way. He was largely correct. Ryan's acceptance speech at the Republican convention was riddled with enough falsehoods to draw the notice of reporters who would otherwise default to traditional horserace narratives about how well Ryan advanced the campaign's tactical goals; still, the mainstream press was reluctant to dismantle Ryan or his speech. Instead, they euphemistically referred to it as "misleading"[20] and "factually shaky."[21] The Associated Press noted that Ryan "took some factual shortcuts,"[22] while CNN's Wolf Blitzer spoke of seven or eight points he felt "fact checkers will have some opportunities to dispute"[23]—as if the job of holding politicians to the truth belonged to someone else. Bloggers on the left may have pounced on the candidates' fabrications and chastised traditional reporters for treating them gently, but Romney understood their protests would never reach the voters he needed.

In addition to the assistance Romney expected from the mainstream press, his playbook depended on maximizing the right's advantages in money and television advertising. Unburdened from campaign finance restrictions by *Citizens United*, the Romney campaign could count on the largesse of wealthy supporters to flood the airwaves with ads repeating the campaign's messages. With television still in the process of being challenged by the Internet and thereby still able to reach fairly large audiences, the Romney campaign could benefit from a saturation strategy waged by wealthy stealth allies to reinforce the statements that traditional reporters would not question.

Where money provided firepower and television provided air cover, institutional efforts to hold back the flood of new voters were implemented by sympathetic Republican governors and legislatures in several important states, with the effect of throwing obstacles in front of voters in the new multicultural electorate. Draconian photo ID laws, restrictions on early voting and purged voter lists could be counted on by Romney to give his campaign a marginal boost in states such as Pennsylvania, Ohio and Florida where these efforts were undertaken—provided he could keep the race close. If Pennsylvania House Republican Leader Mike Turzai was too honest when he said his state's voter ID law "was gonna allow Governor Romney to win the state of Pennsylvania,"[24] he was simply expressing what many on the left and right believed was behind a nationwide effort to stave off the demographic wave that propelled Obama in 2008.

These tools—a mainstream press unable to process deception unless it is committed by both sides, boundless funding from exceptionally wealthy donors, massive television advertising and willingness to use public institutions to political benefit—buoyed the right in the wake of a rising majority resistant to their political agenda. It is noteworthy that, in telegraphing to his base that he would make the 2012 election a choice rather than a referendum, Romney turned the election into a demographic contest where he held the shorter straw, a reality confirmed by the final results. He counted on his money and media advantages to make the difference and permit him to scratch out a narrow victory with a coalition on the verge of receding into the minority, tacitly conceding they were out of step with the rest of the country by trying to hide from view what he was telling his base in plain sight.

Possibilities for Realignment

The coming electoral era will be defined by the occupation of the Republican Party by ideological descendants of movement conservatism and the attempted bottom-up restructuring of the Democratic Party by process-oriented movement progressives. Given the present state of these parallel struggles and the external forces shaping their development, we see two possible combinations of political alignments: A progressive Democratic Party aligned against a conservative Republican Party or a neoliberal Democratic Party aligned against a reactionary Republican Party. We contend that Democrats would be the majority party in the former configuration and Republicans would dominate the latter.

If there is to be a progressive realignment in the United States, it will occur at the intersection of online activism and changing demography. It will require the netroots and Internet Left to continue to mature institutionally, and the emerging electorate to grow sufficiently to overcome the significant advantages enjoyed by declining and unpopular but powerful and determined status quo forces in both political parties. Rudimentary evidence of what this might look like may be found at the electoral level in the coalitions that formed during the two previous presidential elections; institutionally, in the coalitions progressives are forming in Congress; and in the mass public through generational changes in media intake.

Electoral coalitions

The 2008 and 2012 elections provide evidence that online activism coupled with the new demography can win national elections. In both years, an ethnically diverse coalition that closely reflected the changing demographics of America secured victory over the remnants of the Reagan coalition through unprecedented digital organizing strength. Furthermore, in the 2008 Democratic primary campaign, Barack Obama was able to upend New Democrat Hillary Clinton by fusing strong support among African-Americans, youth voters and the netroots, even though Obama himself did not emerge from or identify with the progressive movement.[25]

Although the Obama administration did not depart from the New Democratic philosophy of attempting to achieve liberal ends through market means, from a formal, structural perspective the two Obama presidential campaigns provide a clear blueprint for a potential "new demography plus netroots" progressive electoral coalition strong enough to seize the machinery of the Democratic Party from neoliberals and defeat a declining but resilient conservative coalition in general election matchups.

The diversification of the netroots itself is an important prerequisite to forging this coalition, as we suggested in Chapter 6, and evidence of how that could happen may be found in the response to salient incidents of racial violence in 2014 and 2015. The eruption of protests in Ferguson, Missouri following the shooting dead of 18-year-old African-American Michael Brown by white police officer Darren Wilson, and the later decision by a grand jury not to indict Wilson for homicide, was by far the most tweeted news story in 2014.[26] It had a similar impact on traffic to Daily Kos, which peaked during mid-August because of intense interest in the events in Ferguson.

Even after Ferguson faded from mainstream news headlines, continued Internet Left coverage of the social justice movement against police and vigilante violence under hashtags such as #BlackLivesMatter has had a quantifiable impact on diversity within the netroots. According to Quantcast, starting in late summer 2014, the African-American percentage of overall Daily Kos readership began to increase from historical averages in the 5–7% range to reach a sustained level in the low double digits by mid-2015. *Raw Story* witnessed an even more dramatic increase, with African-American readership increasing rapidly during 2015 and by mid-year surpassing 20% of its total audience, roughly equal to the percentage of Democratic voters who are African-American. These individuals represent new visitors to the two sites, with no evident drop-off in existing readership. Internet Left coverage of, and netroots activist solidarity with, the #BlackLivesMatter movement thus appears to be the first measurable step by the progressive movement toward building rank-and-file diversity.

This is not to suggest that increased interaction between the two movements has always been smooth. At the 2015 Netroots Nation conference, progressive favorite Senator Bernie Sanders faced protests by #BlackLivesMatter activists for not addressing racism outside the context of his populist economic message. As one protester said to Sanders, "[free] public college won't stop police from killing us!"[27] While Sanders adjusted his stump speech to address the need for increased police accountability almost immediately after the conference, some rank-and-file

Sanders supporters who felt their candidate had a strong record on civil rights were incensed by the event. Consequently, numerous "flame wars" ensued on Twitter and in the comments section of Daily Kos diaries, suggesting that increased rank-and-file integration of the netroots may not be an easy process.

Philosophical cohorts on Capitol Hill

Among House Democrats, the Congressional Progressive Caucus (CPC) is now larger than the New Democratic Coalition. In the 114th Congress from 2015–2016, progressives claimed 68 of 188 Democrats[28] versus 46 for the New Democrats.[29] The CPC's 2014 "Better Off Budget" endorsed progressive priorities including expanding Social Security benefits, public financing of federal elections, universally available public health insurance, increasing income taxes on the wealthy, raising capital gains taxes to match income taxes, and reversing all recent cuts to food stamps and unemployment insurance.[30] It marks an unmistakable contrast with the New Democratic market-oriented approach to liberal ends and closely matches public policies championed by netroots organizations.

The natural philosophical alliance between CPC and the netroots is slowly growing into a working relationship. For each of the past four years, before the annual floor vote on the CPC budget, numerous netroots organizations sent action alerts to their memberships urging them to contact their representatives to support the CPC's budget. Representatives from these same organizations attend the annual retreat of Congressional Progressive Caucus members hosted by Progressive Congress, the non-profit organization associated with the caucus. Past Executive Directors of Progressive Congress have included current Democracy for America Executive Director Charles Chamberlain, and long-time netroots activist Darcy Burner, who narrowly lost election to Congress in 2006 and 2008.

A budding CPC/netroots alliance has the potential to provide mutually beneficial exposure for both groups to new communities. Progressive backbenchers in Congress can use netroots channels to reach national audiences, benefiting their legislative causes while helping left-of-center Democrats acquire larger profiles that could help propel them into leadership positions or statewide office. For their part, the netroots have an opportunity to make connections with communities where they currently have low supporter density. The ethnically diverse CPC heavily represents areas with similar demographic profiles to the New York City neighborhoods where Andrew Cuomo wiped out Zephyr Teachout in the 2014 New York State gubernatorial primary (see Chapter 6).

The composition of the Congressional Progressive Caucus shows that candidates who are philosophically aligned with the progressive netroots can perform very well in areas where Daily Kos or MoveOn have low supporter density, marking the potential for a new majority coalition within the Democratic Party that could upend neoliberals. In the 113th Congress, 24 of the 43 House members of the Congressional Black Caucus were also members of the CPC, as were seven of the 25 members of the Congressional Hispanic Caucus, and four of ten Asian Pacific Americans serving in the U.S. House. Furthermore, many of the white members of the CPC represent areas with large minority populations, such as Rep. Steve Cohen in the majority African-American ninth district of Tennessee.

Democratic congressional leadership has noticed the growing influence of progressives. In the aftermath of the 2014 elections, incoming Senate Minority Leader Harry Reid invented a new leadership position for Senator Elizabeth Warren, making her, as *Talking Points Memo* reported, "a liaison to liberal organizations."[31] Given Warren's status as the populist, small donor-fueled, anti-Wall Street icon of the second-generation netroots, Reid essentially offered the netroots themselves a seat at the leadership table for the first time.

Generational change

As we discussed in detail in chapters 1 and 3, the demographic groups where the netroots currently have their lowest participation rate represent the fastest growing groups nationally and in the Democratic coalition. No political realignment favorable to the Democratic Party has any significant chance of taking place unless it connects with this rising new generation. This is especially true for progressive Democrats, given that Millennnials are, as the Pew Research Center noted in a 2014 study, "the only generation in which liberals are not significantly outnumbered by conservatives."[32]

To date, the electoral- and legislative-focused netroots have faced challenges connecting with this younger, liberal, digital-native generation. However, *Upworthy* and *Mic* appear to be making inroads. These are Internet Left media companies that produce and "curate" progressive content optimized for social networks such as Facebook that is usually neither electoral nor legislative in nature. With monthly American audiences ranging between 14 and 26 million people in 2014, *Upworthy* and *Mic* each reached more people than Daily Kos and *Think Progress* combined during that year and as many as the largest conservative online media: FoxNews.com, *Independent Journal* and Glenn Beck's *The Blaze*. Americans under the age of 35 compose an absolute majority of both *Upworthy*'s and *Mic*'s audiences.

Younger Americans tend not to engage in the political process at the same rate as older Americans. Voting and news consumption are habits that take time to form; while Millennials are less politically involved than Generation Xers and Baby Boomers, this is typical of political participation among young people. If established life-cycle patterns hold, it is only a matter of time before they start voting and reading the news regularly. Because digital-native Millennials are already consuming progressive content on a scale equal to the audiences of the largest right-wing media outlets, the progressive, digital-native netroots has the potential to provide them with a natural home as they mature.

To the right or left?

The possibilities for the Democratic Party are therefore fairly clear: If the netroots and Professional Left are unable to reorganize the Democratic Party into a more bottom-up, participatory structure, it will continue to look much like it does now. Moneyed interests will continue to dominate both parties, hamstringing the Democrats' ability to appeal with much more than rhetoric to groups that originally flocked to Barack Obama for the promise of left-leaning change, not to mention economically anxious white voters outside the party's core coalition. Business and Wall Street ties, an entrenched consulting class and reluctance to defend a liberal program would leave Democrats unable or unwilling to address economic unease and social injustice with progressive policies. However, if the netroots and Professional Left can capitalize successfully on the rising tide of liberalism within the party, and continue to increase their reach and alliances to the point where they can form a majority coalition within the Democratic Party, then it will look more like the party progressives have long envisioned, powered by interactive online communities and small-dollar contributors, built on bottom-up grassroots activism, and willing to make a play for voters in red states and non-voters from disadvantaged communities with a populist progressive message.

The choices for the Republican Party are less clear, because they hinge on the future effectiveness of the radical faction. With Reagan Republicanism, the conservative alternative, all but gone, after their second consecutive presidential defeat in 2012 the Republican National Committee issued a report on how to get the party back on track—and promptly ignored it. The "Growth and Opportunity Project"—darkly dubbed the "autopsy report" by political insiders—instructed the party to broaden its appeal to the multicultural electorate that twice elected Barack Obama.[33] While the report talked about the importance of connecting with these voters through better messaging and outreach, it tellingly said nothing about renewing the intellectual roots of conservatism or rethinking policies reviled by the groups they were trying to reach. It was at once an honest analysis of the problems facing Republicans in presidential years and an attempt to address them through repackaging a rejected product. When even this proved impossible, the report faded into memory, a victim of an energized right wing. The radicals may prove to have a limited shelf life if they are unable to compete nationally, but who dislodges and replaces them is an open question.

Even if some Republican elites were inclined to challenge the radicals, it's difficult to see what they would offer as an alternative because the political space they would naturally seek to occupy is filled by Democrats, the result of the decades-long partisan shift to the right engineered by neoliberals. Consider the positions taken by Democrats during the two largest policy disputes of the Obama administration: health care reform and deficit reduction. The policy now called Obamacare began life as a market-oriented center-right approach endorsed in the past by such noted socialists as Bob Dole. It preserves the private insurance market and expands the role of government only in mandating that everyone have insurance and through the expansion of the longstanding Medicaid health insurance option for low-income Americans, not in mandating everyone have government-sponsored insurance. A single-payer government plan—the center-left alternative—was never on the table, and even a widely available public option to compete with private insurers failed to make it into the final bill despite the loud protests of progressives.

Deficit reduction efforts followed a similar pattern, with President Obama twice willing to tinker with entitlement programs in futile attempts to reach agreement with congressional Republicans on a grand tax and spending deal. In the debate over the expiring Bush tax cuts, Obama sought only to restore the tax rates in place under Bill Clinton, and then only for the top 2% of wage earners. In neither instance did Obama feel compelled to open negotiations by protecting entitlement beneficiaries from benefit cuts (or at least cuts in the rate of growth), or by suggesting a return to the higher tax rates of the 1950s and 1960s.

Were progressives to come to power in the Democratic Party, one consequence of their success would be to move the party out of space once occupied by conservatives, giving Republicans breathing room and a chance to offer a mainstream alternative to rejectionist policies. But this would require Republicans to concede to playing on the Democrats' turf, much as Bill Clinton was forced to acknowledge the enduring appeal of Reaganism, and Dwight Eisenhower had to embrace the New Deal. Rediscovering support for market-based health care solutions in opposition to progressive Democratic support for government solutions would mean abandoning the position that health care should be a privilege. It would revitalize and moderate the Republican Party and offer an escape from its electoral dead end, but at the cost of being the opposition party in a progressive era.

The alternative scenario would be a well funded, reactionary Republican Party facing off against a Democratic Party still largely responsive to Third Way political approaches. It is easiest to see Republicans as the majority force in this combination if an apathetic popular majority fails to offset the Republican numerical disadvantage in the electorate. Such apathy could lengthen the period during which Republicans at the state level could tilt the playing field in their favor by curtailing voter registration, limiting early voting or tinkering with the Electoral College in blue states where they control the executive and legislative branches, like the aborted 2012 attempt to award Pennsylvania's electoral votes by congressional districts gerrymandered to favor Republicans. This combination of Democratic apathy and Republican control of the electoral rules could support political outcomes resembling what we have seen in recent off-year elections, where the Democratic coalition of single women, young people and people of color is disproportionately disengaged and/or disenfranchised.

For the near term, Republicans enjoy institutional advantages in the Senate owing to the geographic distribution of their supporters; in the House owing to geography and favorable district maps drawn by friendly legislatures in several states in 2010;

in the Supreme Court, which is a lagging indicator of changing public opinion; and at the state level, where they continue to have a significant numerical advantage in governorships and legislatures. If the decline of the New Deal coalition is an apt guide, these advantages eventually will disappear as the country changes, but they can linger for a long time, and while they persist they can give the right great leverage to combat the demographic monsoon that threatens their long-term viability.

But questions remain. How does the right approach governance if it emerges as the dominant voice in a regime supported by a plurality segment of the electorate that does not represent the population at large? Would questions arise about the regime's legitimacy, and to what degree might this constrain its ability to implement its agenda? In power, would it be able to avoid awakening voters whose disinterest enabled its ascendancy, or could it find a way to win over a larger segment of the electorate? Would it tear itself apart trying to broaden its appeal or trying to broker differences between elites and the rank and file?[34] Radicals do not generally support moderation; would they be able to temper their ideology in order to govern? If not, would their ascendancy be a false start? A Republican president presiding over a party at war with itself at this stage in a regime cycle might look less like the start of a new alignment and more like the relationship between Jimmy Carter and the New Deal coalition, the last presidency of a spent regime. Like movement conservatives after Watergate, progressives might find they had another opportunity if they were positioned to take advantage of it.

Alternatively, will the right accept being a minority presence in the next political regime should their institutional advantages prove insufficient to keep Democrats out of the White House? If Republicans continue losing presidential elections, one would expect a backlash by party professionals seeking to purge or neutralize the Tea Party, but if this were to happen, how could the Republican Party be expected to win without its base if it can't find a way to win with it? Would money continue to flow to the right from deep-pocketed interests, as it has in the election cycles since the *Citizens United* decision, and would it be enough to compensate for a party increasingly out of touch with a changing country? Can that money be spent effectively in a media environment increasingly defined by convergence between television and the Internet?

For their part, the netroots face a host of questions in their quest to reshape the Democratic Party. While progressives have been building institutions and attempting to unify disparate groups on the political left, building a robust, mass participatory movement infrastructure takes time. If the Obama years represent a pivot to the left in the way that the Nixon years represented a pivot to the right, can progressive institution building occur quickly enough to take advantage of a moment when political realignment is up for grabs? Or will the right, with its established, well funded infrastructure, be able to re-establish its dominance in national politics?

Progressives have expanded their influence in the Democratic Party but still face inertial forces that limit their ability to break through. Like others who have challenged the status quo, the potential success of the netroots and Professional

Left rests with their ability to outorganize and outmaneuver elites using whatever tools they have available. Movement conservatives leveraged direct mail and Jacksonian Democrats built a national campaign organization around inexpensive printing technology. If there is a progressive takeover of the Democratic Party, the realignment will not be televised. But it will be blogged, subject line tested and memed.

The emergence of the Internet gave birth to a second progressive movement. The social networking revolution enabled it to explode in size, reach and capability. We are on the verge of finding out whether the netroots, Internet Left and Professional Left, like other insurgents before them, can parlay their facility with the technological advances of our day into a dominant place in a new political order.

Notes

1 Kos. 2014. "The Electoral Boom-Bust Cycle, and Why Parties Have No Incentive To Change." *Daily Kos*, November 6. Retrieved from www.dailykos.com/story/2014/11/06/1342652/-The-electoral-boom-bust-cycle-and-why-parties-have-no-incentive-to-change.
2 Sullivan, Peter. 2014. "Dean, In Break With Group He Founded, Endorses Hillary Clinton for President." *The Hill*, December 10. Retrieved from http://thehill.com/blogs/ballot-box/226598-howard-dean-endorses-hillary-clinton.
3 Kos. 2014. "The Real Primary Fight of 2016 (And It's Not An Alternative to Hillary)." *Daily Kos*, February 17. Retrieved from www.dailykos.com/story/2014/02/17/1278315/-The-real-primary-fight-of-2016-and-it-s-not-an-alternative-to-Hillary.
4 Institutional support for the Tea Party has come from libertarian-leaning, pro-market individuals such as Charles and David Koch, and organizations such as the Heritage Foundation, FreedomWorks and Fox News. For an overview of the emergence of the Tea Party and a discussion of the views of its adherents, see Skocpol and Williamson (2013).
5 Unlike some of their institutional backers, rank-and-file Tea Party supporters—being generally older—are not opposed to Social Security and Medicare, which they regard as benefits derived from having worked. Instead, they object to government benefits going to those they regard as undeserving. See Skocpol and Williamson (2013).
6 See Bingham, Amy. 2011. "Mitt Romney's Top 5 Contradicting Comments." *ABCNews.com*, October 25. Retrieved from http://abcnews.go.com/Politics/mitt-romneys-top-contradicting-comments/story?id=14805513.
7 Stein, Sam. 2011. "Large Portion of GOP Thinks Obama is Racist, Socialist, Non-U.S. Citizen: Poll." *The Huffington Post*, May 25. Retrieved from www.huffingtonpost.com/2010/02/02/large-portion-of-gop-thin_n_445951.html.
8 "The Esquire Survey of America's Republican Elite." 2010. *Esquire*, February 16. Retrieved from www.esquire.com/features/republican-party-survey-0310#slide-1.
9 Galloway, Jim. 2013. "Paul Broun: 'I Was the First to Call Obama a Socialist.'" *The Atlanta Journal-Constitution*, February 13. Retrieved from www.ajc.com/weblogs/political-insider/2013/feb/13/paul-broun-i-was-first-call-obama-socialist/.
10 Llewellyn, Frank and Joseph Schwartz. 2009. "Socialists Say: Obama Is No Socialist." *Chicago Tribune*, November 1. Retrieved from http://articles.chicagotribune.com/2009-11-01/news/0910310206_1_democratic-socialists-obama-administration-dsa.
11 Not insignificantly, former Pennsylvania Senator Rick Santorum told the CPAC gathering that Republicans should nominate a true hard-right conservative—like him. "Conservatives and tea-party folks … We are not just wings of the Republican Party. We are the Republican Party," Santorum said. See Martin, Jonathan. 2012. "CPAC

148 Resolution

      'Severely' Conflicted Over Mitt Romney." *Politico*, February 11. Retrieved from www.politico.com/story/2012/02/cpac-severely-conflicted-over-mitt-072749.
12 Fahrenthold, David A. 2012. "Mitt Romney Reframes Himself As A Severely Conservative Governor." *The Washington Post*, February 16. Retrieved from www.washingtonpost.com/politics/mitt-romney-reframes-himself-as-a-severely-conservative-governor/2012/02/14/gIQAaMiqHR_story.html.
13 During the months of June and July 2012, Obama led in 24 of 34 polls in the Real Clear Politics polling average, at www.realclearpolitics.com/epolls/2012/president/us/general_election_romney_vs_obama-1171.html#polls. On the eve of the Republican National Convention on August 27, Obama led by 1.5 points in *The Huffington Post*/Pollster tracking average and had maintained a slight but steady lead since the beginning of 2012. Retrieved from http://elections.huffingtonpost.com/pollster/2012-general-election-romney-vs-obama.
14 In the Real Clear Politics average of public sentiment on the direction of the country at the start of the Republican National Convention on August 28, 2012, 62.8% of respondents felt the country was going in the wrong direction. Only 31.4% felt it was on the right track. Retrieved from www.realclearpolitics.com/epolls/other/direction_of_country-902.html.
15 Of middle-class voters, 62% blamed Congress, 44% blamed Bush, and only 34% blamed Obama in a Pew Research survey published in August 2012. See "The Lost Decade of the Middle Class." 2012. Pew Research Center, August 22. Retrieved from www.pewsocialtrends.org/2012/08/22/the-lost-decade-of-the-middle-class/.
16 In surveys taken during 2012, respondents rejected Ryan's plan to privatize Medicare by a wide margin, and became more unfavorable to the budget plan the more they heard about it. See Cheney, Kyle. 2012. "Polls: Ryan Plan Unpopular." *Politico*, August 11. Retrieved from www.politico.com/story/2012/08/polls-ryan-plan-unpopular-079607; and Singal, Jesse. 2012. "Conservative Talking Heads Love Paul Ryan's Budget, But Polls Tell Another Story." *The Daily Beast*, August 14. Retrieved from www.thedailybeast.com/articles/2012/08/14/conservative-talking-heads-love-paul-ryan-s-budget-but-polls-tell-another-story.html.
17 For a longer list of assertions about Obama from the Romney campaign, along with a rebuttal to each, see Eichenwald, Kurt. 2012. "The Five Reasons Why Romney/Ryan Must Be Defeated in 2012—And Why Conservatives Should Hope They Are." *KurtEichenwald.com*, September 2. Retrieved from http://kurteichenwald.com/2012/09/the-five-reasons-why-romneyryan-must-be-defeated-in-2012-and-why-conservatives-should-hope-they-are/.
18 Halperin, Mark. 2014. "Puzzle, Enigma Riddle." *Time*, October 10. Retrieved from http://thepage.time.com/2012/10/10/puzzle-enigma-riddle/. Of course, in keeping with the way the mainstream press covers politics, Halperin regarded Romney's tactics as a problem for *Obama*, who was forced to combat Romney's shape shifting.
19 Or perhaps not. One analysis of post-debate polls (Sides and Vavreck 2013) found no change in perceptions of Romney's ideological positioning, attributing his brief political renaissance to an uptick in perceptions of Romney's leadership attributes.
20 "Mr. Ryan's Speech: Effective Maybe, But Definitely Misleading." 2012. *The Washington Post* (editorial), August 30. Retrieved from www.washingtonpost.com/opinions/mr-ryans-speech-effective-maybe-but-definitely-misleading/2012/08/30/a9b4e690-f227-11e1-adc6-87dfa8eff430_story.html.
21 LoGiurato, Brett. 2012. "The Biggest Mistake in Paul Ryan's Factually Shaky Republican Convention Speech." *Business Insider*, August 30. Retrieved from www.businessinsider.com/paul-ryan-speech-fact-check-on-aaa-credit-rating-2012-8.
22 Woodward, Cal and Tom Raum. 2012. "Fact Check: Romney's Deficit Vow Lacks Specifics." *Associated Press*, August 30. Retrieved through http://news.yahoo.com/fact-check-romneys-deficit-vow-lacks-specifics-004029587–politics.html.

23 Noted in Marshall, Josh. 2012. "Great Moments in CNN Euphemisms." *Talking Points Memo*, August 29. Retrieved through http://talkingpointsmemo.com/edblog/great-moments-in-cnn-euphemisms. The exchange with CNN anchor Erin Burnett featured this comment: "There will be issues with some of the facts. But it motivated people."
24 Reilly, Ryan J. 2012. "Pennsylvania GOP Leader: Voter ID Will Help Romney Win State." *Talking Points Memo*, June 25. Retrieved from http://talkingpointsmemo.com/muckraker/pennsylvania-gop-leader-voter-id-will-help-romney-win-state.
25 Once the 2008 nomination campaign became a two-person field following the withdrawal of John Edwards, both MoveOn and Daily Kos endorsed Obama. Exit polls also showed Obama strongly outperformed Clinton among most (but not all) demographics where the netroots is overrepresented relative to the rest of the Democratic coalition: men, liberals, high-income earners and the well educated.
26 Lopez, German. 2014. "America Tweeted About Ferguson More Than Any Other News Story in 2014." *Vox*, December 29. Retrieved from www.vox.com/2014/12/29/7463663/twitter-news-2014.
27 Bouie, Jamille. 2015. "More Than A Food Fight: Why Hillary Should Take The Black Lives Matter Netroots Fracas Seriously." *Slate*, July 20. Retrieved from www.slate.com/articles/news_and_politics/politics/2015/07/netroots_nation_black_lives_matter_protest_hillary_clinton_needs_to_take.html.
28 See the Congressional Progressive Caucus at http://cpc.grijalva.house.gov/caucus-members/.
29 See the *New Democrat Coalition* at http://newdemocratcoalition-kind.house.gov/.
30 See the *Better Off Budget* at http://betteroffbudget.squarespace.com/.
31 Strauss, Daniel. 2014. "Senate Dems Invented A Leadership Spot for Elizabeth Warren." *Talking Points Memo*, November 13. Retrieved from http://talkingpointsmemo.com/livewire/elizabeth-warren-senate-democratic-leadership.
32 "Millennials in Adulthood: Detached from Institutions, Networked with Friends." 2014. Pew Research Center. Retrieved from www.pewsocialtrends.org/2014/03/07/millennials-in-adulthood/.
33 Republican National Committee. 2013. "Growth and Opportunity Project." Retrieved from http://goproject.gop.com/rnc_growth_opportunity_book_2013.pdf.
34 For instance, over privatizing Social Security, a policy supported by some of the Tea Party's financial backers. See Skocpol and Williamson (2013).

References

Bowers, Christopher J. and Matthew Stoller. 2005. "The Emergence of the Progressive Blogosphere: A New Force in American Politics." Research Report. Washington, DC: New Politics Institute.

Sides, John and Lynn Vavreck. 2013. *The Gamble: Choice and Chance in the 2012 Presidential Election*. Princeton, NJ: Princeton University Press.

Skocpol, Theda and Vanessa Williamson. 2013. *The Tea Party and the Remaking of Republican Conservatism*. New York: Oxford University Press.

INDEX

Entries in **bold** refer to tables; entries in *italics* refer to figures.

abortion 135–6
access strategy 23
ACORN 101
ActBlue 117
advocacy organizations: conservative 15, 17; email-based 74, 76; in inside-outside coalitions 58, 60–1; progressive 57
Affordable Care Act (ACA): as 'big government' 17; and blogosphere 66; CBO report on 84–5, 100; fight for public option in 9, 52, 70, 134; insurance sign-ups under 111; as neoliberal policy 120–1, 144–5; progressive and conservative views of 13; and Romney campaign 136–7
African-Americans 13, 37, 141
Alliance for Justice 59
Alternet 6, 72
Americablog 67
American Enterprise Institute 106
American Family Voices 58
AmericansElect.org 7, 28nn3–5
Americans for Prosperity 95–6
American Telegraph Company 23
anti-communism 40, 44, 51
anti-government attitudes 16–17, 29n8, 90, 98n11, 136
apathy 91, 145
Appalachia 15
Armstrong, Jerome 81, 118–19

Associated Press 23, 139
Atkins, Dante 48–9
attack ads *see* negative advertising
audience fragmentation 96

Baby Boomers 14, 77–8, 143
balance, and objectivity 101–2, 106, 109
Beck, Glenn 86, 143
Benen, Steve 100–1
Biden, Joe 120–1
big government 1, 17, 29n10, 37–8, 40, 51
big media 97
BlackLivesMatter 141
Blitzer, Wolf 139
blog advertising 69, 119
Blog for America 98n17
Blogger 67
bloggers: among netroots 11; as left-wing opposition 69; partisan affiliation of 105, 110–11
blogging: community 11, 51, 86–7; early adopters of 63; political 3 (*see also* blogosphere)
blogosphere: conservative 64, 86–7, 97n5; progressive *see* progressive blogosphere
blogrolls 66–7, 69, 73
blue-collar workers 15
Blue Dogs 69
Blue State Digital 74–5, 82n46
Boehner, John 60

bottom-up communication 112
Bowers, Chris 81–2n32
Bradley, Bill 15
Broder, David 29n7
broderism 29n7
Brookings 106
Broun, Paul 137
Brown, Sherrod 58, 62, 65
Buckley, William F. 38, 44–5
Burner, Darcy 142
Bush, George H. W. 41, 135
Bush, George W.: 2000 election of 41; and birth of progressive movement 42, 44; compromise under 13; conservative media under 89; and Howard Dean 1; and Iraq War 64; Lieberman as close to 47; and Obama 51–2, 56; tax cuts under 145; wrongdoing by officials under 64–5
business interests 61, 108, 115, 117–20; *see also* wealthy interests
Byrd, Robert 64

cable companies 60–1, 96
cable television 86, 88, 92–3, 95–6, 104
California 36, 118
Calmes, Jackie 101–2
Campaign for America's Future 58
candidates, personal qualities of 26
Cantor, Eric 107, 113n13
cap-and-trade 121
Carlson, Tucker 86
Carter, Jimmy: and blue-collar constituencies 15; defeat of 118; as late regime affiliate 54n1; and New Deal coalition 35–6, 146; and southern states 39–40
CBO (Congressional Budget Office) 84–5, 87, 91, 97, 100, 102
Cecil, Guy 90
center, missing 3–4, 7–10, 15, 19, 101
Center for American Progress 71–2
Chamberlain, Charles 142
Change.org 76, 82n45
Cheney, Dick 65
Citizens United decision 2, 9, 15, 95, 139, 146
civil liberties 134
Civil War 4, 20, 23
Clinton, Bill: and blue-collar constituencies 15; and DLC 118–19, 121; fundraising by 66; impeachment of 63; as pre-emptive leader 36, 41; on role of government 17; as triangulator 132–4, 145

Clinton, Hillary 15, 27, 52, 134–5, 141, 149n25
CNN: ratings of 95; website of 72
Code Pink 60
ColorofChange.org 58, 60–1, 82n41
Comcast 96
communication models: centralized 86; many-to-many 27, 87, 93; many-to-one 76, 87; one-to-many 11, 27, 76, 87, 93; one-to-one 27
communication strategies *see* media strategies
Communications Workers of America 59
communication technologies: convergence of *see* convergence; political impact of 1–2, 10
communities, virtual 87, 92–4
compromise: governing process requiring 10; radical rejection of 8, 13
Congress: 2014 elections for 125–6; blamed for economic climate 138; , Democratic control of 21; and Iraq War 63; journalistic expertise on 106; netroots in 142–3; personal wealth of members 117; public views of 90; Republican control of 36, 62; and trade agreements 61
Congressional Black Caucus 142
Congressional Hispanic Caucus 143
conservative movement: and business elites 136; in Congress 106; and the courts 131; and FDR 37; mainstream reaction to 48–9; media infrastructure of 4, 44, 53, 85–6; and negative advertising 15–16; in Obama era 35; in post-television era 95; and progressive movement 42, **43**, 111; and Reagan coalition 40; and Republican Party 5, 13, 38, 45–50, 52, 62
conservative self-identification 77
conventional wisdom 50, 85, 96–7
convergence 3, 92–4, 96–7, 146
Coolidge, Calvin 24
CPAC (Conservative Political Action Conference) 137
CPC (Congressional Progressive Caucus) 142–3
CREDO: in inside-outside coalitions 57–8, 60–1, 74; in midterm elections 126; organizational model of 82n41
Crooks and Liars 67
cultural values 14, 102
Cuomo, Andrew 122–4, 129n27, 142

Daily Caller 85–6, 88
Daily Kos: and 2014 New York gubernatorial primary 129n32; and Affordable Care Act 100; beginnings of 63–4; and Democratic Party 46; demographics of audience **124**, 125; discussion of Obama on 51, 55n9; endorsing Obama 149n25; in inside-outside coalitions 57–61, 74; in midterm elections 126; and Netroots Nation 76; RedState as conservative equivalent of 87; and Sanders campaign 134; in second-iteration blogosphere 71–2; sources of traffic to 67, **68**, 71; and Third Way 120
dark money 6, 117
Dean, Howard: alumni of campaign 71, 74, 79, 98n17, 122; defeat by blue-collar constituencies 15; demographics of support 123, 125; and elite dominance of Democrats 118–19; fundraising tactics of 76; as Internet insurgent 11, 53, 65–6, 69–70; and Iraq War 63–5; and progressive movement 8, 49–50; support for Hillary Clinton 134; and 'taking our country back' 1
deception 25, 140
deficits 19, 41, 132–3, 135
DeLauro, Rosa 62
Demand Progress 61, 82n41
Democracy for America 58, 61, 82n41, 120, 142
Democratic National Committee 50, 74
Democratic Party: composition of Congressional delegations 121, 142–3; dominance of presidential elections 2; elite/neoliberal dominance of 4–5, 8–9, 54, 112, 115, 117–22, 132; email campaigning in 75; future of 144–5, 147; and Iraq War 63–4, 70; mainstream media views of 108; mobilizing base of 89–90; outside group spending for 6n3; Professional Left employed within 73–4; socially diverse base of 14–15, 35, 37, 78, 123–5; turnout for mid-terms 125–7, 131–2; under Bill Clinton 41–2; *see also* progressive movement
Democratic Party presidential nominations: 2004 65–6; 2016 134–5
demographic shifts: Democrats gaining from 14, 78; and political instability 3, 10, 12, 140
Digg 71

digital campaigning 11, 73–6
digital departments, in-house 75–6
digital media: multiple platforms of 94; new politics of 2–3; time spent on 79
digital natives 72, 143
DINOs (Democrats in Name Only) 46
direct mail 30n15, 43, 53, 74–5, 147
direct mail
DLC (Democratic Leadership Council) 69, 117–21, 128n17, 132, 134
donations *see* fundraising
drones 134
Drudge Report 86, 88

'echo chamber' 49
economic elites: and conservative movement 136; in Democratic Party 109, 119; political influence of 115, 117; progressive struggle with 106; resentment towards 17
Edwards, John 149n25
Edwards, Lee 38, 40, 48–9, 51
Eisenhower, Dwight: and conservative movement 45–7; military record of 37; as pre-emptive leader 38, 41, 145; and television 25
elections, critical 19–21, 37
Electoral College 14, 40, 145
email campaigning 2–3, 11, 27, 53, 74–5
email lists 65, 74–6, 126
Eschaton 63–4, 67
establishment Democrats 47, 50, 56, 89, 108–9, 127
establishment Republicans 9, 50, 107, 109, 144
evangelicals 40, 135

Facebook: emergence of 11; frequent users of 92; left- and right-wing uses of 87, **88**; political engagement on 18–19; traffic to blogosphere from 70–3
factual consensus, breakdown of 12–13, 29n9, 101, 104
FAIR (Fairness and Accuracy in Reporting) 62
family values 26, 135
'farm team' 46
Fast Track Trade Authority 61–2
FCC (Federal Communications Commission) 60–1
Federal Reserve Board 57–8
Feingold, Russ 120
Ferguson, Missouri 141

filibuster reform *see* Senate reform
FireDogLake 65, 67
fivethirtyeight.com 110
"Fix The Senate Now" 59–60
Ford, Gerald 39
foreign policy: Cold War consensus on 12; of George W. Bush administration 1, 41–2; Millennials on 14; narratives of 26
Fox News 13, 72, 85–6, 88, 95, 143, 147n4
framing choices 102, 106–8
Franken, Al 60
From, Al 118–21
fundraising: of large donations 117; and new media 18; of small donations 64, 66, 75–6, 82n33, 117, 119, 133, 144

Gabba, Charles 111
Gandhi, Mahatma 48
Gawker Media 72
gays 14, 136
Geithner, Timothy 52
generational changes: and ideological self-identification 77–8; and political alignment 19, 136, 140, 143; in social attitudes 10, 14
Generation X 77–8, 143
Gephardt, Dick 63, 118
gerrymandering 5, 127, 132–3, 145
get-out-the-vote (GOTV) 9, 125–6, 129
Gibbs, Robert 56
Gilded Age 8, 12, 132
Gilens, Martin 115, 117, 119
Gingrich, Newt 34, 36
global financial crisis of 2008 17
global warming 13
Gobright, Lawrence 23
Goldwater, Barry 3, 38, 47, 49–51
Google: and decline of newspapers 104; emergence of 11; as source of traffic 71
Google Analytics 67
Google searches 67–9, 115
Gore, Al 14–15, 118–19, 121
Graham, Lindsey 85
grassroots, opening political process to 9
grassroots activism 11, 57, 60, 89, 126–7
grassroots participation, progressive 4–5
Great Depression 12, 20, 37, 40
Great Society 29n8, 39, 42
Greenwald, Glenn 71, 110–11
Guantanamo Bay 134

Hagan, Kay 95
Hagel, Chuck 107
Harding, Warren 24
Harkin, Tom 59
Hart, Gary 15
health care reform 8, 34, 138, 144
hedge funds 7, 28, 132
Heitkamp, Heidi 58
Hogue, Ilyse 82n44
Hoover, Herbert 24
'horserace' paradigm 85, 107–10, 139
Huffington, Arianna 71
Huffington Post: growth of 67–8; and Iran sanctions 59; and Lawrence Summers 58; outside netroots 72–3; supportive content in 57
Humphrey, Hubert 20–1, 51
Huntsman, Jon 107
Hussein, Saddam 62, 64
hyperlinks 66–7, 69

ideological self-identification 77
Ideopolises 14–15, 138
image-making 26
immigrants, undocumented 29n9, 136
immigration, G. W. Bush on 41
immigration reform 107
income inequality: moneyed interests protecting 132; and political instability 3, 10, 12; rising 16, *116*
incompatible worldviews 13, 29n9
information, monopolizing flow of 23
information economy 18; *see also* new economy
information technology 10
'inside–outside' coalitions 57–61, 74–6, 78, 106
institution building 74, 146
interest groups 39, 115, 119
International Day of Action against war in Iraq 62–3
Internet: advertising on 96; in American life 57, 75, 78–9; community-building on 91, 98n14; conservative infrastructure on 86–8; and contemporary journalism 111–12; decentralized structure of 3–4, 11, 27–8, 89, 133; generational increase in use **79**; impact on television 92–3; models of communication via 76; partisan content on 105; progressive movement on 2–5, 9, 11, 44–5, 53; reshaped by social media 18, 71–3

154　Index

Internet activism 2–4, 11–12, 87, 92, 132–3, 140
Internet freedom organizations 61
Internet Left: and Affordable Care Act 91, 100; community structure of 28, 97; and convergent technology 95; and Democratic Party elites 54, 89, 135; and digital-native generation 143; institutional maturity of 140, 147; limits of reach 122–5, 127; and participatory democracy 133; and partisan journalism 112; and racial violence 141; and social media 72–3; use of term 6, 11; victories under Obama 59
Internet television 94
intramural conflict 69, 106–8, 122
Iran 57, 59–60
Iraq War: Howard Dean on 49, 119; movement against 9, 42, 44, 62–3, 65; Obama on 52; and progressive blogosphere 67; and Republican coalition 41

Jackson, Andrew: populist movement of 2–3, 11; and the press 20–3, 28; as reconstructive leader 36
Jacksonian realignment 4, 112
Jefferson, Thomas 36
Johnson, Lyndon 29, 38–9, 49, 51
journalism: and blogging 111–12; professionalization of 23, 103; and progressive movement 109; traditional 5, 101–2, 104–5, 108
Just Foreign Policy 60

Kennedy, J. F. 25, 90
Kennedy, Ted 15
Kerry, John 15, 46–7
Kissinger, Henry 51–2
Klein, Ezra 71, 73, 120
Koch brothers 15, 95, 120, 147n4

labor unions 57, 74–5, 118
laissez-faire conservatives 37, 40–1
Lamont, Ned 47–8, 70, 82n33
Latinos 13
lead generation 76
left-of-center self-identification 57, 77
Libby, Scooter 65
liberalism: in 1970s and 1980s 13; in current Democratic Party 77–8, 144; FDR's use of term 37; and the New Left 39; Reagan coalition built against 40

liberals: classical 37, 40–1; in Congress 106
liberal self-identification 14, 77–9
Lieberman, Joseph 47–8, 63, 69–70, 82n33, 89, 119
life-cycle effects 78, 143
Limbaugh, Rush 86
Lincoln, Abraham 10–11, 20–4, 27–8, 36
link exchanges 68–70
Lippmann, Walter 103
lobbying, professional 60
Lott, Trent 64–5
Lugar, Richard 29n6

mainstream media: continuing strength of 96–7; objectivity of 101; political narratives of 105–12, 132; reactions to movement politics 48–50, 105–6; Republican dominance of 85; right-left equivalence in 12–13, 29n7, 102–3; Romney's approach to 139–40; websites of 72
majority–minority communities 10, 14
Malkin, Michelle 86
Mann, Thomas 106
marijuana legalization 78
marriage equality 78, 135
matching funds 66
McCain, John 41, 51
McGovern, George 40, 119
McKinley, William 20
media: changing environment of 3–4, 72, 95; consolidation of ownership 96; consumption patterns 19, 79, 96; decentralized 96, 105; *see also* digital media; mainstream media; new media; traditional media
media events 25
media narratives 53
media strategies 24, 89, 91, 94, 96–7
Medicare: market role in 8; Obama's changes to 35, 70; proposal to privatize 148n16; and Tea Party 147n5
Meetup.com 65
Merkley, Jeff 58–9
message control: FDR's use of 24; Republican use of 85
Mic 72, 143
micro-targeting 96
midterm elections 95, 120, 123–4, 126–7, 131–2
Millennials: ideological self-identification among 77–8, 143; religious beliefs of 29n13; social engagement of 91–2; values of 14

Mitchell, John 53
mobile viewing 104
moderate self-identification 10
moderation, mushy 50
Mondale, Walter 15, 36, 118
money in politics 9, 12; *see also* wealthy interests
moral flexibility 138
Mother Jones 72
Moulitsas, Markos 46–8, 64, 118–19, 132, 134–5
MoveOn.org: and 2016 Democratic nomination 134; alumni of 71, 76, 79, 82n44; conservative version of 87; and Dean campaign 66; endorsing Obama 149n25; endorsing Teachout 122; in inside-outside coalitions 57–61; and Iraq War 63, 65; in midterm elections 126; name of 81n23; and netroots 6, 45, 76; organizational model of 74–5, 82n41
Moynihan, Daniel Patrick 51–2
MSNBC 13, 95–6, 100
multiculturalism 40
Murtha, Jack 64
MyDD 63, 67, 81–2n32, 118

The Nation 60, 122
National Journal 59, 75, 107, 120
national online primary 7
National Organization for Women 58
National Review: challenge to Nixon 47; and conservative movement 44–5, 52; foundation of 38
negative advertising 15, 18, 85, 101
neo-conservatives 40–2
neoliberals 8–10, 41, 108, 118, 140–1, 144
Netanyahu, Benjamin 60
net neutrality 9, 57, 60–1, 81n14, 133–4
netroots: community structure of 78, 94, 97; in conflict with Republicans 125–6; in Democratic Party 61, 69, 71, 79, 108, 115, 118–19, 135, 144; demographics of 5, 122–3, 125–7, 141–3; and digital campaign teams 75; first-generation 62, 70, 76, 87, 89, 119; in inside-outside coalitions 57–61; institutional maturity of 140, 146–7; lack of conservative equivalent 88; low-tech precursors to 22; mainstream attitudes to 3–4, 48, 56; in nomination campaigns 66; and Obama administration 52, 133–4; and oligarchy 115–16; and rebirth of progressive movement 11, 44–5, 141; role of blogosphere in 73; second-generation 76–7, 143; support for Howard Dean 28, 50; two iterations of 56–7; use of term 6
Netroots Nation 76, 98n17, 141
New Deal: bipartisan consensus on 12–13; conservative reaction to 38, 44–5; Democrats rejecting 42; Nixon's version of 51–2; as unique realignment 54n2
New Deal coalition: decay of 38–9, 53, 54n4, 69; end of 20–1, 29nn8,10, 34–6; life cycle of 19; and new communication technology 2, 4, 10, 25; origins of 37
New Democrats 41, 108, 118, 120–2, 125, 141–2
new economy, cultural values of 14–15
New Left 39
new media: political impact of 1, 96, 112; progressives and 5–6, 64, 73
New Organizing Institute (NOI) 76
newspapers: decline of 4, 101, 104–5, 113n6; partisan 22, 112
news stories, as socially constructed 102
New York Times 28n3, 97n4, 107
Nixon, Richard: 1968 election victory 20–1; center-right alignment under 10; conservative movement and 38, 42, 47, 50–2; as inflection point 34–5; as pre-emptive leader 35; and television 25–8, 85
Nixon–Reagan–Bush era 4, 16, 19
non-Christian populations 78
nonprofits, progressive 57, 61, 74–5
non-white populations 12–14, 78, 125–7
North Carolina 14, 63, 95

Obama, Barack: 2012 election polling of 148n13; and Blue State Digital 74–5; composition of support base 5, 14–15, 19, 135–6, 141; Dean campaign as forerunner of 66; and Fast Track Trade Authority 61–2; as inflection point 34–5; judicial nominations by 58–9, 110; liberal and conservative views on 13; limitations on leadership of 36; media strategies of 89; as New Democrat 121, 144–5; progressive movement under 50–2, 56–8, 133–5; Republican beliefs about 101, 137–8, 148n17; use of the Internet 21, 27–8
Obamacare *see* Affordable Care Act (ACA)
objectivity: in mainstream journalism 5, 100–4; as value choice 108, 110–12

Occupy Movement 17–18; 30n16
oligarchy 115
'one percent' 17–18
open-source communication patterns 88
open-source information 101
Ornstein, Norman 106
Orszag, Peter 52
The Other 98% 58

PACs 117
Page, Benjamin 115, 119
Pajamas Media 86
Palin, Sarah 41, 137
Pariser, Eli 72
participatory democracy 3, 8, 133
partisan realignment 4
Perry, Rick 137
petitions 9, 57–8, 65, 81n26
political asymmetries 106, 109, 111
political elites: breakdown of consensus among 8–9, 29n9, 112, 136; concentration of power 117; impact of technology on 18; movement pressure on 48–50, 56; and news framing 102–4, 108
political engagement 19, 89, 99
political instability 2–3, 6, 11–12
political polarization 3, 12, 21, 106
political realignment: in 1932 37; elections in 4, 19–20; and media technology 11–12; possible future 5–6, 10
political regimes, ebb and flow of 1–2, 5, 35–6
Political Wire 63
Politico: and conservative Internet movement 87; and Obamacare 85
populism, left- and right-wing versions 5–6
post-industrial economy 54n4
post-television era 95–6
preemptive leaders 35, 38, 41
Presente.org 61, 82n41
presidential elections: campaign spending **16**; coalitions forming in 140–1; conservative problems with 131; get-out-the-vote for 126
presidential leadership 35
printing, inexpensive 2, 11, 21–2, 27–8, 147
Priorities USA 15
professionalism, journalistic 100, 102
Professional Left: and 2016 Democratic nomination 134; among netroots 11; employers of 73–6; fundraising by 117;
and future of Democratic Party 144; and get-out-the-vote campaigns 126; Gibbs' use of term 56; institutional maturity of 146–7; reach of 79; rise of 57, 76, 132–3; Third Way opposed to 120; use of term 6
professionals 14–15, 101
progressive blogosphere: and 'broderism' 29n7; emergence of 45, 52; and establishment Democrats 47–8; first iteration of 3–4, 66–71; generating content for 57; and Howard Dean 50, 66; importance of 2; Internet activism predating 45; and Iraq War 63–4; and Ned Lamont 70; and Obama judicial nominations 58–9; second generation of 71–3
Progressive Change Campaign Committee (PCCC) 61, 82, 120, 122, 126
Progressive Congress 59, 142
progressive movement: in Congress 142–3; and democratic process 9, 15, 133; demographic challenges for 125; goals of 106; limits of 80; mainstream reactions to 48–9, 108–9; media capability of 44–5, 53; mobilizing and messaging tactics of 108–9; original 103, 108, 132–3, 145; struggle within Democratic Party 4–6, 8–10, 45–7, 50, 57–62, 69, 122–3, 132–3, 140, 146–7; twenty-first century rebirth of 11, 42, **43**, 147
Progressives United 82, 120
Progressive Voices 59
public financing of elections 133, 142
publishers, progressive 76
Putnam, Robert D. 90–1

Quantcast 72, 82n35, 124–5

racial violence 141
radio, impact on politics 2, 4, 10, 21, 24–5, 27–8
Raw Story 67, 71–2, 88, 124–5, 141
reactionaries 107–8, 111, 136–7, 140, 145
Reagan, Ronald: 1980 election of 20, 53; as alternative to Nixon 47, 51; as movement president 35; and New Deal coalition 36; on role of government 16–17; and television 10, 26–7
Reagan coalition: decay of 10, 29n10, 41, 136; defeat by Obama coalition 141; life cycle of 19, 40–1; presidential campaign spending and **16**; uniting factors of 40

Reagan Democrats 36, 40
realigning periods 3–4, 28, 54n2; *see also* political realignment
reconstructive leaders 36
red/blue political framework 1, 7, 10, 97, 109
Reddit 71
RedState.com 87
Reed, Bruce 118–20
regime flux 36
Reid, Harry 62, 70, 74, 143
relationships, virtual 27, 94
Republican National Committee 144
Republican Party: coalition of 2, 14, 135–6; dominance of mid-term elections 2; future of 144–6; internal struggle in 9, 106–7; and Joseph Lieberman 70; media strategy of 85; and Obamacare 84–5; origins of 20, 23; outside group spending for 6n3; presidential successes of 41; radical dominance of 3, 5, 8, 12–13, 19, 106, 140; in southern Congressional districts 21; voter turnout for 96
right-wing factionalism 106–7
RINOs (Republicans in Name Only) 46
Rockefeller, Nelson 50–1
Roemer, Buddy 7
Romney, Mitt: 2012 campaign of 136–40, 148n19; and income inequality 17–18, 30n16; negative ads for 15; white support for 14
Roosevelt, Eleanor 25
Roosevelt, F. D.: 1932 election of 20; and compromise 13; and New Deal 37; and radio 10, 21, 24–5, 27–8
RootsAction 60, 82n41
Rootscamp 76
Rosen, Jay 111, 113n1
Rove, Karl 15
Rusher, William 38, 44, 49, 52
Russert, Luke 85
Ryan, Melissa 117
Ryan, Paul 138–9, 148n16

Salon: demographics of audience 124–5; in Internet Left 6; and social media 72
Sanders, Bernie 66, 123, 134, 141–2
Santorum, Rick 147n11
Sargent, Greg 106
Schrum, Bob 47–8, 54n6
Schudson, Michael 103–4
Schwartz, Allyson 120
scientific method 103, 113n2

search engines 45, 66–7, 69–71
second round innovators 39
secular realignment 20–1, 34
self-publication 105
Senate Banking Committee 58
Senate reform 9, 57–9
September 11, 2001 19, 62
Silver, Nate 71, 110
simple messages 86, 91
single-payer health care 134, 145
smartphones 18, 93
Smith, Al 37
Snowden, Edward 110–11
social capital 66, 90–2, 94, 98n14
social diversity 14
socialism 134, 137, 144
social media: blog traffic from 71–2; characteristics of users 92; and decline of newspapers 105; explosion in 11, 18, 70–1, 87; progressive movement and 4; pushback against televised messaging 91; and young people 30n19
social networks: among Millennials 92; deterioration in 90
social programs 39, 135–6
Social Security: Eisenhower expanding 38; Goldwater on 49; in New Deal 37; Obama's changes to 35; privatizing 149n34; progressive victories on 57; state and market role in 8; and Tea Party 147n5; and Third Way 120
southern states: in New Deal coalition 37, 39; Republican growth in 29n10, 36
spin control 23
stenographic fairness 104
Stoller, Al 121
StumbleUpon 71
Summers, Lawrence 52, 58
SumOfUs 61, 82n41
Supreme Court 35, 41, 90, 146

tablets 104
Taft, Robert 38
'taking our country back' 1
"Talking About This" 87, **88**
talking points 85
Talking Points Memo: Gilens talking to 115, 117–18; origins of 63; as part of blogosphere 67, 72; under Bush administration 64–5
talk radio 104
taxes, lowering 26, 40

Teachout, Zephyr Rain 122–4, 129nn26,32, 142
Tea Party: establishment backlash against 146; and global financial crisis 17; institutional support for 147n4; possible lasting dominance of 10; as Reagan Democrats 40; struggle within Republican Party 41, 106–9, 132, 135–6
telegraph, impact on politics 2, 4, 11, 21–3, 27–8
television: and 1968 presidential campaign 21, 25–6; continuing dominance of 80, 95–6, 112; decentralization of 92–4, 97, 104; and diminished engagement 19, 90–1; generational decline in viewing 79; image-making via 26–8; and negative advertising 16; in right-wing messaging apparatus 2–4, 10, 85–9; Romney campaign and 139–40
Tester, Jon 58
Think Progress 71–2, 124–5, 143
think tanks 85, 106
'third way': A. Cuomo as 122; Bill Clinton as 36, 41; bloggers as opposition to 69; and Democratic future 145; Eisenhower as 38
Third Way (think tank) 120, 132; Board of Trustees *121*
ticket splitting 10
Todd, Chuck 85
top-down politics 96
TPP (Trans-Pacific Partnership) 61
Traditionalists 77–8
traditional media: and Affordable Care Act 100; decline of 93, 101, 104; and Democratic Party 69; dismissal of partisan media 105, 110; negative advertising in 15–16; in political process 4–5
transparency, journalistic 110–12
Truman, Harry 37
Tsongas, Paul 15
Twitter 11, 28, 71, 93, 142
Typepad 67

Udall, Tom 59
Ultraviolet 58, 82n41

unemployment insurance 37, 84, 136, 142
universal health care 8, 52, 136
Upworthy 6, 72–3, 87–8, 143
USaction 60

value judgments, journalists avoiding 108–9
VCRs 93
Vietnam War 39, 90, 98n11
Virginia, new economy in 14
voter suppression 139–40

Waldman, David 59
Wall Street, influence on politics 58, 122, 133–4, 144
Wall Street Journal 86, 120
Warren, Elizabeth 58, 62, 66, 120, 134, 143
Washington Post 107
Watergate 39, 42, 90, 98n11, 101, 146
wealth, concentration of 5, 15, 133
wealthy interests: and conservative movement 53, 136; and Democratic Party 117–18; political power of 9, 79, 116, 118, 133, 144; and Romney campaign 139–40
websites, front pages of 70–1, 73
welfare state: bipartisan acceptance of 7–8, 37; and Reagan 40
Wellstone, Paul 118–19
Whigs 2, 20
white voters 14–15, 29n10, 35–6, 40, 135, 144
Win Without War 60
wire services 11, 23
Wittmann, Marshall 89
women: in Democratic base 124–5; single 14, 145
Women's Donor Network 58
working-class communities 29n10, 54n4, 117, 125–7, 138
Wu, Tim 129n32

Yellen, Janet 58
YouTube 11, 94

zero-sum games 2, 8, 105, 112